# DAWN TO DUSK

*Jonathan P. Scott*

# DAWN TO DUSK

## A Safari Through Africa's Wild Places

### JONATHAN SCOTT

BBC BOOKS

IN ASSOCIATION WITH KYLE CATHIE LIMITED

For my wife Angela, with love and gratitude

Drawings by Angela and Jonathan Scott

This book is published to accompany the BBC television series entitled
*Dawn to Dusk*, which was first broadcast in1996. The series was
produced by the BBC Natural History Unit for the BBC.
Series producer: Robin Hellier
Producers: Robin Hellier (three programmes),
Keith Scholey (one programme), Michael Gunton (one programme),
Sara Ford (one programme)

Published by BBC Books,
an imprint of BBC Worldwide Publishing,
BBC Worldwide Limited, Woodlands,
80 Wood Lane, London W12 0TT
in association with Kyle Cathie Limited,
20 Vauxhall Bridge Road, London SW1V 2SA

First published in 1996

Copyright © 1996 by Jonathan Scott

The moral right of the author has been asserted.

ISBN 0 563 37195 1

A Cataloguing in Publication record for this title is available
from the British Library

Designed by Geoff Hayes
Edited by Caroline Taggart
Map by ML Design
The quote from *Through a Window* by Jane Goodall at the beginning
of Chapter 4 is reproduced by permission of Weidenfeld and Nicolson
The photograph of Victoria Falls on pages 180/181 is by
Roger de la Harpe/Planet Earth

Set in 11/16 ITC Galliard
Printed and bound by Butler and Tanner Ltd, Frome and London
Colour reproduction by Radstock Reproductions Ltd,
Midsomer Norton
Jacket printed by Lawrence Allen Ltd, Weston-Super-Mare

# CONTENTS

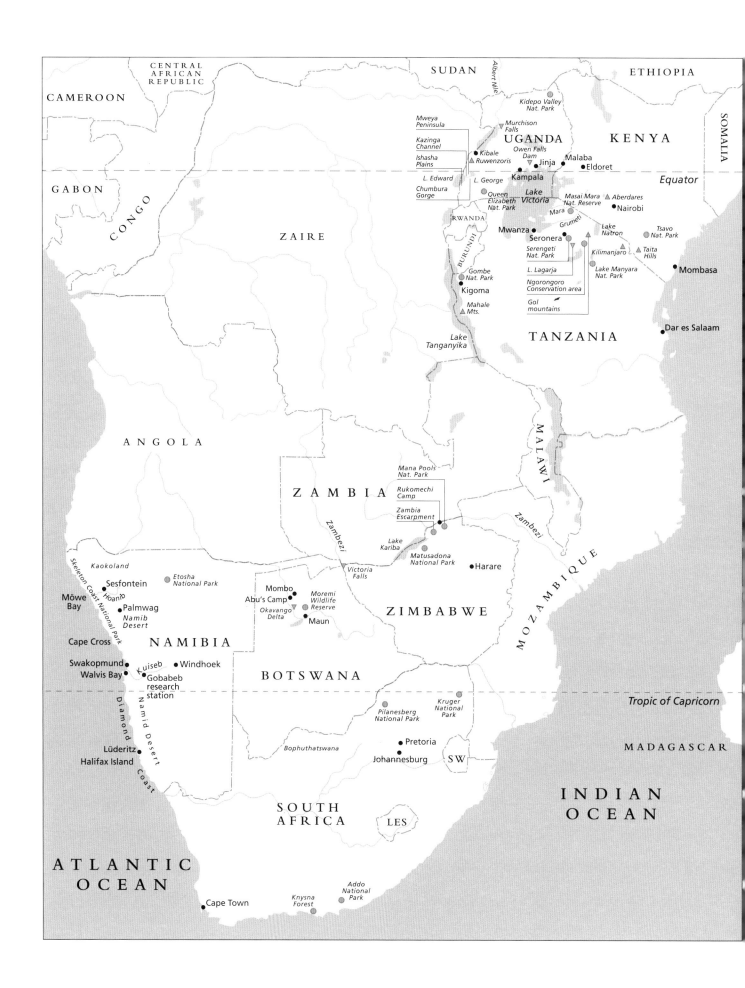

# INTRODUCTION

At some time in their lives everybody must have dreamed of Africa – the same dream that Karen Blixen lived and then immortalized in her book *Out of Africa*: a vision of flying like an eagle over the green hills of Ngong, swooping low across the soda-encrusted lakes of the Great Rift Valley where 2 million flamingoes gather at the water's edge, the vivid pink of their plumage dazzling the eye. Onwards you fly, reaching out to that far-flung corner of Masailand, the Mara, dry-season refuge for more than a million wildebeest, watching now as the herds surge onwards, ox-like heads tossing this way and that, long tails streaming behind them as they move remorselessly towards the Mara River, heading south once more to the wide open spaces of the Serengeti in Tanzania.

Africa's wilderness areas are as important as the great museums and art galleries of the world – genetic treasure troves holding the secrets of times past and a key to our future. A journey to Africa is a journey of the soul – an ancient voice stirs deep within us, reconnecting us to the very essence of our being, for it was here, in Africa, that our ancestors became men. The sage and poet Laurens Van der Post talks of Africa as 'the bush, the plains, the great free mountain tops and immense skies, about a life that was a continuous trek, a journey without walls or streets to hem it in.... I realized then how deep, how life-giving and strengthening was the vision of Africa in my blood.'

In the autumn of 1925, Carl Jung, the great Swiss psychiatrist, visited Kenya and Uganda. Jung always referred to Africa as God's country and found insights here into the archetypal nature of mankind. He describes waking one morning at sunrise while travelling on a train, to see a slim brownish-black figure standing motionless on a steep red cliff, leaning on a long spear. The sight of that lone figure gave him an intense sense of *déjà vu* and Jung said, 'I could not guess what string within myself was plucked at the sight of that solitary dark hunter. I knew only that his world had been mine for countless millennia.'

Certainly Africa is many things: the cool air of the high savanna blending with the night sounds of tree frogs and mole crickets. The landscape is infinitely varied, whether you are driving across the rolling grassy plains of Kenya's Masai Mara or trekking through the harsh thornbush country to the north in Samburu District, where reticulated giraffe look outrageously beautiful when matched against a deep blue sky, and dust-red elephant trundle down to bathe in the muddy waters of the Uyaso Ngiro River. The blistering heat of the Sahara Desert and the cloying dampness of the equatorial rain forest, where water pours from your body as fast as you can drink it, are just the extremes, helping to define every possible type of landscape and climate – different worlds in a land of contrasts. But who can forget the evil and sadistic buffoonery of Idi Amin or the slaughter of one million Rwandans – horror stories written in the blood of a whole nation, tribal blood-lettings of such ferocity that they make Bosnia pale by comparison? Yet I have never met friendlier or more forgiving people. Africa is now my home.

Wild animals have always featured prominently in my life, though my own dream of Africa was nurtured far from these shores. I was brought up on a farm in England, where as a child I kept notebooks full of sketches, pressed wild flowers and grasses between newspapers, clambered up trees and fell into bramble bushes – anything for a glimpse of a new bird species or the chance of discovering the shape and colour of its eggs. I fished for sticklebacks and collected tadpoles in jam-jars and I still remember how anxiously I awaited the occasional parcels of bird feathers – grouse and pheasant, quail and partridge – saved from my uncle's restaurant in London. I ran barefoot through the fields and stalked among the woodlands in search of rabbits and squirrels. There were badgers and foxes too, and occasionally a deer or a kestrel – just as rare and exciting to glimpse in those days as the leopard and hunting dog I would one day search for in Africa.

Having graduated with a degree in zoology from the Queen's University of Belfast in Northern Ireland, I quickly discovered that career opportunities in the wildlife field were few and far between. I was warned by one of my lecturers that the study of natural history was a pastime, not a career, and that unless I had a private income (which I didn't) I had better concentrate on getting a 'proper' job. I spent the next year in North America, exploring such wilderness areas as the Grand Tetons, Yosemite and Yellowstone National Park. There were encounters with brown bear and bison, elk and caribou. I saw Aspen in its autumn coat of colours and the Rockies resplendent with winter snowfall. The fog-shrouded coast of Nova Scotia and sunbaked deserts of Arizona were stunning to behold. But at night, in the far corners of my mind, lurked bigger fare – lion and leopard, elephant and rhino. Africa and its great cast of animal characters beckoned.

I returned to England determined to save up enough money to travel to Africa. Africa spelled adventure – a journey into the wilderness; a step back in time; a chance to take risks. In Africa there is more than a touch of the Wild West, of being able to be yourself more honestly and easily, in just being. To journey to Africa is to experience times past – a retreat, a reconnection; a being something other. Even the word 'safari' has magic to it, and not just because of the animals. It is a truly African experience. A safari outside Africa is not a safari at all.

My first safari began in 1974 and took me the length and breadth of Africa, an overland journey of almost four months' duration – and we hurried. I have vague memories of being bogged down under canvas in France, huddling in snow-covered tents that were designed for better weather. Our old Bedford army truck had seized up

before we really got going, forcing us to wait for spares, cursing whoever it was back at the workshop in London who had fitted the wrong part or applied the wrong oil. Finally we boarded the ferry taking us from Spain to Algeciras. Suddenly we were in Africa – or were we?

Like many people, I inherited a typically stereotyped view of Africa. The individual countries seemed to be the continent itself; only when you drive through Africa do you realize just how vast it is. Certain places, particularly those in the north – Morocco, Tunisia, Algeria, even parts of Niger – were at odds with my idea of Africa. Africa to me had always been as black as night, muscular-bodied men and elegant robed women carrying baskets on their heads, mist-shrouded rain forests and animal-speckled savannas. North Africa is an enigma, cut off from the body of the continent. I had visited Tunisia and Morocco as a teenager – all golden sand and camels, bustling street markets and spicy coffee. Even Tarzan seemed confused at times, swinging through the rain forest on a canopy of vines to come face to face with lions more suited to the open savanna. I was hungry for the real Africa, whatever that might be.

It wasn't until I reached East Africa that I began to feel at home – here were the animals that I had watched on film and read so much about. This was the land of the Serengeti and Ngorongoro Crater, the Masai Mara and Amboseli, Mount Kenya and Kilimanjaro, just as I had seen on Armand and Michaela Denis's ground-breaking television series *On Safari*. Now I knew what Karen Blixen meant when she wrote:

> *I have just emerged from the depths of the great wide open spaces, from the life of prehistoric times, today just as it was a thousand years ago, from meetings with the great beasts of prey, which enthral one, which obsess one so that one feels that lions are all that one lives for.*

I could hardly bear to drag myself away from East Africa as the old Bedford truck hurried us remorselessly down the Pan-African highway to our final destination in South Africa. All thoughts of continuing my travels by boat via Cape Town to Sydney in Australia had long since disappeared. I was determined to try and transform my safari experiences into a job. I spent the next year and a half working with wild animals in Botswana, including a memorable few weeks with wildlife photographers Tim and June Liversedge on their houseboat in the Okavango Delta, before returning overland to East Africa in 1976. Within a few months I had made my base at Mara River Camp in the Masai Mara, and was busily collecting material for my artwork and detailing the lives of the animals which in 1982 resulted in my first book *The Marsh Lions* (co-authored with Brian Jackman). My dream of living in the bush had become reality.

When Keith Scholey and Alistair Fothergill from the BBC Natural History Unit suggested to me a six-part TV series on Africa's wild places, I jumped at the opportunity of presenting it.

The locations for the series were to be chosen to demonstrate a number of key points. We wanted to show the continent's incredible diversity of habitat and scenery, while also trying to provide people with a glimpse of the extraordinary variety of Africa's wildlife. There had to be lions and elephants, of course, and despite the number of times they have been featured in the past the splendour of the Serengeti Plains and the wildebeest migration never fails to send a tingle down my spine. The equatorial rain forests are a world of their own, so they had to be included, with gorillas an obvious choice. But they had been given plenty of coverage in recent years, with David Attenborough and Julian Pettifer showing how extraordinarily trusting these giant apes could be in the presence of human beings. The murder of Dian Fossey in the remote forests of Rwanda in 1985 robbed the mountain gorillas of their greatest human ally. Her years of work at the Karisoke Institute had helped to focus people's attention on the plight of all the larger primates. In the end we all agreed that perhaps it was time to feature Africa's other great primate and man's closest relative, the chimpanzee. Alistair had made a highly acclaimed film on the work of a Swiss biologist, Christophe Boesch. He and his wife, Hedwige Boesch-Achermann, had been studying a group of seventy chimpanzees in the Côte d'Ivoire's Tai forest since 1979. One of the study groups that Christophe had been following was a coalition of adult males who regularly set off to hunt red colobus among the canopy of the forest. To film this it was necessary to try and keep up with the great apes as they loped through the forest. It all sounded incredibly exciting.

Sadly, in the end we were unable to film at that location as a mystery disease struck while Christophe was on a rare spell of leave. By the time he returned a number of the males had died, victims of the deadly Ebola virus. This would inevitably lead to the group territory being taken over by one of the rival coalitions of male chimpanzees.

With the loss of the Côte d'Ivoire as a filming location for chimpanzees our attentions switched to Tanzania. There are two sites along the shores of Lake Tanganyika where chimpanzees can be seen relatively easily: the Mahale Mountains and Gombe National Park. Gombe is the location of the thirty-five-year chimpanzee research programme that Jane Goodall started in 1960. Today much of the research is conducted by Tanzanian students and scientists. Jane continues to work tirelessly on behalf of chimpanzees, lobbying for the banning of the use of primates for medical research and trying to halt the exploitation of young chimpanzees by street photographers who use them as tourist curiosities in countries such as Spain. We decided to film at Gombe.

For many people the quintessential setting for a safari is among the savannas of East Africa: wide open spaces dotted with flat-topped acacia trees; places such as the Masai Mara and Serengeti. It is here that one often finds predators such as lion and cheetah, hyaena and jackal – wild dog even. East Africa is certainly blessed with the pick of the world's finest game-viewing areas. Who wouldn't relish the chance of driving down into the gigantic volcanic caldera known as Ngorongoro Crater, in Tanzania, sometimes spoken of as the eighth wonder of the world. The crater is one of the last places in Africa where the endangered black rhino still prospers and where elephant bearing massive ivory seek shade among ancient stands of yellow-barked acacia trees. The lion here are black-maned and big-bodied, the finest in Africa, competing for their share of the food with large clans of spotted hyaena.

There are many similarities between the Ngorongoro Crater and Kenya's Masai Mara, where I have been based for most of the last eighteen years. Both areas have attracted film-makers from around the world; few other places can provide such a variety of animals in a relatively small area. Another bonus is that the animals are so approachable. This is particularly true of the lion, which are so accustomed to being viewed that they sometimes seek the shade of a vehicle to escape the sun. Added to this is the fact that the terrain is open and easy to navigate: not only can you often spot the predators at a great distance, but you can usually reach them with comparative ease without getting stuck. The fact that it is still permitted to drive off the roads in the Mara makes filming even easier; you can drive wherever you please.

But these benefits have to be balanced against the legitimate complaints of animal harassment by safari vehicles in the Mara, and the sheer volume of people visiting these remarkable locations. In the end we decided that both the Mara and the

*Following pages: The Serengeti Plains are vast – 10,000 square km (3,860 square miles) in extent, and stretch from the southern Serengeti all the way east to the foot of the Ngorongoro Crater Highlands, in the Ngorongoro Conservation Area. During the rains, which last from November until June, the wildebeest and zebra leave the woodlands where they have spent the dry season and move en masse on to the plains: 1.5 million wildebeest and 250,000 zebra, as well as hundreds of thousands of gazelle. It is the largest and most spectacular land migration on earth.*

Ngorongoro Crater were already too familiar to viewers, and we should opt instead to make a film in the Serengeti, of which the Masai Mara is the northern extension.

Until the 1970s Uganda's parks and reserves were an integral part of many people's safari to East Africa. Now that peace once again prevails in that beautiful country it was one of the areas that we had hoped to include in our series. There are a number of parks and reserves in Uganda which are exceptional primate habitat where you can trek in search of gorillas or chimpanzees. The Kazinga Channel and Murchison Falls both offer the chance of game-viewing from the water, something of which I had little experience. Unfortunately, though we visited Uganda, we were unable to find an area that could provide us with the right mix of wildlife and adventure at a single location.

In any case, we didn't want to feature only East Africa. With the abolition of apartheid, South Africa's tourist industry has blossomed and many people who five years ago might have chosen to visit Kenya or Tanzania for their safari are now packing their bags for a journey to Table Mountain and Kruger National Park. For years a bastion of Afrikanerdom, the Kruger is Africa's oldest national park. There was a time when blacks and whites were prohibited by law from sharing food or sleeping under the same roof, as I had found to my chagrin when visiting the Kruger in 1974 with Simeon Nkoane, an old friend of my family's. Nobody could have imagined then that twenty years later Nelson Mandela would lead the country towards the year 2000. As a child I had fallen under the spell of Percy Fitzpatrick's epic tale *Jock of the Bushveld*, which was set among farmland that ultimately became part of Kruger National Park. But the Kruger proved a disappointment, partly because it was so well run. The roads were tarmacked and the authorities laid speed traps and swooped down in helicopters

to enforce their regulations. Worse still, much of the game stayed safely tucked away behind the thick cover of thornbush or was viewed only at waterholes. It all seemed somewhat tame, notwithstanding the excitement of a huge bull elephant crossing the road and a pair of sleepy lions that had us craning our necks for a better view over the long grass. I felt cooped up inside a vehicle with no roof-hatch: the sights and sounds of Africa seemed too far away. One could argue, of course, that this was all in the best interests of the animals; here at least they are free to determine how closely they can be approached. But for filming the Kruger was never a consideration.

Most wildlife films take months or even years to complete, whereas our programmes had to be completed in a maximum of two weeks each, a tough assignment by anyone's standards. We weren't just looking for places that would provide wonderful images of animals for our cameras. We also wanted to show the variety of landscapes and habitats and to capture the sense of adventure by travelling by land, air and water. Tourism is destined to be the world's largest industry within the next decade, and we hoped to reveal the whole range of safari options now available to visitors as individual countries compete for their share of the tourist trade.

Wildlife-based tourism has proved to be one the most lucrative forms of generating foreign exchange and in the process of helping to fund conservation. The variety of safaris now being offered is almost endless. You can take a camel safari to savour the harsh beauty of northern Kenya, or travel by hot-air balloon in places like the Masai Mara or Serengeti; some choose to fly over the herds in a microlight at the foot of Mount Kilimanjaro in Amboseli. Why not take a scenic flight in a helicopter over the Okavango Delta or float quietly through the papyrus in a dug-out canoe? In Zimbabwe you can walk on foot among elephant and buffalo or canoe past hippo along the great Zambezi. Further north, Uganda, Zaire and Rwanda all offer the chance to hike through tropical rain forest for a glimpse of a mountain gorilla. And though many people now find the idea of hunting animals for sport distasteful, certain countries such as Tanzania and Botswana still allow overseas visitors to hunt big game under the experienced eye of a professional hunter.

The Okavango Delta in Botswana is often referred to as the Jewel of the Kalahari. It was here, in 1975, that I first had the opportunity to live among wildlife on the Liversedges' houseboat at Shakawe, in the northern part of the delta. So when it was decided to make two of the films in Botswana it was a little like coming home, and I was able to revisit one of Africa's true wilderness areas. The first of our films was to be an elephant-back safari with the American zoologist Randall Moore. He and his herd of African elephants promised to provide us with a unique view of the delta. The second film would feature predators, and would concentrate on a pack of wild dogs, one of Africa's most endangered large carnivores. I had studied wild dogs in East Africa, where numbers have been seriously diminished in recent years by diseases spread by domestic dogs. So this would be a wonderful opportunity for me to reacquaint myself with one of my favourite creatures.

*The Namib – meaning endless expanse – has been in existence for perhaps 55 million years and is one of the oldest and driest deserts in the world.*

One country that I haven't mentioned up to this point is Namibia, formerly South-West Africa. Namibia conjures up vivid images of towering sand dunes with desert-hardened gemsbok trekking across the copper-coloured mounds. I had visited Namibia in 1984 to make two wildlife documentaries with ex-park ranger and professional hunter Jan Oelofse. During my visit I had hoped to make a safari to Etosha Pan, one of Africa's most famous parks. Much of the game-viewing at Etosha is at the waterholes which attract a great variety of animals during the dry season – the best time to visit. Not only do the wildebeest and zebra, kudu and impala come to drink, but the predators stake out the waterholes as ambush sites. During the rains when water is freely available the animals have no need to trek to the waterholes and disperse far and wide to feed on the succulent grasses which spring up almost overnight, swathing the area in a green carpet speckled with a multitude of colourful flowers. But for this series we weren't just looking for locations where you could most easily view wild animals. It was always our aim to try and capture the essence of the word safari – not just a journey, but a journey full of adventure and excitement. Namibia could certainly offer that, but not at Etosha Pan. Our safari would take us from the jackass penguins and fur seals of the bleak Atlantic Ocean, deep into Kaokoland, where desert elephant and rhino eke out a living in seemingly impossible circumstances. We would use light aircraft or microlights to give us a bird's-eye view of the vast Namib Desert, travelling as far west as the Skeleton Coast, whose name derives from the many shipwrecks that bear stark testimony to man's attempts to conquer this inhospitable land. Etosha would just have to wait.

While we were wracking our brains to think of the best locations, series producer Robin Hellier suggested Madagascar. An island safari would certainly be different, and Madagascar undoubtedly had a wealth of smaller creatures for us to look at, including the world's largest variety of chameleons (some as big as a plate) and fourteen species of lemurs, which are endemic to the island. One idea was for me to explore an area in the south called Ankaramena with spectacular caves deep within an extraordinary outcrop of limestone formations where crocodiles could be seen.

But after much deliberation it was decided that we might not be able to film enough good material in the relatively short period of time allocated to each programme. Instead we went back to our original idea of including a canoeing safari at Mana Pools in Zimbabwe combined with white-water rafting along a stretch of rapids below Victoria Falls.

The working title for the TV series was *Dawn to Dusk*, as this was the timescale within which we would be telling our story. Dawn in Africa is like the moment of creation. Colours range from the deepest orange to the soft pink of ash-filled skies during the dry season. Bird song fills the air; white-browed robin chats sing with liquid voices, forest hornbills bray like donkeys, francolins cackle and doves coo – a fitting reward for dragging yourself bleary-eyed from the warmth of your tent to be sure of being on the road by 6 a.m.

Anyone who has been on safari soon adapts to the well-worn routine of dawn rises. It is essential to be among the animals by first light if you don't want to miss the best of the game-viewing (even earlier if you are really keen and can persuade the driver of your safari vehicle to take you out when most people are still snuggled up in bed). The early hours of the morning are undoubtedly the most productive time to be looking for predators, particularly the big cats – the lion, leopard and cheetah that visitors to Africa most want to see.

There is certainly some validity to the idea of 'dawn to dusk', as it very much mirrors human activity cycles or rhythms. Like our close relatives the great apes, our early ancestors on the African savannas would have awakened and become active with the dawning of each new day, huddling around the dying embers of their campfires, discussing in which direction they would choose to hunt or gather food. Darkness would have been a fearful time, alive with demons and predators of the night. Each evening, before the light had faded, the hunter-gatherers would have hurried back to the safety of their encampments or caves.

The still of the night can be an uneasy time for all primates, and certainly most human beings feel safest hidden away behind closed doors once darkness falls. Baboons retire to the security of the treetops and chimpanzees and gorillas slumber in a bed of leaves in the forest canopy, avoiding terrestrial predators who might otherwise try to kill them, venturing to the ground again only when dawn arrives once more to illuminate their world.

For humans, with limited physical strength with which to defend ourselves, the best way of avoiding being eaten is to seek safety in numbers and shun the darkness. The habit of living together in groups provides real benefits for the individual: the power of numbers is one way of counteracting the threat of predators. A single baboon is no match for a leopard, but when challenged by a mob of baboons the leopard must flee for safety or risk serious injury, even death. For humans the fear of being taken by the unseen predator has been replaced by the fear of our fellow men, who often choose the dead of night as the moment to strike. There is an uneasiness that settles across our spirit at night, filling us with irrational fears as well as bringing real ones.

Our habit of being active during daytime and sleeping at night has tended to warp our perception of how other animals live. Take the hyaena, for example – long reviled as a slovenly scavenger, the garbage collector of the animal world. Until quite recently the spotted hyaena was thought to be incapable of killing for itself, skulking around the fringes of a lion's kill in the hope of picking over the scraps once the 'king of beasts' had departed or bullying and intimidating leopard, cheetah and wild dogs over possession of their hard-earned food. It was only when scientists adopted the noctur-

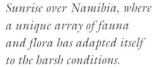

*Sunrise over Namibia, where a unique array of fauna and flora has adapted itself to the harsh conditions.*

nal ways of these much-maligned predators and observed them night and day that it became apparent that a grave injustice had been committed. Spotted hyaena are in fact the most adaptable of the larger predators, capable of foraging singly or in groups and killing animals the size of full-grown wildebeest and zebra.

The plant-eating species or herbivores must spend a far greater proportion of their time searching for food to sustain themselves than the predators with their protein-rich diet. Elephants feed for up to sixteen hours a day to gather the 140-250 kg (300-550 lb) of vegetation that they need to maintain their huge bulk. For them the time scale of dawn to dusk has little bearing and they are active intermittently day and night. An elephant's eyes are the least important of its senses, though they probably see better than many people give them credit for. They certainly don't need the kind of vision that enables a lion to recognize prey at a considerable distance, nor do they have much to fear from predators. Weighing anything from 3 to 6 tonnes, the ability to spot a predator from afar is hardly a priority for an elephant (unless the predator is in the form of a human being carrying an automatic rifle).

Though 'dawn to dusk' would be the timescale within which each film was created, we hoped to be able to reverse the format and do some photography at night during our visit to the Moremi Game Reserve in the Okavango Delta, where we intended filming the pack of wild dogs at their den. Wild dogs are often active on moonlit nights, which we hoped would allow us to follow them when they hunted. But in the end things didn't work out quite the way we had expected.

# BOTSWANA: ELEPHANT-BACK SAFARI

*Of all African animals, the elephant is the most difficult for man to live with;*
*yet its passing – if this must come – seems the most tragic of all . . . There is*
*mystery behind that masked grey visage, an ancient life force, delicate and*
*mighty, awesome and enchanted, commanding the silence ordinarily reserved for*
*mountain peaks, great fires, and the sea.*
**Peter Matthiessen, *African Silences***

Elephants are among the best loved and most familiar of all the earth's animals. They are creatures of our childhood, stars of the circus and lovable giants of the zoo. In a world which for many people is detached from nature, where the sound of bird song is a rare event, elephants still retain their noble aura. They are goliaths among living things – unworldly, prehistoric of shape but sharp of mind, with the longest childhood of any animal except man. The largest of all the land mammals, dwarfing the hippo and rhino, they are an echo of the time when dinosaurs roamed the planet. To see a herd of elephants emerging from the dust of the African plains is to watch a mighty phalanx moving silently towards the ends of the earth.

I could see the elephant browsing deep within the forest; grey shapes merging with the shadows. We edged closer. 'Come here, Kathy – Kathy, come here.' Joseph, the African mahout, spoke the words gently, but insistently. I knew from the tone of his voice that a long-established rapport existed between him and the fully grown cow elephant standing barely 15 metres (50 ft) away. I held my breath. At first Kathy ignored us and continued feeding. Then suddenly and without a sound she turned towards us. I couldn't believe how quickly she covered the ground, although she was still only walking. For a moment I wasn't sure that she would stop. She was right in front of me, towering over us. I could smell the pleasant, earthy, elephant odour, count every long eyelash fringing her extraordinary brown eyes. Kathy sniffed Joseph with her trunk, prompting him to reach into the canvas bag that every mahout carries around his waist and pull out a handful of horse cubes, which he poured down her outstretched trunk – as if he were giving sweets to a child. 'Good girl, Kathy, good girl.' Kathy rumbled with satisfaction. The two of them stood there for a moment – man and elephant – each speaking to the other in their own language, yet both understanding. Then Kathy turned and walked quietly away from us to continue feeding.

'Come here' was just one of the commands that I would hear spoken over and over again during the next few days, together with 'Stretch down', 'Move back' and 'Trunk up'. That first glimpse of Randall Moore's elephants told me that this was going to be one of the most memorable experiences of my life.

When I was told that we were going to make a film about elephant-back safaris in Botswana's Okavango Delta, I couldn't help wondering if it was all just a high-priced gimmick, a novel way an enterprising individual had found to make a quick buck. I wasn't sure what to expect – I had heard some people refer condescendingly to Abu's Camp as Randall Moore's elephant circus. But the mere thought of an African elephant allowing anyone to ride on its back filled me with wonder. Wasn't the African elephant supposed to be impossible to domesticate?

Suddenly I was transported back to my childhood: the annual Christmas visit to Olympia in London to see Bertram Mills's circus had been a part of my life. It was only much later that I began to question the morality of keeping animals in captivity and forcing them to perform for a human audience. How I loved the circus. My sister and I would sit totally en-

*The mahouts supervise the elephant's drinking – Abu is the big tusker in the centre of the picture.*

grossed in the glamorous, make-believe world of the big top. The smell of fresh sawdust, popcorn and toffee apples, bright lights and the big band playing. The death-defying skills of the high-wire act and the trapeze artists, the bravery of the animal trainers, the marvellous skill with which they controlled the lions, tigers, leopards and bears – all larger than life – right there, in the flesh. But it was the elephants that I loved best as they deftly picked objects up in their trunks or paraded around the ring – sheer size matched by incredible gentleness.

What I didn't realize until much later was that all of these circus elephants were Asian elephants, instantly recognizable (once you knew what to look for) by their smaller ears and humped back, and the single lip at the tip of their trunk. African elephants are much larger – and more aggressive – with huge ears and a sway back.

Even today it is still widely believed that the African elephant is far too big and aggressive to be domesticated, and that they are difficult to tame fully. In circuses and modern zoos, handlers are especially wary of sudden changes in mood in even the most submissive females. But the truth of the matter is that African elephants have been used by man for almost as long as their Asian cousins.

The Asian elephant (*Elephas maximus*) takes readily to captivity and training, and has been used for at least 5,000 years, both in war and as a beast of burden. It seems likely that it was initially domesticated for its prowess in warfare and for tiger hunts, as well as being the prestigious mount of chiefs. In China elephant were tamed for transport and military purposes as far back as the second millennium BC, and they were in continuous use throughout the Ming and Manchu dynasties – that is, until the early part of the twentieth century.

All over Asia, wherever they were found, elephant provided the backbone of the timber industry. In some areas they found service ploughing farmland and pounding rice. They are the jungle's perfect four-wheel-drive vehicle – though they seldom work more than six hours a day, and require substantial amounts of food, upkeep and care, they rarely break down.

The Asian elephant is still found in parts of Bangladesh, Bhutan, Burma, Cambodia, China, India, Indonesia, Laos, Malaysia, Nepal, Sri Lanka, Thailand and Vietnam. But suitable habitat has shrunk to an area of less than 500,000 square km (200,000 square miles), and that is disappearing at a rate of 4,000 square km (1,500 square miles) a year. In the eighteenth century Thailand had 200,000 working elephant, half of them in military service. Today there are only 5,000 at work in the whole country – mainly in the forestry service, but a few are still used by the army for ceremonial occasions. Loss of natural habitat and traditional migration routes has meant that wild elephant in both Africa and Asia are increasingly coming into contact with humans. The mushrooming human population – the majority of whom depend on subsistence farming – would be happy to see elephant eradicated to protect their crops. Both continents will be hard pressed to preserve their surviving elephant in the face of the human population explosion that threatens to overwhelm them.

Elephant from the northern parts of Africa were used in war in North Africa in classical times – most famously by Hannibal when he took them across the Alps during the war between his native Carthage (a city in what is now Tunisia) and Rome. The North African elephant were said to be no match for big Indian bulls that were highly trained for warfare. Nevertheless, the might of a party of war elephant must have been a terrifying sight for the most battle-hardened adversary. For those who had never seen an elephant, let alone been charged by one, they were a potent psychological weapon.

After Hannibal, nothing much was heard about domesticating African elephant for almost 2,000 years. Then during colonial times King Leopold II of Belgium became obsessed with the idea of using the African elephant in the manner of its Asiatic cousin. He sponsored an ambitious attempt to trek from the coast of East Africa to what was then the Congo Free State (now Zaire) involving four Indian elephant and 600 porters. But disease and the arduous nature of the journey took their toll on man and beast, and the effort failed. However, Leopold later succeeded in establishing an elephant training centre at Api, in a remote corner of north-eastern Zaire, near its border with Sudan. By 1925 there were over fifty African elephant at Api, trained largely by Ceylonese (Sri Lankan) mahouts. In 1927 the centre moved to the edge of Parc National de Garamba.

For thirty years, elephant numbers at Garamba fluctuated between fifty and a hundred. The elephant were employed in agricultural and timber operations. Self-replacing, needing no spare parts, independent of fuel requirements, they proved the perfect solution in an area thousands of kilometres from the sea, with appalling roads and only limited and unreliable river transport.

But by the time independence came in 1960, only fifteen elephant were left, and during the Simba rebellion that followed independence the area around Garamba was overrun by rebels. The *cornacs* (mahouts) took what elephant they could into the forests, where they remained in hiding until the rebel armies had been defeated. Only four of the original herd remain – Lwiru, Kukutu, Kiko and Zombe. The first three were captured as calves while Zombe was bred in captivity; their average age is about forty. A rehabilitation project for Garamba has been in effect since the early 1980s, funded by the World Wide Fund for Nature and the Frankfurt Zoological Society, to

*Opposite: The view across the Okavango from Abu's Camp. David Livingstone was the first European to report the existence of this great expanse of inland water, having journeyed across the Kalahari in 1849.*

try and encourage tourists to visit the park, the only place in Africa where the northern white rhino survives in the wild.

But the elephants at Garamba were working with mahouts whom they knew and who knew them. Now I was about to meet a man who had trained African elephants to carry complete strangers on safari.

At the outset I didn't know quite what to make of Randall Moore. First impressions can so often be misleading. He certainly didn't fit easily into the cliché of the passionate conservationist dedicating his life to 'saving' a species; nor did he come across as someone who loved animals more than people. With his long dark hair pulled back in a pony-tail, thick moustache and a Havana cigar clamped between his teeth, Randall had the air of a showman combined with the strong features and brooding good looks of a fashion model. He readily admits that his heritage – an Italian mother and a Irish father – could well explain his mixture of fiery temper and laid-back charm. When there were no clients in camp, the Okavango's swampy reed-beds reverberated to the sounds of the Doors, Jimi Hendrix and the Grateful Dead. Here was a character right out of the Swinging Sixties if ever I had met one.

However, my uneasiness about the whole idea of elephant-back safaris was quickly dispelled when I heard the story of how Randall became involved with elephants. His book *Back to Africa*, which I read at every spare moment while we were at Abu's Camp, races along like a first-rate adventure novel, except that this story is true. It is a gripping account of courage and adversity, of someone looking for a foothold in life, something to anchor themselves. For Randall the answer turned out to be elephants.

Randall was twenty years old and going nowhere when a chance meeting with animal trainers Morgan Berry and Eloise Bercholt provided the stimulus he had been searching for. The couple presided over a menagerie of more than a hundred species of exotic creatures, including lions, tigers and bears. But it was the elephant Randall was asked to help unload from their trailer which gave a focus to his life. Randall was captivated by them – particularly by Durga, Owalla and Tshombe, the trio of young African elephant to which he was introduced that day. Looking back, Randall remembers sensing that one day he would visit Africa and that the elephant would come with him. He left his telephone number with Morgan and Eloise, begging them to employ him at Elephant Mountain, as he had christened their farm. A few days later he received a call from Eloise offering him a job. There was one condition, but Randall was too eager to work with the elephant to object. He duly cut off his waist-length hair.

That was almost twenty-five years ago. As we talked, Randall gave his pony-tail a mischievous tug, dark eyes twinkling at the memories. He had achieved something unique when he returned those three wild-born African elephant to the bush. Nobody could dispute the man's determination. He had sold the idea to an American film

*Randall Moore has twenty years' experience working with African elephants, both in the field and in captivity. He achieved something unique when he returned three wild-born African elephant (raised in the United States) to the land of their birth, a project completed in 1983. Towards the end of 1990, Randall began leading elephant-back safaris in the Okavango Delta.*

company to help pay the costs of shipping the elephant to Kenya. But a story he told me about their journey across the Atlantic helped to dispel any lingering doubts I may have had that he was in it mainly for the money.

In the course of the voyage they encountered a pod of pilot whales. Randall described the excitement of this strange meeting between the giants of land and sea:

*Long before we spotted the whales, Tshombe, Durga and Owalla had their trunks fully extended over the ship's rail, trying to identify the scent of these other strange mammals. All three were emitting excited guttural sounds and at one stage Owalla let rip with a strident trumpet blast which must have carried for miles across the ocean . . . It could have been fanciful, but I was convinced there was some form of communication between these two groups of endangered mammals . . . It was only a few minutes before the whales peeled off and disappeared beneath the waves, but it had been a moving and humbling experience.*

Initially the elephant were corralled at Taita Hills Reserve, bordering the vast Tsavo National Park, formerly the home of Kenya's largest elephant herds. Then tragedy struck. Tshombe, the male, became ill and died of salmonella, an aerobic bacteria that attacks the stomach and is invariably fatal in captive elephant. This left just the two females, Durga and Owalla, who were by now fifteen years old.

That wasn't the end of Randall's problems. After months of wrangling with the authorities he was told that he could no longer keep his elephant in Kenya. The reason: they had been born in apartheid-ruled South Africa. Fortunately, the South African authorities proved more obliging, and Randall persuaded them to provide a home for his elephant in the Pilanesberg National Park in Bophuthatswana, one of the newly 'independent' homelands. But first the elephant would have to be shipped back to America to comply with veterinary regulations. This would ensure that they had not contracted foot-and-mouth or any other contagious disease during their stay in Kenya. A year later the elephant were given a clean bill of health by the US Disease Control Centre. At long last they were free to return to Africa.

For years South Africa has been in the forefront of game-ranching and utilization of its wildlife resource: management figures prominently in the country's conservation philosophy. The creation of Pilanesberg National Park is a case in point. The park is situated in the crater of an extinct volcano, and in earlier times it teemed with wild animals. But then the hunters arrived, and the farmers with their fences, and the wildlife dwindled.

In 1970 the Bophuthatswana government agreed to redevelop the area as a game reserve. Covering an area of 200 square km (78 square miles), it has become a veritable Noah's Ark, with more than 6,000 animals recruited from parks and game ranches all over South Africa and Namibia, including black and white rhino, hippo, buffalo, giraffe, cheetah and a variety of plains game – all of which had at one time inhabited the region.

In 1979 five young elephant were introduced from Addo National Park in Natal, the first elephant to roam this area for 150 years. Only one of the five survived – three died and the fourth was returned to Addo after escaping and killing a farmer. The fifth elephant shunned the company of more recent arrivals introduced to Pilanesberg in August 1981 – eighteen calves spared from culls in Kruger National Park.

The Pilanesberg babies were a pathetic sight to behold. Without the security of older, more experienced elephant to lead and protect them, they found it hard to adapt to their new surroundings. Three had died in the holding pens prior to release into the park. The survivors wandered off, keeping well out of the way of people, and were rarely seen.

Then came Randall and his elephant. For the first week Owalla and Durga where kept at a *boma* (fenced enclosure) where they were fed on hay and could sleep in safety. During the second week Randall rode Owalla into the park with Durga following behind. After many adventures and close encounters with rhino and buffalo he decided it was time to let the two cows wander off by themselves. He felt confident that they would be safe and able to find sufficient food.

It wasn't long before Durga and Owalla made contact with some of the orphans. By November 1983 – a year after they were released into the park – they were reported in excellent health and had adopted all fourteen of the Kruger babies. By reintroducing the two cows to Pilanesberg, Randall had not only lived out his dream of returning them to the wild, he had provided the adult elephant so vital for the future prosperity of the young Kruger orphans. With Owalla as their matriarch the calves had integrated into a proper herd. Without Randall's help life would have been very different for all the elephant.

Now Randall was the owner of a lucrative safari business based around a group of thirteen elephant. The glossy brochures and posters promoting his elephant-back safaris perfectly captured an impossible dream – vignettes of a Garden of Eden in which man is both protector and manipulator. In the new age of wildlife utilization, Randall had trumped them all.

Until Randall Moore came into their lives none of his elephant had much of a future – only one of captivity in a foreign land. Now they had the chance of a life back in the wilds of the Okavango Delta. As part of a man-made herd, certainly, but it was freedom of a sort.

Despite their obvious 'elephantness', Randall's elephant were as individual in their temperaments as the men who rode them. While there is little to be gained by comparing elephant to humans, they can certainly be described in similar words. Some were adventurous, natural leaders; others were shy; some were more intelligent than others, judged by the yardstick of how difficult or easy it was to train them to do something. And some were more aggressive, quick to respond to a challenge, real or perceived.

Bibi, the old cow elephant with the broken tusk, was a no-nonsense character: take her for granted and she was liable to knock you flying with a dismissive flick of her trunk. She had languished for years in a zoo in Sri Lanka, and even though Randall knew that she would have to be watched carefully, he decided to buy her, hiring the two Sri Lankan mahouts who looked after her and bringing all three of them back to Africa. The other adult female was a twenty-five-year-old Ugandan elephant called Kathy, whom Randall had acquired from a safari park near Toronto. Kathy was gentle and well-behaved, and had taken easily to training.

The largest of the bulls, Benny, was instantly recognizable by his floppy right ear, which had been damaged during his fifteen years in captivity at a zoo in Texas, and now fell limply forwards across his face. Benny had endured a miserable life enclosed in a tiny cage before Randall intervened and brought him back to Africa. Alone and

frustrated, Benny had continually rubbed his tusks against the wall of his cage, breaking one and causing the other to become infected. Randall felt so sorry for Benny that he offered to buy him from the zoo and in the end they let him go for nothing. Benny was still a very shy, nervous individual; Randall warned us to be careful with him and only approach him when the mahouts were in attendance. It wasn't that Benny meant anybody any harm – just that if he was frightened or alarmed he might panic and in the process hurt someone.

The other flop-eared elephant was Nyakanyaka. Both he and Mthando Bomvu had been brought from the wilds of Zimbabwe. Randall felt sure that the two elephant had been trained at some time in their life – probably as youngsters. One of the mahouts had been overly rough with Nyakanyaka and had damaged his ear cartilage, causing it to flop over. The elephant had lost a lot of weight, but was beginning to pick up again.

And then there was Abu, the big bull after whom the camp was named. Buoyed by the success of releasing Owalla and Durga back into the wild, Randall had brought Abu, Kathy and Benny to Africa to star in a film about the elephant of the Knysna Forest in South Africa, based on Dalene Matthee's book *Circles in a Forest*. Up until then Abu had been languishing at a small park in America where he was employed to give rides to children. One day he made a bid for freedom and tried to run away. As a result he was branded as dangerous and left for weeks on end locked up in a barn. Randall was horrified at Abu's condition. He had met the bull a few years earlier and remembered him for his even temperament. Now Abu's face was caked with dung through lying in his own faeces, and large callouses had formed over his temporal glands and become infected. Far from being in 'musth' – the somewhat mysterious condition of adult bulls when they display increased aggression and heightened sexual activity – as his owners had thought, what Abu needed more than anything else was a good bath and some proper care and affection. Randall immediately bought him.

The filming of *Circles in a Forest* was a great success and Abu in particular gave a remarkable performance. From his experiences with the company that filmed his own story, Randall was well aware that people in the film business – particularly those making feature films – were prepared to pay handsomely for the chance of employing the talents of elephant such as Abu. Abu was a star – stunt artist and character actor rolled into one – with the rest of the herd as highly willing extras. Abu could perform on command. He could shake his head and flap his enormous ears, he could charge as convincingly as if he were genuinely being challenged in the wild, scooping a person up with his tusks and curling his trunk around their midriff, hoisting them skywards as deftly as a man lifting a bale of hay with a pitchfork. Abu could play the part of a circus elephant as easily as that of a wild bull. When he broke his magnificent ivory tusks, Randall had a new pair made to measure and cast in life-like plastic: they fitted perfectly over the stumps of Abu's own tusks.

Eventually Randall was given permission to move the elephant to Botswana and the elephant-back safaris began. The elephant slept in a clearing at the edge of camp, a 3

*Bibi giving herself a bath. In the wild, elephant follow a daily routine of feeding, drinking, resting, mud-wallowing, dust-bathing and more feeding. They not only drink large quantities of water, they also use it to keep cool, by showering themselves with trunkfuls of it. Where possible they complete the routine by blowing dust over themselves.*

*Abu stands 2.7 metres (nearly 9 ft) at the shoulder, weighs 5 tonnes, and used to sport 1.2 metre (4 ft) perfectly matched tusks...until they were broken after the making of the film* Lost in Africa. *A Hollywood special-effects man made Abu a replacement set of plastic tusks, which fit perfectly over his broken stumps. Abu's own tusks will grow back at the rate of about 7.5-12.5 cm (3-5 inches) a year.*

metre (10 ft) high wall of mopane branches ringing their sleeping quarters. Here each night the elephant were fed and the seven youngsters were given a brief training routine before retiring. Meanwhile the mahouts inspected the adults, checking for any signs of cuts and scratches. If a wound was discovered, it was treated with antibiotic powder or ointment. The massive ears were scrutinized with particular care to ensure that the bull hooks used to guide the elephant were not damaging the skin.

*An elephant-back safari lasts for five days and one of the highlights is travelling along the narrow channels of the Okavango Delta in a mokoro – the traditional flat-bottomed dug-out canoe used by the local people to navigate a way through the long reeds and papyrus. Sitting at water level with the elephants towering over you is the perfect way to appreciate their size, and a comfortable alternative to sitting on their backs.*

Business is thriving for Randall, even though the price of leasing a wildlife concession in Botswana has skyrocketed. For many years rich deposits of industrial diamonds provided the backbone of the country's economy. Though tourism generated a steady income for privately run safari companies, the government failed to see the long-term importance of wildlife tourism both to the economy and to conservation. In the past, large areas of wilderness were leased to hunters and safari operators at knock-down prices. Now things are changing.

To help pay the concession fees Randall has sub-let parts of his concession area to other people offering a variety of safari-based activities, each with its own camp and area of operation. Visitors looking for something a little more exciting can combine game-viewing from four-wheel-drive vehicles with a horse-riding safari, and for £1,000 a day you can hunt big game under the watchful tutelage of a professional hunter. Each hunting concession has to provide a special camp for citizen hunters, catering for the local Botswanan people who are entitled to hunt certain species of game on payment of a licence fee. And if an elephant-back safari isn't to your liking, you can always view the Okavango Delta from a helicopter based at an exclusive family-sized camp. Equally exciting is to travel in a *mokoro* – the traditional flat-bottomed, dug-out canoe used by the local people to navigate through the narrow channels that spread like a cobweb through the long reeds and papyrus of the delta. A mokoro is low to the surface of the water, so when the elephant pass by it feels as if a giant army were ploughing through the water alongside you, huge feet rising and falling in unison, the water glinting in the sunlight as it cascades off their wrinkled skin.

Having spent twenty years watching elephant in the Masai Mara in Kenya, I had begun to feel that I knew quite a lot about them. But getting to know Abu and his companions provided me with a far richer and more intimate experience than I could possibly have hoped for. Until now most of my encounters with elephant had been made from the safety of my Toyota Landcruiser. There were times when I could have reached out and touched these huge, gentle animals as they passed silently alongside my vehicle, and once in a while one of the cows would stretch out her trunk towards my open window to catch my scent, before shaking her great head from side to side, ears flapping with the sound of someone slapping a pair of Wellington boots together. There was always something of interest happening: the small calves, pink and hairy, hugging the underside of their mother's belly while struggling to figure out what a trunk was all about; the young bulls suddenly erupting with wild screams or trumpeting at the tops of their voices; blustery youngsters beginning to exercise their awakening power. But until now I had never really spent time getting to know elephants as individuals.

*Little Miss B, the youngest elephant at Abu's Camp. In the absence of her own mother she is bonded with Bibi, the oldest of the females.*

The core of elephant society is a group of related females and their offspring. These family units number from five to twenty individuals, and it is usually possible to pick out the lead cow within each group. The matriarch, as she is known, is always the oldest member of the family, and because an elephant continues to grow throughout its lifetime, she is usually the biggest of the cows. These old females are extraordinary creatures, embodying the wisdom of an ancient sage with the bravery of a gladiator if they feel their family is threatened.

If the decline in numbers of Asian elephant is largely due to pressure on their living space, the tusks carried by both sexes of African elephant have caused vast numbers of them to be slaughtered. (Only male Asian elephant have tusks, and they tend not to be so magnificent.) The people of Africa have always seen the elephant as being more valuable dead than alive – a monumental provider of meat, with the hide used to fashion armour, the hair from their tails for bracelets and the ivory for carvings, jewellery and above all export. The whole of the elephant's head could be stuffed and mounted on a wall, the ears turned into coffee tables or drums, the feet into stools or umbrella stands; the hides might be used for leather, breastplates and now cowboy boots.

But above all it is the elephant's ivory which has brought about its downfall. For as long as man has been associated with elephant he has used their ivory. The demand has always come almost entirely from non-African countries, much of it from China and Japan. For centuries Arab sultans from Zanzibar to Oman channelled the flow of ivory and slaves used to transport it from the heart of Africa. Now the trade is organized through large-scale networks. It is ironic that Africa itself has had very little use for ivory.

Africa's elephant population is estimated to have plummeted from 1.3 million in 1979 to 609,000 in 1989. But the true number of survivors can only be guessed at – a species that is dispersed across a third of Africa, with 40 per cent of them being forest-dwellers which are almost impossible to see from the air, is difficult to count accurately. Poaching has undoubtedly accounted for the great majority of losses.

In recent times the elephant has crystallized conservation issues. In 1989 the Convention on International Trade in Endangered Species (CITES) imposed a total ban on ivory trading. When the ban was reviewed by CITES during its biennial meeting in Japan, Zimbabwe and five other southern African countries – Botswana, Namibia, Malawi, South Africa and Zambia – lobbied hard for a partial relaxation, to allow a strictly controlled trade in ivory. Their argument was that revenue from legally obtained ivory – from elephant that had died of natural causes or from culls of managed populations – had long been a major source of revenue for their conservation policies. But the fear is that such a proposal would simply provide a new incentive to the poaching gangs which the ban has so effectively thwarted. This is borne out by the fact that the possibility of a relaxation of the ban caused the price of ivory on the black market to soar. How is anyone going to ensure that poached ivory doesn't infiltrate the system?

Nowadays more and more people take the view that wildlife must pay its way if it is to survive. 'Sustainable utilization' and 'consumptive use of wildlife' are the words on every-one's lips. For years South Africa and Zimbabwe have in effect farmed their elephant on a sustainable basis to reduce the pressure on the vegetation, utilizing not only the tusks but also the meat and hides from culled animals. Kenya has so far resisted this option and is a leading advocate of the ivory trade ban.

Part of the reason for this is that during the 1970s and '80s poaching decimated elephant and rhino populations in East and Central Africa – unwittingly alleviating pressure on the habitat – while in Botswana, Zimbabwe and South Africa elephant numbers multiplied inside national parks and reserves to the point where they began to destroy their environment, and that of some of the other animals too. Elephant's method of feeding can certainly be destructive – they strip the bark from branches, gouge great holes in the trunk, and sometimes push the whole tree over to get at the foliage. In the old days, when there was plenty of room for elephant and people, the elephant were able to roam widely, seeking new sources of food and allowing areas to recover as part of the normal cycle of change in an ecosystem. But that is no longer possible, and Zimbabwe, for example,  has for a number of years culled elephant in Hwange National Park on an annual basis to reduce the pressure on the vegetation and to try to maintain the status quo.

Though culling is a less emotive word than killing, no one who has witnessed the slaughter of a family of elephant will ever forget it. A team of men with high-powered automatic weapons kill the animals with a well-aimed shot to the head. It is a terrible sight to see such a huge creature collapse so suddenly and emphatically into a quiver-ing heap of flesh. But those involved see it as a necessity and prefer not to dwell on the emotional issues.  After all, they say, no slaughterhouse is a pretty sight.

It was an eerie feeling to approach quietly and watch the elephant at first light. The mahouts would be busy getting them ready before the clients arrived for the early morning ride. Soft rays of light filtered through the leaves, casting a golden glow around the place where the elephant stood waiting, their feet anchored by chains.

Bibi was always kept at one end of the clearing, where she was joined by Little Miss B, to keep the youngster out of trouble. Little Miss B was bonded to Bibi and these two elephant – the oldest and the youngest of Randall's troop – were the charges of the Sri Lankan mahout Gunasena. There was a picture in my tent of the other Sri Lankan mahout, Sumandasa, long dark hair flowing, balanced on Bibi's outstretched foreleg. The Sri Lankans used this method to mount Bibi. At the given command the elephant would raise and straighten her foreleg, allowing her mahout to climb ceremoniously up to her neck and then straddle her. It was a wonderful sight.

The first thing you must do if you are going to ride an elephant is to climb on board. At the command of 'Stretch down', the elephant kneels on its back legs and

*Camp manager Sandor Carter prepares Abu for the early-morning ride.*

rests with its belly on the ground in a crouch position. With the mahout straddled over the elephant's neck passengers are assisted to step up on to the frame of the saddle and on to the elephant's back. The elephant then rises to its feet – a surprisingly gentle movement. But doing the splits was never one of my favourite stretching exercises, and sitting astride Abu's back vividly reminded me of that fact. The most comfortable way to travel was side-saddle, with both legs lolling over the side of the elephant – perfectly secure with the cushioned frame pressed against your chest. Alternatively, you could sit up on the back of the frame – like squatting on a low chair.

Though it may well be true that an elephant never forgets, it is essential to maintain a routine to ensure that they work properly. This was clearly illustrated one day when Randall was riding Abu. For much of the previous year Randall had been preoccupied with formulating the management plan for his concession, leaving his able assistant Sandor to lead the safaris and ride Abu. Abu was a gentle elephant, easy to handle and intelligent, but recently he had taken to 'goofing off', as Randall put it. Once Randall was up in the saddle he soon began to show signs of frustration with the elephant. For the past few months Kathy had been taking the lead and setting the pace for the rest of the herd. Abu had grown unaccustomed to leading the walks and Randall talked to him as one might a naughty child. He scolded Abu for his laziness, lecturing him about how he had been having an easy time of it. With a less experienced rider on his neck Abu had been able to take things at a more leisurely pace, just ambling along, pausing as and when he felt like it to grab a trunkful of palm fronds or pull down a branch from one of the mopane trees. There had been no need to 'jump to it' quite as quickly as when the 'boss' was in the saddle. Now Abu was having to do what he was told, and from the occasional growl of protest it was quite obvious that he didn't like it. But Randall was having none of it and after a while Abu settled down.

While I was ruminating on the nature of man's relationship with these gentle giants, particularly as to why such huge creatures should tolerate being told what to do by a mere human being, Randall suddenly asked me to take a turn at riding Abu. My mind flashed back to the time when I was four years old and tried to make friends with the wrong end of my sister's pony, which had promptly kicked me in the eye. Now I was being asked to ride an elephant. I scrambled past Randall and straddled Abu's neck. It felt a little like being placed in the turret of an army tank with the engine running and nothing to steer with. But I need not have worried – this particular elephant seemed unlikely to bolt.

Abu's massive ears enveloped my legs like a pair of customized riding chaps. I instantly felt secure. The top of his head jutted out in front of me like the flat surface of a coffee table. I reached forward to feel his skin; the insides of his ears were smooth and silky, particularly the folded edges, revealing the extensive network of blood vessels that helps elephant to keep cool. Abu stood absolutely still, waiting for instructions. It was obvious from the way the tip of his trunk kept reaching up and gently but insistently grasping for the bag of cubes resting in my lap that he knew he had a novice on board. His trunk was heavy and rubbery, like the tentacle of a giant octopus, its moistened tip reaching out to test my scent – the 'sniff test' that identified me to the elephant. I pushed Abu's trunk aside and told him to 'leave it' – that much I knew already. Coercion was all part of the routine, and if Abu behaved he would be rewarded.

There are about half a dozen basic commands that I needed to master if I wanted to ride Abu. 'Move up' meant move forward, 'Move back' meant move back, and 'Steady up' meant stop. 'Move over' meant move to the right, and was said while tapping the elephant on the left ear with the wooden shaft of the bull hook. 'Come here' meant move to the left and was reinforced by tapping the elephant's right ear. To begin with I managed to confuse Abu totally by giving the correct verbal command with the wrong hand signal. I was glad we were in the open; sitting on top of an elephant's neck as it lumbered through a patch of forest would be the last place I wanted to find myself. Careful as the elephant might be, it was my responsibility to look out for myself, pulling my legs out of the way when passing through a narrow passage among the tree trunks and avoiding low branches armed with thorns.

Sitting up there behind Abu's great head as he strode through the shallow water, I felt as if I could conquer the world. Riding an elephant certainly gives you a perfect aerial view of the surrounding countryside, although in fact an elephant's eyesight is perhaps the least important of its senses, far inferior to its sense of smell, taste and particularly hearing.

Scientists have been studying elephant in the wild for many years, revealing a whole new world of elephant behaviour. It is now known, for instance, that elephant sometimes communicate with voices that we cannot even hear. Like some marine mammals, such as pilot whales, elephant transmit low-frequency sounds that travel for 5 km (3 miles) or more, opening up a network of communication with elephant in other herds and allowing them to communicate over distances far beyond the visual range of any living creature. These infrasounds, as they are known, have a frequency beyond the hearing of the human ear. They vary according to the elephant' degree of excitement, with the higher frequency sounds being correlated with high states of excitement such as during aggressive displays. Researchers have documented some thirty different sounds used by elephant in their day-to-day activities.

There is plenty of variety to an elephant-back safari. On two out of the five days we stayed out all day, breaking off around noon for lunch at a private picnic site in the bush. Here among the shade of palm trees the elephant could spend the next two or three hours doing what they like to do best – feeding, dozing, drinking and mud-wallowing. Meanwhile clients could enjoy a long cold beer or iced fruit drink, stretch out on canvas-covered blankets for a quiet zizz or try their hand at fishing from one of the nearby pools. Lunch was a feast washed down with wine. The tablecloth, cutlery, food and drink belonged to the best safari tradition – even the wealthiest and most demanding clients would have been churlish to have found fault. And tucked away discreetly among a palm grove was a bush toilet with wooden seat. Nothing had been forgotten.

While the elephant browsed on the foliage within a patch of forest, some of the mahouts whiled away the time by huddling together beneath a leadwood tree to play cards. Others took a catnap, but there was always someone keeping a close eye on the

*Following pages: Abu feeding on palm fronds. Elephant consume about 5 per cent of their body weight daily. A 5,000 kg (11,000 lb) bull therefore needs about 250 kg (550 lb) of food per day. They are mixed feeders, taking more grass and herbs during the rains and concentrating on woody plants in the dry season.*

elephant to make sure they didn't get tangled up in the foot chains which stopped them from wandering too far away. A wild elephant must spend most of its time feeding, consuming approximately 140-250 kg (300-550 lb) of vegetation daily – around 5 per cent of its body weight. Eating is the single most important activity in an elephant's life, apart from the inevitable need to reproduce. The composition of the diet varies from one area to another, but where lush vegetation predominates grass may make up more than 80 per cent of the total.

A wild elephant can cover 50 km (30 miles) at a comfortable walking pace as it searches for food, constantly rotating round a familiar home range. Given the choice, Randall's elephant would indulge their voracious appetites for hour after hour, tearing off the spear-like leaves of the ilala palms or stripping the bark from the branches of the mopane trees. It was remarkable to see how skilfully they used their trunks, first tearing off a suitably leafy branch and then neatly stripping the leaves from the stem by pulling their trunk along the branch and collecting a handful of leaves which they carefully transferred to their mouths. They then place the branch in their mouths and methodically grind their teeth over the bark, freeing it along the length of the branch before neatly pulling the bark off, as if they were peeling a banana.

During times of drought families sometimes break down into sub-units of individual cows and their calves. By contrast, at the height of the rainy season, when pools of water are available throughout their range, elephant often gather together in large herds, following time-honoured migration routes to areas providing the best forage.

With such prodigious appetites elephant cannot afford to be bashful about their toilet habits, particularly when around 45 per cent of the food they eat ends up as waste. It is hard not to notice. Urinating with the force of a fire-hose and dropping dollops of dung the size of a volley-ball are pretty impressive by anybody's standards, and a great shudder could be felt rippling up through the elephant's body as it emptied its bladder. Elephant are very clean animals and the mahouts were constantly removing piles of droppings when the elephant were corralled back at camp.

Randall and the mahouts monitored the 'movements' of their charges carefully. When an elephant paused but did not feed or stop to test the wind, it was presumed that it needed to relieve itself. 'Is he dumping?' Randall would ask, as he tried to keep Abu moving. If he was, then words of encouragement would quickly follow. 'Gooood boy, Abu, good boy, let it out, let it all out.'

Whenever possible I tried to steal some time alone with the elephant and the mahouts in an attempt to get to know them a little better. In particular when we were in camp in the afternoon I made a point of joining the elephant for their mud bath and drink at around 2.30. Randall was well aware of what was required to keep the elephant in prime condition and a mud bath – particularly when it was hot – was much appreciated by the herd.

The elephant were led from the forest where they had been feeding, and then released from their foot chains before they entered the water. Usually they would pause

*Three of the 'brat pack' cavorting in the clear waters of the delta. Young elephants love frolicking in the water. Elephants are strong swimmers, submerging completely at times and using their trunk as a snorkel to enable them to breathe.*

for a drink, sucking up the water in their trunks and then squirting it into their mouths. Then they got down to the wonderfully messy business of plastering themselves with mud. The youngsters seemed particularly to relish this activity, rolling on their sides and covering every inch of themselves with the delicious cooling mud. They squirmed with delight, wriggling their massive backsides back and forth, at times balancing on their heads and using their tiny tusks to prise out some mud, or kicking and sploshing their feet to enlarge the hollows and make a more comfortable wallow. It wasn't just for the fun of it. Mud and water are vital ingredients in an elephant's cooling mechanism and help maintain their skin in tip-top condition, keeping the ticks and biting flies at bay. Later, as the herd trundled back to the forest to saddle up for the afternoon's ride, they often paused for a quick dust bath, blasting trunkfuls of fine powder over their backs.

The mahouts took pride in their work and were always smartly turned out in identical grey overalls. They were as different in looks and temperament as the elephant. There was Joseph with his ready smile, the most outgoing and confident of them – a natural with people and elephant. Big Joe was a giant man with one squiffy eye and a quiet, pleasant manner. He was more than a head taller than Old Bester, who carried one of the rifles – a .458 that could stop a buffalo at full charge. Bester loved to chat and had bright, twinkling eyes that you could rely on. I had complete confidence that he would stand his ground and use the gun to good effect if there was a problem. Then there was Boise, who was small and prone to moodiness. Randall rated him highly and said he was a natural with the elephant, but needed to watch out. He was almost too cocky, something that Randall knew from years of working with elephant could be dangerous.

It was hard to tell how much the mahouts actually liked the elephant. Their feelings for their charges were not the same as the great affection many people have for a dog or cat. There is something very soothing and reassuring about stroking a cat or a dog which both parties obviously find satisfying. Elephant aren't like that. You can touch them, scratch their skin, tickle their ears, pat them on the backside – and in return they may reach out their trunk to smell who you are or rumble softly at you. But for the most part they are just themselves, exuding a quiet dignity and wisdom that need no elaboration. Among their own kind they undoubtedly enjoy physical contact, whether touching with their trunks or simply leaning against one another. Greetings between elephant involve placing their trunks in each other's mouths, vocalizing with excitement and generally running about and flapping their ears.

What was evident was that the mahouts and the elephant shared an easy acceptance of one another, devoid of the more emotional outpourings that the elephant elicited from many of the visitors. The mahouts' relationship with the elephant was much more businesslike – essential if they were to sustain a safe working rapport with the animals. They were well paid by local standards, earning US$300 a month plus board and lodging, with the two senior mahouts earning $1,000 and $1,500 respectively. There was real status to their work. Anyone who had learned to ride an elephant for a living was worthy of respect in the village community.

Some of the mahouts liked to show off, hanging from Abu or Kathy's tusks and letting them lift them high above the ground. And sometimes one of them would raise his voice at an elephant, verbally dressing it down. But beneath all the bravado was a lingering fear – the very real fear that an elephant might some day exact its revenge, perhaps remembering a time when a mahout had been unnecessarily rough with the bull hook.

A bull hook could inflict serious damage in the hands of an inexperienced or angry mahout, and Randall had made sure that the spiked ends of the hooks were filed down. He also ensured that each mahout took it in turns riding different elephant, a necessary part of their training and a sensible precaution in the event of a mahout going on leave or being ill. But this meant that none of the mahouts developed the kind of relationship that the Sri Lankans, Sumandasa and Gunasena, had nurtured with old Bibi. And unlike their Sri Lankan counterparts the African mahouts were not bonded to their charges by the deep-rooted links between man and elephants which are so enshrined in eastern religion and philosophy.

Abu and Benny epitomized the grandeur that humans see in African elephants. They looked huge – they were huge – until you came face to face with a wild Botswanan bull, which was positively thuggish in comparison.

During our safari we had seen wild elephants virtually every day, both breeding herds of cows and calves and bachelor herds – temporary associations of adult bulls. One particular herd of bulls numbering some half-dozen individuals was often encountered feeding along the palm-fringed luggas bordering Warthog Plain, where we used to drive in the evenings looking for kudu and leopard. Kilo for kilo Botswanan elephants are probably the largest and heaviest of all bush elephants. They exude awesome power, their massive heads and the thickness of their trunks making them quite unlike the elephants I had seen in East Africa. Abu himself was born in South Africa, a survivor of one of the Kruger Park culls. His face was long, his body less robust in its proportions. He had been challenged by one of these wild bulls in the past in a battle to test his prowess, and he emerged with a nasty wound below one of his eyes where a tusk had been rammed into his face.

In the wild, young bulls constantly measure their strength against one another. They spar with other youngsters, jousting head to head like baby juggernauts. By the time they are fifteen years old they will have left their family unit, forced on their way by the increasing antipathy of their mother and aunts, who sometimes jab at their behinds, letting them know in no uncertain terms that it is time for them to move on. This exodus of young bulls from their natal herd helps to prevent inbreeding. They now join the ranks of bachelor society, a fluid population of bulls ranging in age from fifteen to sixty. Through the constant process of sparring and testing their strength against one another bulls organize themselves into a dominance hierarchy within each population. Though they are capable of mating when they are quite young, in general it is the musth bulls that dominate the breeding opportunities within a particular population of wild elephant, with each mature bull coming into musth at a different time during the year. This helps to prevent fights between adult bulls which might otherwise lead to serious injury or death, and ensures that any cows in oestrus are covered by the fittest members of the male population when they conceive.

I asked Randall what would happen when Abu started to come into musth. Domesticated male Asian elephant are taken out of circulation during this period to prevent them from injuring people or other elephant, whereas females work year-round unless they are pregnant. Male African elephant come into musth for the first time at around thirty years of age – Abu's age.

Randall's answer was that visitors would not be allowed to ride him. Never make the mistake of thinking of the elephant as anything other than wild animals with their own imperatives, he warned us. However much Abu and the rest of the herd had become accustomed to being around people, they must still be treated with respect. Abu would be kept apart from the herd unless any of the females was in oestrus and ready to mate.

One of Randall's biggest worries was that, due to the success of his elephant-back safaris, other safari operators were now trying the same thing. It wasn't that he resented the competition – rather, he was concerned lest others fail to maintain his high standards of safety. Training an elephant took years, and it was best to start when they were very young, like Little Miss B; nothing must be left to chance when entrusting people's lives to such enormously powerful animals. If and when someone was injured word would spread like wildfire; people would panic and the authorities might decide that it was all too dangerous. Over and over again Randall reminded both the visitors and the mahouts to pay attention to what they were doing – to be on their guard. The mahouts were ever-vigilant when people were in the vicinity of the elephant, always making sure that one of them quickly positioned himself between the client and an elephant if either of them got too close. Only when the elephant was stretched down would they call us to mount up.

If an elephant decides to attack it follows a well-established pattern. Charging forwards faster than any human being can run, it keeps its trunk curled up until it is within striking distance, before sending its victim sprawling with a whip-like blow from its trunk. Dropping to its knees, the elephant then stabs down with its tusks, using the full force of its forehead to crush its adversary. There have been lucky escapes with people hanging on to the elephant's leg or where the elephant's tusks have been so long that they prevented it from crushing its victim. People have even been picked up and hurled through the air and lived to tell the tale. But Randall was taking no chances. Both of his mentors from the early days at Elephant Mountain had been killed by elephant, despite many years of working with captive animals. Eloise Bercholt had been killed by an Asian circus elephant, when she tripped and fell in front of him in the ring. The elephant had immediately dropped to its knees and impaled her with its tusks, disembowelling her before throwing her 10 metres (33 ft) across the ring. The elephant had been in musth, and though Morgan Berry had advised Eloise not to risk using the bull for her performance she had ignored his warning. Morgan was still grieving over the death of his partner when he too was found dead, lying crushed on the ground in the barn where another Asian bull, also in musth, was housed.

When it was time to leave, I found it hard to extricate myself from the emotion of my visit to Abu's Camp. What Randall Moore had given us was an extension of the experience of wonder that I had felt as a child when I saw an elephant in the zoo or performing in a circus. For me, it was an awakening of sorts. To have stood next to Abu, reached up and touched his skin, stood beneath his tusks and realized how small and frail I was by comparison; to have become part of the herd, walking among their pillar-like legs; to have got to know something of the individual characters of these elephant – stroppy, no-nonsense Bibi, gentle Benny; to have seen the 'brat pack' of youngsters testing their strengths and weaknesses, becoming elephant – had been a deeply moving experience, and the most exciting start possible to our series of safaris.

The elephant faces a difficult future. Africa's human population is expected to double over the next two decades and the demand for land is relentless. If current trends continue there is little hope for the survival of Africa's large mammals – most of them are likely to be extinct within a century. The arguments about sustainable utilization and trade in wildlife products versus tourism and international aid as the means to protect their habitat will continue. Ultimately it will be the people of Africa who decide what happens to the wildlife. Perhaps if the African elephant can be seen as an economic asset, as it is in Asia, paying its way by working in forests or on farms as well as being a tourist attraction, then the value of its continued existence on commercial grounds, if not simply because it is an integral part of the natural order, might secure its survival.

# BOTSWANA: PAINTED WOLVES

*Throughout my life I have tried to heed the ancient call that demands contact
with nature, foregoing security for pleasure. I prefer a life of quiet, of conscious-
ness with beauty around me, a life where my scientific endeavours are enriched
by a sense of unity with the animals I study.*
**George Schaller, *Golden Shadows, Flying Hooves***

Around the campfire at Mombo Camp that night, Keith Scholey, Diana Richards and
I discussed how we were going to overcome the challenges posed by our next programme – the predators of the Moremi Game Reserve. All of us realized just how
lucky we had been with Randall Moore and his elephant. The elephant were the ideal
subjects to work with, as highly trained and co-operative as any human actors. With
Abu and his co-stars you were always assured of a second take, a rarity when filming
wildlife. All you needed to do with Randall's elephant was to give the right command
and roll cameras. The 'sync' crew (the most expensive part of the shoot) had been
with us for five days, just sufficient for our needs. But Keith was worried that this
might not be enough when we returned to the Okavango Delta in eight weeks' time.
Here at Mombo Camp we would be working with wild animals over whose behaviour
we had no control.

Our main reason for choosing to film at Mombo was the presence of a pack of wild
dogs, or hunting dogs as they are sometimes known. But if the dogs decided to hunt
and the light wasn't just right for our cameras we wouldn't be able to get them to
wait, and worse still they could all too easily disappear over the horizon and enter areas
where it would be impossible to follow them. We also hoped to focus our attention on
the other predators – lion, leopard and cheetah – none of which could be relied on to
appear on cue. Keith wisely decided to advise series producer Robin Hellier to extend
the time that the sync crew would be with us to ten days.

Everyone I spoke to about our safari to Botswana agreed that Mombo tented camp
was one of the best places to see wildlife. Mombo is located at the north-western edge
of the Moremi Game Reserve, an area that has been set aside for protection by the
indigenous people. For the past three years a pack of wild dogs known as the Mombo
Pack have chosen this area for their den site. We were told that the pack numbered

thirty-eight dogs, bringing back memories of the 'super pack' that I had watched hunting around the Aitong Plains in the Masai Mara in the 1980s. Packs of this size are rare indeed these days. It was fascinating to watch the Aitong Pack prosper over the years, growing in number from nine adults in 1985 to more than forty adults and young by 1989. But suddenly, as so often happens, the pack was struck down by disease. Epidemic diseases are known to be an important factor in the decline of wild dog populations, and distemper, anthrax and parvovirus are all known killers. But it was an outbreak of rabies in the domestic dog population that led to the demise of the Aitong Pack.

The wild dogs are the wolves of Africa, the only continent where they exist. They are similar in many ways to the dingoes of Australia and the dholes of India, both of which also hunt as a pack and disembowel their prey. Shock and loss of blood serve to kill the victim, which is eaten alive.

Like all wild canids, the dogs have been persecuted for as long as their paths have crossed with those of humans. Farmers, professional hunters, even park wardens and game rangers have been implicated in their demise, and they have been shot and poisoned throughout their range. We have never quite been able to forgive the wild dogs for their gruesome method of killing. They have been perceived as an

*It is not unusual for a pack of wild dogs to hunt twice in a day – in the early morning and late afternoon. But there are times when they seem to prefer to huddle together for warmth and wait out the chill mornings. Litter-mates often rest together, even as adults.*

abomination, and together with such creatures as hyaenas, crocodiles and vultures, wild dogs have long been characterized as a blot on the landscape, an aberration on the part of the great creator. Their hunting prowess and rapaciousness became part of folklore. People insisted that the dogs were capable of decimating whole prey populations; that a hunt was invariably successful, that once a 'target' animal was marked out there could be no escape. Only when scientists began to undertake more rigorous studies of the wild dogs' habits in the 1960s and '70s did a more balanced picture begin to emerge, refuting some of the wilder claims of years gone by, and highlighting the extraordinary social behaviour of the pack.

It was inevitable, I suppose, that I should be a little disappointed with my first visit to Mombo. The staff were friendly, the beds comfortable and the food excellent, but I had arrived with expectations built on stories told to me by professional safari guides, film-makers and visitors who had been fortunate enough to see the area during more favourable times, when the Okavango Delta receives the annual blessing of floodwaters from the Angola Highlands, to the north. But for the past two years the Okavango had been drier than usual. The local people shook their heads in despair, wondering what was happening to the time-honoured rhythms that guided their lives. There was talk of the thinning of the ozone layer, of warm ocean surges; some even said that the drought was the result of man's greed and wastefulness come to mock his technological extravagance.

Flood and drought are part of the age-old cycles that define many of Africa's greatest wildlife areas. Over countless eons the animals have adapted to a regime of intermittent scarcity and plentitude. I had experienced this for myself while trying to follow the migratory wildebeest and zebra on their annual pilgrimage through East Africa's Serengeti-Mara ecosystem. In Africa there are no guarantees as to when the rains or the floodwaters will arrive. Humans and their domestic stock can only look and wonder, incarcerated within fences, shackled to the dams and waterholes, growing thinner by the day. Meanwhile the wild herbivores continue doing what they do best – moving from place to place to harvest the vegetation at its most nutritious. But there are times when even they succumb, helping to maintain a balance between animals and plants that preserves the environment.

During the late 1980s and early 1990s southern Africa suffered the most appalling droughts, the worst in living memory. Cereal production dwindled in Zimbabwe, Lesotho, Swaziland, Malawi, Mozambique, Zambia and parts of South Africa. Some of these regions lost a larger proportion of their crops than either Ethiopia or Sudan in the devastating drought of 1985. In Zimbabwe almost half the communally owned cattle died. Hundreds of thousands of people faced starvation, as did many of the wild animals. Not a blade of grass remained. Hippo and warthog tottered about the dust-bare plains, bone thin. The stench of death was overpowering. Vultures huddled together in the tree-tops, their crops bloated with carrion. Buffalo, those fiercest of adversaries, could barely raise their heads in defiance as the lions pulled them down, eating them alive.

Mombo in May 1995 did not look very promising. The area was nothing like as rich in animal numbers as we had hoped, and predators were hard to find. The majority of the wildlife was still entrenched further north, the herbivores hugging the green-fringed islands where the best grazing was to be found, drawing the predators to them. Even those people who assured us that the floodwaters were on their way qualified their predictions by saying that the water-table was so low that when the water did arrive it would quickly disappear beneath the surface, sucked down, down, down by the insatiable thirst of the land.

If only we could be sure of finding and following the wild dogs, we would rest a little easier. Of all the larger predators, wild dogs are the most easily habituated and the least disturbed by human presence, whether on foot or in a vehicle. During our elephant-back safari one of the visitors to Abu's Camp had told us about the beautiful male leopard she had watched feeding on an impala kill stashed high up in a tree. She sounded a touch less excited when mentioning the pack of wild dogs they had seen hunting a herd of wildebeest. Apparently the visitors had found the dogs purely by chance – the only way one generally manages to find wild dogs unless a member of the pack has been radio-collared and can be followed on a daily basis using a receiver.

The other way of being sure of finding wild dogs is when they establish a den, an annual event in the life of each pack. For the past three years the Mombo Pack had denned in June, with the puppies emerging for the first time in July. It was our intention to return to Mombo during the full moon in mid-July in the hope of catching a glimpse of the dogs during the hours of darkness. It is not uncommon for wild dogs to hunt on moonlit nights, and there was always likely to be something of interest going on at the den. The interplay between the adults and puppies is a delight to watch and there would no doubt be confrontations between the wild dogs and the many spotted hyaenas found in the area. Spotted hyaenas and lions pose the greatest threat to young wild dog puppies, and both species sometimes steal a pack's kill.

Though we saw no sign of the wild dogs during our short visit, we were assured by everyone who knew the Mombo Pack that the dogs would have denned by the time we returned. Brave words, I thought to myself, having experienced first-hand the unpredictability of such events in the Mara and Serengeti, even though wild dogs do tend to synchronize their breeding activity to when prey is at its most abundant (which varies from one region to another). If the puppies failed to emerge during our two-week stay they would still provide the pack with a focus of activity – the den. So as the time to start filming drew closer we waited anxiously for news of the dogs.

*Opposite page: Wild dog puppies are dependent on an underground burrow for the first three months of their lives, after which they follow the pack on their nomadic wanderings. Though they continue to suckle for the first two months, puppies begin eating meat when they are three or four weeks old, fed with regurgitated meat brought back to the den in the stomachs of their older relatives. The adults, all of whom are related to the puppies – older brothers or sisters, cousins, aunts or uncles – maintain a close watch over them, mobbing any hyaenas or lions who come too close to the den.*

In the distance I could see the dusty town of Maun, an ugly, characterless place, with row after row of bland, tin-roofed houses, set all too neatly in a criss-cross of tired patterns on the threadbare soil. The town nestles right at the edge of wilderness, the last outpost before you enter the Okavango Delta. It is the hub of life for the safari operators and professional hunters; a resupply depot and vehicle service centre, the headquarters for air charter companies ferrying clients in and out of the delta. But despite all the conveniences, it was hard to find anyone with much good to say about Maun; living there seemed a matter more of necessity than of choice. People complained that the water made you sick, and most preferred to eat at home. The old-timers propped up the bar at the local pub and winged about how much better it used to be, when Maun's reputation for partying and philandering was legendary. The younger generation – many them were Zimbabweans and South Africans – seemed full of energy, buoyed by the challenge of making things work, regardless of the difficulties. Tourism has undergone a welcome revival throughout southern African ever since the dark cloud of apartheid was swept aside by Nelson Mandela's ascent to the presidency.

Almost as soon as we lifted into the blue aboard our four-seater charter flight to Mombo, we were back in the wild. People had been right in their predictions. The floodwaters had pushed south, fingers of reddish brown water reaching almost to Maun. There were those who said it would be on the outskirts of the town within the month; others disagreed, arguing that the floodwaters were insufficient and that they

*The dominant female generally gives birth once a year, with the average litter containing ten or twelve puppies. Groups of females emigrate from their natal pack when they are two or three years old to try and find unrelated males with whom to breed.*

*Each wild dog pack contains a dominant or alpha pair which monopolizes breeding. The alpha pair spend much of their time together, and regularly perform what is known as the 'pee ceremony'. First the female urinates or defecates; then the male cocks his leg and urinates over her scent.*

would soon vanish again. But for the moment it was as if a magician had waved his wand over the dry land. Palm trees wavered like green windmills in a desert; islands moulded in sand emerged at every turn; beneath the clear waters, termite mounds looked like yellow pimples. Here, indeed, was the Jewel of the Kalahari.

The delta was alive with animals. A solitary bull sitatunga – the shy, swamp-dwelling antelope of the Okavango – grazed among the watery vegetation alongside a half-submerged island, unconcerned by the familiar drone of yet another aircraft passing overhead. Giraffe stood motionless, stilt-legged giants with lightly patterned coats, gathering to drink from the reddish waters. Herds of wildebeest and zebra grazed on the proceeds of the flood, while buffalo – black and brooding, less hump-backed than the wildebeest – gathered in herds 200 strong. And every so often a solitary elephant would stride into view, ambling past thickets of dead trees, as it headed for water.

The flight to Mombo took less than an hour. We were met at the airstrip by our guides from Wilderness Safaris (who own Mombo Camp), Alan Wolfromm and Ian Mitchener. Alan looked as if he had stepped straight out of the Australian outback with his wiry black beard and lean, weather-beaten features. He wore a crumpled black hat that must have seen a thousand safaris. There was mischief in his smile, and he would keep us amused throughout our safari. He was a keen ornithologist who really knew his birds, and whenever the vehicle faltered he could fix that too. Ian wore his long brown hair in a pony-tail, and had an open, friendly manner.

Introductions complete, I asked for news of the wild dogs. Ian told us that the dominant female in the Mombo Pack had disappeared, though no one knew when or how; perhaps she had been killed by a lion or had succumbed to disease. The pack had denned a few weeks before our arrival – there were thirty-eight adults and yearlings. Four of the females were pregnant, including the new dominant female. Shortly after-wards, one of the subordinate females had given birth to puppies, but these had either been killed by the dominant female or died of natural causes. The pack then split, with the mother of the dead puppies leaving the area accompanied by fourteen of the other dogs. The main pack now numbered twenty-three dogs, and I was relieved to hear from Ian that he had seen the dominant female transferring one of her own puppies to a new part of the den. So there definitely were puppies. We decided to visit the den later that afternoon.

By the time we arrived the wild dogs had already departed to hunt. The den was located in a broad clearing among a ribbon of woodland. The dominant female had selected the same burrow that the pack had used the previous year, a darkened tunnel beneath the arches of a massive fallen tree which rose from the ground like some der-elict castle. Alan and Ian pointed out the position of two other burrows occupied by subordinate females. One was right next to the vehicle track and both were far less suitable than the place chosen by the dominant female.

The distinctive spoor of wild dog was imprinted everywhere we looked. We sat for a while, watching the hooded vultures scuffing about among the dusty soil. This species is a familiar sight around wild dog dens, congregating in small parties to feed on the scraps of meat regurgitated for the dominant female and her puppies, as well as feast-ing on the dogs' droppings. In this way the vultures help to keep the den site clean and reduce the number of flies. Hooded vultures are similar in size to Egyptian vultures, sharing the bottom rung in the vulture 'pecking order'. Both species have relatively weak bills and are unable to compete effectively with the more powerful grif-fon and lappet-faced vultures which are armed with powerful bills and feet, and can dominate at a carcass by their size and sheer force of numbers. In such circumstances the hooded vultures are reduced to the status of bystanders, inhabiting the fringes and picking up the scraps missed by the other species. But here at the wild dog den they could find food without having to compete with their larger relatives.

Though there is only a single species of wild dog in Africa, there is some variation among populations. Southern African dogs are said to be larger on average than their East African counterparts, and have more white in their coat markings, making them look paler in colour. The two populations have been geographically isolated for long enough to be genetically different and to have adapted to local conditions, and in par-ticular to the various diseases to which they have been exposed. It is for this reason that biologists have been resistant to the idea of introducing dogs from southern

*Overleaf: The Mombo Pack setting out on their morning hunt. A crocodile might lurk in the shallow pool they are about to cross, so they treat it warily.*

Africa to repopulate areas in East Africa, where numbers have been depleted. As most of the wild dogs held captive in zoos and safari parks around the world are from southern Africa, they would not be suitable for introduction into East African parks and reserves. Arguments still rage among the experts as to how best to help this endangered species to survive.

Later that afternoon we drove to the edge of the plains, following the hooded vultures which had suddenly taken to the sky. Over the two-way radio in Alan's vehicle, one of the drivers from camp reported that he had found the dogs. The pack was on the move and headed for the flood-plains. We hurried to catch up with them.

People often express surprise when they first see a wild dog. They are certainly extraordinary-looking creatures, with outlandish bat-ears and a tussled, rather scruffy blotched coat of black, yellow and white. They look almost frail, with their skinny marathon-runner legs, but they can move as fast as a greyhound, white-tipped tails flowing behind them as they gallop along, and they will menace a spotted hyaena twice their size, ripping at its backside with their razor-sharp teeth.

The dogs emerged from a thicket, backlit against the golden grass, trotting along in twos and threes. Some came over to the car and sniffed around the front bumper, bobbing their heads, bold and curious, quite fearless. Despite their reputation as ruthless killers, wild dogs are far more social than Africa's other large predators. There is nearly always something happening, from the frenzied greeting ceremonies

pack members before going off to hunt, to the ganging up on some luckless spotted hyaena caught alone and in the open. Co-operation is the key to the dogs' survival. Individuals must work together for a hunt to be successful, and when there are young puppies each pack member must help provide them with regurgitated meat. A wild dog cannot survive on its own for long.

The Mombo Pack regrouped, pausing to look around them. The sudden appearance of a small herd of wildebeest provoked an immediate response. The dogs stopped and stared as one, ears twitching with anticipation. Some unspoken command moved them forwards in unison, a new purposefulness to their stride. They advanced with ears back, necks stretched out, in the rather stiff-legged approach that I had seen so often in the Mara and Serengeti when watching a pack closing with its prey. This creates an element of surprise, buying time before the prey realizes what is happening; the dogs bound forwards only as their quarry turns to run.

The sheer speed of the dogs never fails to draw gasps of admiration as they wind up the pace – 30, 40, 60 kph (20, 25, 40 mph) – racing like the wind. Not as fast as a cheetah, but able to maintain their speed for far longer and deadly effective in extended pursuit of impala, reedbuck and gazelle.

The wildebeest raced away, kicking up dust into the faces of the dogs, milling around, then stopping, bunching in a tight knot of animals, the sun skimming the horizon, red as blood behind them. The dogs nipped at the wildebeest's heels, keeping them moving, darting in and out between the crush of legs, searching for a calf; but there was none. Reluctantly the pack moved on. There would be other wildebeest.

Some of the yearlings tarried a while, not yet ready to abandon their quarry, revealing their inexperience. The adult dogs knew when to continue a pursuit and when to give up. Perhaps the younger dogs were simply enjoying the excitement of it all. One big bull broke away, forsaking the security of the herd. He crested the rise, his head held high, nostrils flared, black mane rising stiffly in the wind. A dog challenged him,

*Red lechwe fleeing from wild dogs. Red lechwe are highly gregarious and similar in appearance to the Uganda cob, but are somewhat bigger and shaggier, with plumper hind quarters and longer horns. Along with impala and reedbuck, they are an important prey species for wild dogs in the Okavango Delta.*

testing for any sign of weakness. Neither dog nor wildebeest was prepared to give way; neither looked intimidated. At last the young dog turned and trotted way, breaking into an easy loping stride as the rest of the pack merged with the distance. Suddenly they were off again – this time chasing in three different directions as a party of reedbuck scattered ahead of them, bounding high through the long grass, showing a surprising turn of speed.

A pack of this size, numbering more than twenty individuals, allowed the dogs to adapt their hunting strategy to different types of prey. When hunting large herds of lechwe (a common antelope in the delta, related to the waterbuck) or impala they would pursue two, three or even four animals at the same time. Not uncommonly this led to multiple kills – so long as there were enough dogs to pull the prey down once it was exhausted. But occasionally during such chases a dog would find itself isolated from the rest of the pack as it closed on its victim. Without other dogs to help anchor the prey and pull it apart a lone dog may find it impossible to make the kill and begin feeding – unlike members of the cat family, which generally hunt on their own and by necessity use a single killing bite, strangling or suffocating their prey while holding it firmly with their retractable claws. This enables them to overpower their prey single-handed and begin feeding without relying on the help of others. But pack-hunting animals like wild dogs and hyaena simply pull their victim apart – killing it in the process of eating, as ruthlessly effective as the solitary killers. Larger prey such as adult wildebeest and zebra need the co-operation of all the dogs, if a hunt is to be successful. Earlier in the evening the Mombo Pack had half-heartedly harassed a family of zebra. Invariably it was the yearling dogs who took such attempts most seriously. But with no adults in the pack experienced in catching such dangerous prey, which involves one of the male dogs leaping up and grabbing the zebra by its upper lip to help immobilize it, they had little chance of success.

It was the golden hour: the colours of Africa suffused with a warm glow, dusty back light picking out the distinctive bat-eared shapes of the dogs as they came through the spiky fronds of the palm thickets. Gold turned to soft-tinted orange, then a deeper red. The pack gathered up once again, regrouping along the water's edge where red lechwe stood watching, ready to run for their lives the moment the dogs moved towards them. Suddenly there was a great crashing from the thickets as a female reedbuck burst into the open, pursued by one of the dogs. Her only hope of escape lay in the water. The pack closed in behind her, with one dog running fast and wide across dry land to cut her off. She bounded through the water, spray flying high into the air, half a dozen dogs hard on her heels as others stood and watched. The reedbuck reached a spit of dry ground almost at the same moment as the lead dog. The two animals collided in a blur of bodies. Before the reedbuck could escape, the dog fastened its jaws around her hind leg and yanked her to her knees. The rest of the pack were there in an instant.

The reedbuck disappeared beneath a scrum of dogs, all pulling and wrenching, thrusting their faces into the carcass, tearing out chunks of meat and bolting them down. This is how pack members compete with one another for food; there is little time for squabbling – no biting, just eating. Within minutes there was nothing left except skin and bones. This was the dogs at their most efficient, their prey surprised among cover and cut down in a chase lasting less than a minute. Every so often a dog looked up, bat ears boldly outlined against the sky, the shapes of the palm trees reflected in the water. The sun was gone, the moon rising fast in its wake, casting an eerie light across the flood-plains; the rawness and beauty of Africa mirrored in the shallow waters of the Okavango Delta.

I thought about the kill. It had been so perfunctory. There was no cruelty – just the wild dogs doing what they must to gain a meal. Surely this was not something to be condemned. Surely they deserved better treatment than they had received in the past.

As we drove back to camp we were elated. We could not have hoped for a better start to our safari. Our biggest worry was over – the Mombo Pack had established a den, so we would be able to keep track of their movements. Added to this, there were at least two prides of lions with young cubs for us to watch. And on our way to the wild dog den we had seen three cheetahs – a female with two cubs as large as herself, almost ready to strike out on their own. A second group of three male cheetahs had also been seen hunting in the area, and leopards were being sighted almost daily. What more could we ask for?

I awoke around 5 a.m. and pulled the blankets a little tighter around my neck. The chill night air had stolen into the bed as I lay there listening to the sudden and somewhat early outburst of sound from the cockerel of the bush, the red-billed francolin. A pair of black-backed jackals barked, a harsh, high-pitched yelp that I had heard many times before. Almost immediately, another sound cut through the air, deeper and more authoritative, so close that it sounded as if it were right inside my tent. It was the wood-rasping cough of a leopard. The hair on the back of my neck tickled with excitement. I thought it was a male, but I could not be sure. So they *were* here – nearby. In my dreams I followed the leopard, slipping stealthily through the forest with him to his daytime resting place.

The next thing I knew it was 6 a.m. and time to get up. A cup of steaming coffee and a bone-hard rusk were all we had time for as we scrambled into the Ford control and headed for the den.

'You get to like rusks after a while,' chuckled Alan with an evil grin on his face.

There are not many places in the world where you can rise early each day and know that a clear blue sky awaits you. Barely a cloud forms from one day to the next at Mombo from July until November, when towering thunderheads blot out the sky and herald the onset of the rains. Sunrise and sunset are magical times, red and orange outlining the palms and the acacias, creating a tapestry of tree shapes reflected in the silvery waters. But the coldness of the mornings comes as a shock, especially when driving in open vehicles, a feature of many game-viewing areas in southern Africa. Being out in the open certainly has an immediacy to it, though it was not uncommon to see visitors with blankets clasped around their knees until late in the morning.

The den was less than ten minutes' drive from camp, and when we arrived we found the dogs still huddled together for warmth. There was no sign of the dominant female – she must have been curled up with her puppies deep inside her den.

Two of the other females in the pack were known to be pregnant. They were thought to be sisters of the dominant female, and both of them had chosen burrows less than 100 metres (330 ft) from the main den. These subordinate females rigorously guarded their dens from other pack members, and both of them spent a considerable amount of time digging at the entrance to their burrows, scuffing earth into the air and raising clouds of dust before entering. Other pack members quite

*Hooded vultures* (Neophron monachus) *waiting for the chance to scavenge on scraps of meat regurgitated by the wild dogs; they also feed on their droppings! Hooded vultures do not have powerful bills and cannot compete with the larger vultures at kills, so are obliged to feed on scraps left or dropped by the others.*

often visited these dens; and every so often the females would emerge and be greeted by their relatives. But there were times when they remained below ground, uttering protective growls and squeals to deter others from entering.

The forest surrounding the den echoed with the sound of bird song. The exuberant bubbling calls of red- and yellow-billed hornbills, rising then falling; the harsh clicks and whistles of a pair of swamp boubous helping to soften the grating dry country sounds of crested and red-billed francolins. Woodpeckers drilled noisily against the towering stumps of dead trees, and parties of Burchell's glossy starlings chattered and squeaked, competing with the harsh 'Go-away, go-away' call of grey louries. I recognized many of the birds, though I knew them by different names. A quick glance through the local field guide helped resolve any confusion. If the birds had the same scientific names then they were indeed the same species.

Suddenly it was as if the whole pack had gone berserk, erupting in a frenzy of activity. The cause of all the fuss was the emergence of the dominant female from her den. She was 'queen' among the dogs and her appearance was always guaranteed to cause a riot of activity. The younger dogs – some of whom were her puppies from the previ-

*A wild dog begs for food from a fellow pack member who has just returned from a hunt. When wild dogs establish themselves at a den, any animal that stays behind to help protect the puppies may solicit regurgitated food from the hunters by begging – just as puppies do, 'wittering' and jostling other individuals who have already fed, to force them to regurgitate.*

ous year's litter – seemed beside themselves with excitement, mobbing their mother. They circled around the courtyard of the den like some royal procession, exhibiting a mixture of submissiveness and indulgence, excitement and reverence, all desperately vying for her attention. They swarmed alongside her, reaching forward to lick at her open mouth, pressing her to the ground and nuzzling her belly, licking the drops of milk from her twelve swollen teats. She 'yittered' – a high, loud, yakking noise repeated over and over again. This was her way of begging for a share of the food that was hidden in the stomachs of the hunters.

First she begged – no, demanded – food from her mate, the dominant or alpha male, father of her puppies, a dark, stocky dog with a prominent throat ruff of matted hair. Having received a mouthful of meat from him she ran from dog to dog, salivating profusely and chattering incessantly, circling, pushing her nose into the face of each dog, forcing them to respond as they twisted and turned, until they regurgitated some food. It was her right. She had stayed at the den to protect her puppies rather than leave them exposed to danger when the other dogs went off to hunt; so now she was entitled to a share of the food. No dog could refuse her – their stomachs heaved involuntarily, unable to resist the puppy-like begging, until a pile of meat appeared at the female's feet and was greedily gobbled up, both by the female and by the dog that had regurgitated it.

The hooded vultures watched from the trees. They had learned the signs, knew the sounds. Even before the food hit the ground they were on the wing. Hopping and dancing around the dogs, wings flailing, the vultures were anxious to be first to snatch up any scraps. Glossy starlings perched on a stump, beady-eyed hornbills watched from the ground, all eagerly awaiting the chance to pick up the leftovers, as columns of army ants, black as treacle, marched towards the scent of food.

A pattern began to emerge. While the Mombo Pack were always going to be the primary focus of our programme, we wanted to try and see as many of the other large predators as possible – some of the smaller ones, too, if time permitted. Just as the herbivores are adapted to try and avoid competition with one another, so too are the predators. Some, such as civet and caracal, are nocturnal in their habits, avoiding contact with the larger predators by hunting smaller prey. Others, such as cheetah and wild dogs, usually hunt during daylight when competition from lion and hyaena is at a minimum. Leopard, too, must avoid these larger predators, and by employing their superlative climbing skills are able to carry their kills high into trees, out of reach of less nimble competitors. But there is always the possibility of conflict between creatures which have evolved to kill, and which will scavenge from others whenever the opportunity arises. There is a fine balance between avoiding potentially harmful confrontations with other predators and capitalizing on each other's strengths and weaknesses when food is at stake.

Of all the African animals the leopard is my favourite. It took me six years to compile a book about this elusive predator in the Masai Mara, so I knew better than to assume that we might find a leopard during our short stay in the Okavango Delta. But as we travelled through the dust and darkness early one night, we came upon a magnificent male leopard known as Gimpy. Like all adult male leopard Gimpy's head was broad, his muzzle square. His neck was so thick and muscular that his head sat squarely on his broad shoulders, perfectly adapted for hauling his kills up into the trees. He seemed totally unconcerned by our presence, rolling sinuously on his back, itching his beautifully marked coat against the dusty ground, sitting up and licking a massive forepaw before wiping it across his spotted face.

There was a stiffness to Gimpy's stride, an arthritic twist to his hindquarters – sufficient to make him look somewhat uncomfortable when he walked. If Gimpy's indisposition affected his hunting ability, it did not show; there was a lustre to his coat, solid bands of muscle rippling beneath his skin. This was a prime male leopard on his early evening prowl, pausing to investigate and mark his territory, searching out

*Opposite: Leopard are solitary in their habits, and a female must raise her cubs on her own; males play no part in rearing their offspring. Like all predators, leopard are opportunists, stalking as close to their quarry as possible before launching a rush of lighting speed and pouncing on their victim. They are creatures of legendary strength, and pound for pound probably the most powerful of all the big cats.*

prominent bushes and arches formed by fallen trees – the same 'scent posts' to which any leopard would be drawn and which they might investigate and mark. Gimpy was looking for signs that would indicate whether other leopard had passed through his territory, signifying by their individual odour whether they were male or female, young or old, a threat to his domain or a simply a transitory vagrant.

Gimpy turned and arched his spotted tail, revealing the pure white underside to its tip. Urine tainted with powerfully scented anal gland secretions arched upwards, the droplets forming a shower of reflected crystals in the beam of our spotlight, leaving an pungent oily mark on the tree.

Gimpy moved from one scent post to another, reaching up and stretching his serpentine head high enough to sniff and rub his face where scent – his own scent, perhaps – had been deposited on a previous visit to the area. I wondered what he could smell – the provocative scent of an oestrus female, or the different odour of another male, an interloper who might need to be challenged at some time in the future. Gimpy had been seen a few months earlier fighting with another adult male. His withered leg was perhaps the result of a spat over territory; a bite in the hindquarters from a leopard's dagger-like 6 cm (2½ in) canines could leave an opponent paralysed, doomed to a slow death by starvation – unless the hyaenas finished him off first.

We followed Gimpy's paw prints along the track, clear pugmarks etched in the soft, sandy soil – smaller and more compact than those of a lion. I listened, hoping that he might call into the moonlight. But he didn't, losing himself deep within the green interior of a dense island of bush and tangled palms. We circled, waiting for Gimpy to emerge before reluctantly abandoning our vigil and heading back to camp. It had only lasted a few minutes, the briefest of glimpses into the secret world of the leopard, but it would be replayed in minutest detail around the campfire that night.

My co-host for this programme was South African wildlife cameraman Richard Goss. Richard had won universal acclaim for *Meerkats United*, filmed in the Kalahari Gemsbok National Park in South Africa. This was followed by *The Sisterhood*, an intimate portrait of the much maligned spotted hyaena, filmed here at Mombo. Much of *The Sisterhood* was filmed at night, and as we hoped to follow the various predators by both day and night, Richard would be the perfect guide. Not only did he know the area intimately, but he was also familiar with some of the individual predators we were likely to see. Apparently the Mombo Pack had used the same den area eight years ago; a favourite site. By now the sync film crew had arrived and we could begin to record both sound and pictures.

There were always two cameramen with us for each of the programmes, so that one of them could concentrate exclusively on filming the wildlife, while the sync cameraman filmed dialogue between myself and my co-host. Wildlife cameraman Hugh

Maynard had been spending as much time as possible with the wild dogs before the sync crew arrived and had managed to film many of the social activities that bind members of a pack together – the greeting ceremony, regurgitation of food, grooming and resting together. But the emergence of the puppies was a key event that loomed large in everyone's mind. We were all hoping that the pups would appear above ground before we departed. The dominant female was thought to have given birth approximately two weeks before our arrival. I knew from watching wild dogs in the Serengeti and Masai Mara that it was unlikely that the puppies would appear before they were three weeks old, perhaps even four weeks. The emergence of the puppies would provide a fitting climax to our film, though the pack would remain with the puppies at the den until they were ten to twelve weeks old and mobile enough to be able to follow the adults.

It wasn't long before trouble started at the den. Four days after our arrival at Mombo, Hugh reported that the dominant female had stolen two puppies from the den of one of her sisters – a subordinate female. She had moved quickly and purposefully from the main den where her own puppies were safely hidden, and without any warning had disappeared down into her sister's burrow. When she emerged again she had a puppy clasped in her mouth. She carried it halfway to the main den and then dumped it on the ground. Some of the yearlings sprang to their feet, twittering with excitement. Together they rushed to where the tiny puppy – no more than a week old – lay prostrate on the ground. This prompted the dominant female to pick the puppy up again and hurry to the den, disappearing beneath the wizened stumps. No sooner had she done so, than she re-emerged and headed straight back to her sister's den. Again she went inside – and again she emerged with a tiny pug-faced puppy held firmly between her jaws, carrying it quickly to her own den.

The mother of the stolen puppies emerged and paced around, whining incessantly, obviously distressed. Briefly she solicited food from one of the yearlings before cautiously approaching the dominant female's den, weaving among the fallen branches. A few moments later the dominant female popped her head above ground, ears cocked, eyes fixed on her sister. There was a flurry of appeasement from the subordinate female, as she rolled on to her back, jaws parted, whittering with fear and anxiety as the dominant female jabbed her nose into her sister's upturned throat.

The dominant female trotted, head low, towards her sister's den. The yearlings hurried to their mother's side, pressing themselves against her. She ignored them, barely pausing at the entrance to the den before disappearing from view. But this time she emerged empty-handed, so to speak. Perhaps there were no more puppies to steal. I wondered if it had been only a small litter or if more puppies had been abducted during the night. There was no way of knowing if the dominant female had already killed any of her sister's puppies or what might be the fate of the ones she had transferred. Would she adopt them and treat them as her own, as sometimes happens, or would they perish, unable to compete with the larger puppies for a share of the food?

The monopolization of breeding opportunities by the dominant pair in a wild dog pack might seem to be unduly harsh, but with each female being capable of producing twelve to fourteen puppies annually, there is little opportunity for more than one to breed successfully if the pack is to provide sufficient food and care to ensure that all the puppies survive. By stealing or killing the puppies of a rival, the dominant female helps to ensure that the pack's resources are clearly focused on her own offspring. Under these circumstances it is hardly surprising that female wild dogs leave their natal pack in their second or third year to try and achieve breeding success for themselves, away from the repressive influence of their mother. When new packs are formed between groups of these young females and unrelated males, it is not uncommon for more than one of them to become pregnant. But usually only the dominant female among sisters manages to raise her pups – particularly when food is scarce – and in these cases a subordinate sister will sometimes emigrate again to escape the deadly attentions of a dominant sibling. Unless she does so she may never breed successfully.

Browsing through the latest issue of *National Geographic* at camp that evening I came across a small footnote on wild dogs at the back of the magazine:

*At the turn of the century there were perhaps as many as 200,000 wild dogs or Cape hunting dogs as they are sometimes called. Big game hunter R.C.F. Maugham in 1914 spoke for many people when he stated: 'It will be an excellent day. . .when means can be devised . . .for this unnecessary creature's complete extermination.'*

His wish may soon come true – barely 5,000 wild dogs today battle against habitat loss, disease and human animosity. Although they are not the most endangered carnivore in Africa – that unfortunate label is reserved for the Ethiopian wolf, which numbers fewer than 500 in the wild – they have nearly vanished from 19 of the 34 countries where they once occurred, with strong populations remaining only in southern Africa and in the Selous Game Reserve in Tanzania. Their plight seemed all the more poignant in light of the battle being waged by the three breeding females in the Mombo Pack, the outcome of which would determine the fate of their puppies.

The radio crackled into life from the car parked outside my tent. 'A leopard has made a kill and is dragging the carcass into cover. Looks like a female with a half-grown impala. Are you interested in filming her?' It was one of the driver-guides from Mombo's main camp. I looked at my watch – 6.30 a.m. We had been given a 'lie in', an extra hour in bed and it felt lovely and cosy with two extra blankets to keep me warm. But the chance of seeing another leopard banished any thoughts of sleep. I scrambled into my clothes and grabbed my camera bag.

There were no trees in the area large enough for the leopard to stash her kill, so she

*Leopards are consummate hunters. They are the most adaptable of the big cats, able to survive in the thickest forests and the driest deserts, wherever there is suitable prey.*

had dragged it into a den of dark shadows beneath the tangled thorny branches of an acacia bush. If the spotted hyaenas caught the scent of blood and fresh meat they would immediately try to appropriate the leopard's kill. The impala would be torn apart in minutes and consumed, such is the power of their bone-crushing jaws. Lions will kill a leopard if they are given half a chance, be it a cub or an adult. So the fact that the leopard was accompanied by a six-month-old cub meant that she had to be especially careful to avoid conflict.

A halo of light pierced the tangle of thorns where the young leopard crouched over the impala. The carcass was already partially eaten; 1.5-2 kg (3-4 lb) of nutritious muscle had been gnawed away from the rump. I could just see the mother leopard lurking in the background, a stealthy silhouette, hugging the ground. She slunk away as another vehicle approached, tail held out straight, shoulders rippling beneath her golden coat. Each paw was raised well clear of the ground, then placed carefully down again, stepping in her own tracks, to ensure that she moved without the slightest sound. The leopard vanished – or did she? I could see nothing more of her.

Within days there was a dramatic transformation in the behaviour of the subordinate female wild dog. We watched her emerge from among the pile of dogs clustered beneath a palm tree. Once more her identity was submerged within the pack. She no longer appeared restless, and all signs of distress had vanished – outwardly at least. Already her milk had begun to dry up, her belly looked tighter, her ribcage narrower. The tireless digging at the entrance to her den, the constant toing and froing – all this had ceased. Her lonely vigil was over.

Now the pack's attention was divided between the dominant female at the main den and the third breeding female, who was using an exposed burrow at a crossroad among the tracks. Flop Ear, as she was known, looked somewhat younger and was more slightly built than the other two females, though her coat markings – particularly

*While her puppies are still very small, the dominant female remains behind when the rest of the pack set off to hunt. As the puppies become older their mother may join the hunt, but often one of the other pack members stays behind and is later fed with regurgitated meat.*

around her chest and her forelegs – bore distinctive patches of white and pale yellow similar to those of the dominant female. It seemed likely that all three females were sisters, even if not from the same litter. Flop Ear begged for food from the pack whenever she emerged from her den, though her soliciting was quieter and less frenetic than the dominant female's, almost as if she didn't want to draw undue attention to herself in case her sister emerged and threatened her. She was very protective of her den, and whenever another dog approached too close she would rush back, frantic lest they try to enter the burrow and harm her puppies.

The arrival of the full moon had a marked influence on the dogs' behaviour, enabling them to remain active well into the night. The previous evening the pack had not set off to hunt until it was almost midnight. At some point they had killed a male impala, returning to the den at around 6.30 a.m. Normally, without the moon to guide them, the dogs left the den to hunt during the first hour before sun-up. But we could no longer rely on this. There were times when they decided to hunt as late as 8 or 9 a.m., depending on the temperature and how hungry they were. Frustrating as this might be, it was all part of the fascination of watching wild animals: despite what one might have read there were always surprises; new insights reflecting the ability of wild creatures to adapt to changes in their environment.

Whenever the Mombo Pack hunted successfully, the dominant male was the first to leave a kill, his face bloody from feeding, a belly full of meat waiting to be shared with his mate and their puppies. I had quickly learnt to recognize this male by his dark pelage and black tail – only the very tip was white. He had two flecks of white above his hip and a yellow blotch on his left buttock, matching the white star on his rump.

It wasn't just the breeding females who waited at the den for the hunters to return. Pack members who had become separated during a chase and had failed to kill would often return to the den to await the arrival of their relatives. Every so often the dominant female would emerge from her den and look around, ears cocked expectantly. If she saw the dominant male or any of the other hunters arriving, she would charge out to meet them, hounding them for food. Often she would push her head under the dominant male's belly, lifting his back legs right off the ground, winding herself round him, forcing him to a halt and causing him to regurgitate some food for her. Then she passed from one dog to another – targeting each in turn – yipping like a noisy puppy until she got her way. Any she passed by at first she returned to later. Each individual was expected to provide her with food at some point during the day, sometimes hours after the hunt.

Though much of our time at Mombo was spent watching the wild dogs, we were constantly on the look-out for other predators. We had been incredibly fortunate in filming Gimpy and the female leopard and her cub. The lions, meanwhile, were proving a

little more difficult. Though we had seen four different prides of lions, we were yet to see them doing something worth filming – just lying there being lions wasn't enough, even though 'doing nothing' is what lions engage in for much of the day and some of the night, dozing and relaxing for up to eighteen hours out of the twenty-four. Our best hope was going to be in trying to keep track of a small pride of three lionesses, the oldest of whom was known as Stumpy. One of the other lionesses, known as Tipless, was the mother of the four small cubs that we had seen moving with the pride one night. They were gaining in confidence by the day and were a joy to watch and film – when we could find them.

Stumpy stood bathed in sunlight, immediately recognizable by her short, stumpy tail. She was a grizzled old lioness, her hindquarters shrunken with age, the muscles around her pelvis wasted. Richard Goss remembered Stumpy from seven or eight years ago. Her tail had been severed in a battle with a clan of spotted hyaenas he had been filming. Stumpy was already fully grown at the time, so she was probably eleven or twelve years old by now. Lionesses have been known to continue to breed until at least this age and can live to the age of fifteen or twenty in exceptional cases. The oldest known female in the thirty-year-old lion study in the Serengeti was seventeen.

Small prides such as the one Stumpy belonged to were fairly typical of this part of Moremi Game Reserve, with two or three lionesses hunting predominantly warthog and impala, but also buffalo and some zebra. The abundance of prey varies seasonally – sometimes it is plentiful and at other times scarce, forcing the lions to wander further afield and thus increasing the likelihood of conflict with other prides. Under these circumstances a territory may not be able to support a large pride. Each pride – consisting of a group of related females and their cubs – is accompanied by two or three adult males, and Stumpy's pride was lorded over by two fine males, one of whom I could see sprawled in the shade of a thicket. A partially eaten zebra carcass lay a few metres from where the male rested. He was young, four or five years old, with a magnificent blond mane. With both Stumpy and the male looking replete, and no sign of Tipless and the cubs, we decided to return to the dogs.

It was almost a week since we arrived at Mombo and our attention was still very much focused on the imminent appearance of the puppies. By now they were at least three weeks old. Although it was impossible to get a clear view of the entrance to the den due to the thicket of fallen branches, we could hear the puppies long before they emerged. High-pitched whines and whimpers greeted the dominant female whenever she poked her head into the entrance of the den.

Four of the yearling dogs stood side by side atop the sandy rim overlooking the den. Their huge ears were cocked excitedly, focused like satellite dishes on the sounds emanating from below ground. One of the yearlings stepped forwards and whined softly at the darkened entrance to the burrow. Immediately the dominant female raced back to the den and jostled the younger dogs out of the way, standing protectively over the entrance. She in turn cocked her head and whined, and suddenly there they were, two tiny, pug-faced, four-week-old puppies. One was distinctively marked with white leggings and white blotches on its flanks, rather similar to its mother's markings.

The yearlings could hardly contain themselves, involuntarily regurgitating some meat at the sight of the puppies. Immediately the dominant female darted forwards and pushed the puppies aside, gobbling up the meat. The puppies looked bemused, their bluish eyes slightly cloudy as if not yet seeing clearly. They snuffled about in the dirt, mouthing up the scraps of meat as two hooded vultures hopped around the overhang at the entrance to the den, eager to pick up the leftovers.

The dominant female lay on her side inviting the puppies to suckle. One climbed on to her back, another, even more adventurous, waddled over the rim of the den. The yearlings nudged the puppy with the tips of their noses, rolling it on to its back and licking it clean. As they did so the dominant female jumped to her feet and, picking the puppy up by the waist, carried it back into the den. It was early days yet.

By now we were desperate to film the dogs hunting in good light. But often they did not leave the den until 6 p.m., with the sun dropping fast towards the horizon, relying on the moonlight to act as their guide. And on a number of occasions they departed through thick bush, making it impossible for us to follow them. Only if they headed for the more open country around the flood-plains did we have a real chance of keeping up with them.

The pack made their way purposefully through the forests and thickets surrounding the den site, emerging briefly in a clearing in the bush, bathed in the orange glow of dusk. The dogs paused to sniff the ground. Each squatted to relieve itself, urinating and depositing piles of black faeces coated with strands of hair from their prey. The clearing was a regular latrine for the dogs, used whenever they passed this way. Alan pointed out the place where a side-striped jackal had added his own droppings to one of the piles of the dogs' faeces. They were smaller and packed with brown seeds known as jackal-berries, testifying to the fact that this omnivorous carnivore eats large quantities of wild fruits as well as taking insects, small mammals and carrion.

Suddenly the dominant female trotted into view. Had she heard something that alarmed her? Did she intend joining the pack on the hunt or had she mistakenly thought that they had killed close by? Whatever the reason, she now moved purposefully around the latrine, overmarking each pile of droppings with her own distinctive-smelling urine. When the dominant male saw his mate, he ran back to join her, covering her scent with his own. It was an unequivocal sign of the alpha pair's dominance and a powerful message to any other group of dogs that might pass through the area that there was a breeding pair in residence.

As the dominant female ran back to the den the rest of the pack moved off again. But they had hardly gone any distance when a red-billed francolin alarm-called, causing the dominant male to slow to a walk. When he gruff-barked the whole pack froze in anticipation. A chorus of barks echoed across the pan. Lions! Some of the pack moved forward, keeping well clear of the bushes, wary of being ambushed. It was Tipless, the lioness with the four small cubs, now ten weeks old. The cubs looked nervous; although their mother was there to protect them, they barely resisted the urge to flee for cover. Shielded by the bushes, the lioness and her cubs continued on their way and the dogs soon lost interest and trotted into the distance.

We followed the pack towards the flood-plains, where the largest concentrations of game were to be found. I looked at my watch; it was an hour after sunset and our path was illuminated by the cars' headlights and the beam of a hand-held spotlight. Twice the pack set off in pursuit of impala, but each time they were forced to abandon the chase, losing their quarry among the thickets. Eventually the darkness and an island of dense bush forced us to a halt, and we decided to make our way back towards camp.

Impala sat on their haunches, resting among the tall, spindly vegetation; herds of wildebeest cantered ahead of us, their eyes sparkling green, reflecting the light. This was a chance for us to search for the secretive aardwolf, an insectivorous creature allied to the hyaena and resembling a lightly built striped hyaena. Our other vehicle spotted an aardvark, a pig-like insectivore which, like the aardwolf, is a specialist feeder that preys on termites, using its strong claws to break into the rock-hard earth castles, lapping up the termites with its elastic 30 cm (12 in) sticky tongue. The last time I had seen an aardvark, in the Masai Mara, it was being eaten by a young lioness, which had ambushed it after it had emerged from its burrow. In an attempt to protect themselves against predators aardvark have the habit of exploding from their underground re-treat, kicking backwards as they emerge with the force of a champagne cork popping.

The following morning we arose at five o'clock, huddling briefly around the hot embers of the campfire with mugs of coffee clasped in our hands for warmth. We arrived at the den at 5.45 to find that the pack had already gone. Only the dominant female and her sister Flop Ear remained.

A thin slither of moon cut through the dark sky, casting an eerie light around the den. Fiery-necked nightjars fluttered up from the warm ground, caught in the head-lights. I recognized them by their call – 'Good Lord deliver us'. The palm trees rattled in the wind as a pair of honey badgers gambolled towards their burrow, having feasted on grubs and insects during the night. We searched for tracks in the hope that they might guide us to the dogs. A cluster of damp patches on the ground marked the place where six of the dogs had gathered near the main den and greeted, peeing with excitement before setting off to hunt. Close to the subordinate female's den were more pee marks where the dogs had milled about before departing. We drove to the latrine in the clearing and searched for fresh droppings, but there were none. We must have missed the pack by a matter of minutes. The waning of the moon had reset the dogs' time clock; they could no longer hunt in the middle of the night. The hunter's moon had gone. The pack was probably many kilometres away by now, so we decided to wait for them to return. At least we might catch sight of the puppies again.

The dominant female suddenly appeared alongside our vehicle. She immediately started overmarking the damp patches in the powdery soils, methodically moving from place to place, sniffing then peeing, obliterating their scent – registering her presence. She moved on, stopping by Flop Ear's den and peering into the darkened entrance. She listened intently, her scarred and notched ears twisting imperceptibly to catch the faintest hint of tiny puppies. I could imagine Flop Ear's reaction – she would know who it was by her sister's powerful smell. Curled up with her puppies, Flop Ear could only lie in her burrow, shielding her litter and hoping that the dominant female would leave her alone.

The yearlings were the first to return from the hunt, but they did not rush to the burrow. Instead they lay among the surrounding thickets, signalling that they had failed to kill and had nothing to offer the pups or their mother. It was another thirty minutes before the rest of the pack arrived. Having fed the female, one of the domi-nant male's brothers came and flopped down beside him. Both were dark dogs, with-out strongly patterned coats. They often rested close to one another, exhibiting the strong bonds that bind individuals within a pack together. These bonds are forged among litter mates, from their earliest days, and are witnessed by their preference for close contact with members of their own generation. This helps to ensure that they stay together as adults and promotes a pack-dwelling existence.

Day by day the dominant female relaxed her grip on access to the den. Now the yearlings moved right up to the entrance, calling to the puppies so that they could

*Opposite: The wild dog's scientific name is* Lycaon pictus, *meaning painted or ornate wolf, which aptly describes their distinctive, tricoloured coat markings of yellow, dark brown and white. Each animal has a white-tipped tail and a unique coat colour, allowing experts to recognize individuals. Wild dogs possess only four toes on each foot, lacking the dew-claw of true dogs (though it can be seen beneath the skin on X-rays).*

feed them with regurgitated meat or simply to make contact with these new and intriguing additions to the pack. They sniffed the puppies, rolled them around on the end of their noses, cleaned them, mothered them a little. The puppies seemed quite unperturbed by all the commotion, peering from beneath the adults' spindly legs, milling around the cavernous mouth of a yearling about to regurgitate some food for them or stumbling over a fallen branch, before settling down to suckle from their mother's swollen teats as she lay on her side, encouraging them to join her and feed.

Occasionally it all became too much for the dominant female and she would snap at the yearlings, driving them back. Then she would lie above the entrance to the den, her large notched ears sifting the sounds: the cooing of turtle doves, the chattering of long-tailed glossy starlings, the barking of chacma baboons, the trumpeting of elephant. All of these were part of her world, and when the sounds alarmed or startled her she would get to her feet, alert to the possibility of danger, ready to defend her litter, sending the puppies scurrying for safety.

It was our last chance. A cluster of ten pairs of emerald-green eyes twinkled back at us from the darkness as we arrived at the den. They were still here. The yearlings lay huddled together for warmth at the base of one of the palm trees, a familiar resting place. The older dogs lay to the south of the den, huddled in groups of two or three. The moon stared down at us, a thin-lipped slither of white casting a dim light around us. An hour later one of the dogs got up and stretched, then trotted, head low, towards the den. Another soon followed, and within seconds the pack erupted with the extraordinary high-pitched sounds of the greeting ceremony. Dogs hurdled the maze of fallen branches, wheeling this way and that, joining, gathering, separating – collecting each and every one into their midst. Then, just as suddenly, they lay down again.

Moments later the yearlings began to trot off in ones and twos, then the rest, hurrying so as not to be left behind. We followed. The pack was headed towards the flood-plains. Once in the open the dogs paused, sniffing, peeing, defecating. They trotted onwards – an easy, rather dainty stride that covered the ground effortlessly. Sometimes they galloped – just as effortlessly. Every so often they stopped and listened, ears cocked, or gathered together to sniff the grass stems and bushes, reading the pungent messages left by other predators – hyaenas, lions, leopards.

Red-billed francolins raced each other through the dust, passing close to a pair of side-striped jackals curled up in the feathery grass. I had heard the jackals calling earlier – an owl-like hoot, quite distinct from the call of their relative the black-backed jackal. A small herd of impala – distant shapes – remained hidden from the dogs. The pack gathered in menacing formation, all eyes focused on a lone hyaena. Within seconds the dogs caught up with it. Howls and roars rent the air, testifying to the sharpness of the wild dogs' teeth. The hyaena buried itself in the only cover available, a solitary bush, its fearsome jaws snapping with a mixture of defiance and submission. Satisfied for the moment, the pack moved on, striding out in pursuit of a small herd of wildebeest. One of the bulls ran into the shallow water, pursued by a yearling, while the rest of the herd bunched together, confronting the dogs and moving them on their way again.

Our joy at finally being able to keep up with the wild dogs in daylight soon faded. Ahead of us lay deeper water. As the pack waded across, intent on pursuing a herd of lechwe, one of their favoured prey species in this area, we could only sit and watch them disappear into the distance.

No wildlife photographer is ever satisfied – you always long to see something new, hoping for a better shot. But at least we left in the knowledge that we had enough material to piece together an interesting sequence on the Mombo Pack.

With all the equipment packed away in preparation for our midday departure, I asked Ian if he would take me out on one final game drive. Tipless and her four cubs had been seen the previous evening. Even at this late stage I still had hopes of photographing them.

Ian is a keen photographer and he had been happy to take me out whenever I wasn't needed for filming; that way we could both take some stills. We had spent the previous two evenings trying to capture the dramatic sunsets so characteristic of the Okavango Delta at this time of the year, the dust and smoke transforming the sun into an enormous pink orb. Now, as the sun peeped over the horizon, it silhouetted a giant baobab tree against the brightening sky. I had been longing for the chance to photograph it. Baobabs are startling trees, erupting in front of you like enormous volcanic plants – massive, up-ended shapes, swollen with fluid and nutrients. They look as if they are growing with their roots in the air, and can be bare of leaves for up to nine months of the year. God is said to have uprooted the baobab in a fit of rage and planted it upside down – hence its strange appearance. Baobabs can grow up to 9 metres (30 ft) in diameter and are one of the longest-living trees in the world, living for 2,000-3,000 years – perhaps even longer. It is not uncommon to see a baobab with gaping holes in its trunk where an elephant has plunged its tusks into the soft, spongy wood. Countless generations of elephant must have rubbed their thick hide against this particular baobab's trunk, yet for more than a thousand years it had escaped serious damage.

We continued towards the open ground where the previous day Robin and Alan had come upon Stumpy and her companions stalking three buffalo. The buffalo had been grazing the lush grass near to a thicket when the lionesses had ambushed them. Stumpy, the oldest and most experienced of the lionesses, was the first to react, stalking towards the buffalo as dusk concealed their approach. When she charged forwards the buffalo fled for the forest, with all three lionesses hard on their heels. Alan and Robin, unable to follow, had sat and listened to the sounds of battle as the lionesses struggled to pull the buffalo to the ground.

Now we struggled to find a way through the trees, eventually emerging in a glade of dry land bordering a marsh. The body of a cow buffalo lay on her side at the edge of the pan, with Tipless and her cubs nearby. The lionesses must finally have cornered the buffalo among the maze of fallen trees. They would have circled warily, three against one, keeping well out of reach of the cow's sharply pointed horns until one of them saw the opportunity to leap forwards on to the buffalo's rump. Biting into the muscles over her spine, the lioness would have attempted to pull the cow off balance, sending her crashing to the ground. The cow's bellows of fear and distress would quickly have been stifled as Stumpy, perhaps, grabbed her by the face, clamping her teeth over nose and mouth, suffocating the life from the buffalo. Meanwhile the other lionesses would already have begun to feed.

The last time I had seen the four tiny lion cubs was at the beginning of our visit, two weeks earlier. How they had grown! Now they were sure-footed and more confident, less nervous at being exposed to view in the open. Tipless lay alongside the carcass, guarding it from hyaenas and vultures. The cow's face had been stripped of flesh, giving it a ghoulish, death-mask grin. The cubs picked away at the soft scraps around the neck, using their sharp incisors to tease out the tasty morsels of meat. Their bellies were as tight as ticks, bloated from the feast. Spotted hyaenas lurked in the shadows; a pair of side-striped jackals tarried somewhat nervously on the fringes, wary of the lions. Half a dozen hooded vultures gathered on the ground, while the larger white-backed vultures peered down from the tops of the tallest trees. There was little for the vultures to feed on yet, but the lionesses were taking no chances. The hooded vultures played cat and mouse with their adversaries, gingerly moving closer whenever the lions closed their eyes, scouring the ground for scraps of meat and bits of offal scattered about by the lionesses.

Life for the cubs was one of exploration, of endless play in the company of brothers and sisters – enacted within the security of the pride. All three females tolerated the cubs' antics, though to varying degrees. Two of the cubs played king of the castle on top of the buffalo, cuffing one another, pawing, biting, tumbling backwards over the side of the carcass. As the sun climbed higher into the sky and the cubs tired of feeding, they began to grow restless, wandering back and forth between the edge of the clearing, where the other lionesses rested in the shade, and the carcass, where their mother was busy scraping at the ground with one massive forepaw, sending puffs of choking dust into the faces of her cubs. It looked like a laborious process, but pawful by pawful Tipless covered up the pungent gut contents that lay strewn around the carcass.

It was already well past the time that we should be returning to camp. I kept taking pictures. Just a few more minutes, just one more photograph.

Mombo had been an outstanding success. The film crew had managed to capture some wonderful footage of all of the larger predators as well as of caracal, African wild cat and large spotted genet. We had seen aardwolves and aardvarks, spring hares and honey badgers. The annual flood might not have been as dramatic as in the past, but it had still managed to create a watery haven for lechwe and reedbuck, a sheet of blue water washing the plains; a bird watcher's paradise where yellow-billed egrets and black-winged stilts plied the shallows. But more than anything it had been the wild dogs that made this journey so special. Though their future seems bleak as land and prey become ever scarcer, for the moment Africa's painted wolves are prospering in this distant corner of Eden.

*A Swainson's francolin (Francolinus swainsonii) on a termite mound. Males of this species are often to be heard calling from a tree or termite mound at dawn and dusk, with a very loud, harsh, crowing 'krrraa-krrraa-krrraa', repeated six or seven times.*

# UGANDA: THE PEARL OF AFRICA

The smell of freshly baked cookies filled the kitchen of our house in Nairobi, where cans of beans and yellow corn were stacked in neat lines across the table. Tomorrow Robin Hellier and I would be on our way by road to Uganda, to reconnoitre it as a possible location for one of our safaris. Corned beef and sardines would suffice for lunch or dinner, with the option of spaghetti bolognaise, beef stew or red beans and chili sauce if we were feeling extravagant. The mango chutney and black pepper would help to disguise just about anything and make it edible. There were packets of crisps and salted peanuts, chocolate bars and strips of toffee for when we didn't feel like stopping to eat, and the jars of dried fruit were always welcome (especially the mango) on a long journey.

Outside, the garage doors were flung wide open, exposing a mountain of safari equipment. It would all have to be thoroughly checked before we set off. There were two jacks, two spare wheels, a wheel spanner, planks of wood – which would be invaluable if we got bogged down – as well as coils of wire to strap up an ailing spring or to hold a broken battery bracket in place long enough to have it repaired. Shovel, panga, hand axe, tyre levers, foot pump, spare tubes: I ran my finger down a list that seemed to get longer with every safari. Everything had its place, tucked away within the cupboards and drawers of my Toyota Landcruiser.

I checked the winch at the front of the vehicle. No problems there. In the bush it might be days before help arrived if we got caught in the rains. A canvas bag tied to the roof-rack concealed mattresses and sufficient bedding for us both in case we needed to sleep in the car. Twin fuel tanks, a water tank and a fold-down bed are the most basic requirements that a safari vehicle must provide. We had all of them.

Robin and I were keen for our adventure to begin. Uganda held the promise of something new for both of us. The guide book had boasted, 'Politically stable, safe and friendly...things are changing fast in Uganda, and we expect to do frequent up-dates.' Could this really be the same country that just a few years ago was off limits to all but the most intrepid backpacker or the enterprising businessman ready to take a risk in exchange for quick profits?

For most of the 1970s Uganda had been torn apart by the dictator Idi Amin, who came to power after a coup had ousted President Milton Obote. Amin first focused his wrath on the Asian community, accusing them of being 'paper citizens', loyal only to their own community, not to their adopted home. It is an accusation often heard in Kenya, where the Asians still dominate the economy through their business acumen. In Uganda, 80,000 of them were given just a matter of hours to pack their bags and go, sounding the death knell for Uganda's economy.

After he had expelled the Asians Amin embarked on a reign of anarchy and terror in which hundreds of thousands of people died. In 1979, with the backing of socialist Tanzania, which took advantage of a terri-torial dispute to invade Uganda, Obote was restored to power and Amin went into exile. But Obote's rule was scarred by tribal-based civil war in which his political rivals and some 3½ per cent of the population — 500,000 people — were killed. Now Obote too had gone and Uganda was in the hands of former guerrilla leader Yoweri Museveni, who had proved himself an outstanding president since he came to power in 1986.

Uganda is only 235,796 square km (91,041 square miles) in area, roughly the same size as Great Britain or the state of Oregon. It nestles between the borders of six countries: Sudan and Ethiopia to the north, Kenya to the east, Tanzania and Rwanda to the south, and Zaire to the west. Small though it may be, much of the country remains untouched by human development. Described as the 'Pearl of Africa' by the explorer Henry Morton Stanley, this lush green paradise is blessed with abundant food to nourish its people and could yet become the envy of its neighbours.

One of the challenges posed by *Dawn to Dusk* was to try and film all of the 'sync' pieces within a single day. The optimism which had suggested this was achievable stemmed in part from our experience over the years in the Masai Mara and Serengeti, where the sheer abundance of wildlife amidst varied scenery enables you easily to fill a thirty-minute wildlife programme without travelling far afield. Everything you need is right there in front of you. This is one of the reasons why so many camera crews head for the Mara when time is short and budgets are limited. Spoiled for choice among such places, we were hoping Uganda would focus our attention in a new way. We all agreed that the country desperately needed positive publicity, to help free it from the terrible legacy of Amin and Obote. The rape of Uganda's fabled wildlife parks and re-serves has been well documented. Much of the wildlife was slaughtered during the long years of civil war. The rhino are gone; thousands of elephants were killed for their ivory, the herds of buffalo and hippo butchered for their meat.

But filming rhino and elephants wasn't our priority in Uganda; there were plenty of other things to investigate. We wanted to explore the waterways – riverine environ-ments such as the Kazinga Channel in Queen Elizabeth National Park and the Nile at Murchison Falls, which in the old days were considered essential parts of a successful safari to Uganda. We were to visit Daniela de Luca, an Italian scientist studying troops of banded mongooses that she had habituated during her studies at Queen Elizabeth. Daniela had a Ugandan research assistant called Onen, an elderly man who would be able to tell me about life during the bad years when he had been employed as a park ranger, rising eventually to the rank of corporal. Onen was to be our guide during game drives around the park and would show us the best places to photograph the Uganda kob, a species of antelope which occupies traditional breeding grounds throughout the year. Dominant males strut and whistle as a means of advertising their territory, challenging rival males and mating with oestrus females attracted to the 'lekking grounds', as they are known. And the highlight of our safari promised to be a visit to Chambura Gorge, on the eastern boundary of the park. Here we hoped to make a foot safari in search of chimpanzees. This would be a first for me – I had never seen a chimpanzee in the wild. I could hardly wait.

Our journey had been delayed by two weeks due to Robin's commitments at the BBC, and from the start I fretted about the onset of the long rains. As we travelled west the storm clouds gathered menacingly in the sky. The land looked parched. Paper-dry maize husks littered the ground, while fires set to clear the land licked at the grey sky. Everyone, it seemed, was preparing for the arrival of the rains, which usually begin towards the end of March and continue intermittently through to June. Lines of people – men, women and children – were recruited to the task at hand. Sturdy brown arms rose and fell in unison, backs bent to the sun, the rich red soil breaking up under the flailing hoes. The land was ready, exposed to welcome the harvest of the rains, to feed the people.

The wind hissed angrily through the trees, a noisy messenger snapping at our heels.

*The Ankole of south-western Uganda are famed for their large herds of spectacularly long-horned cattle. The cows are symbols of wealth and prestige, as well as being providers of meat and milk.*

It had taken us five hours to cover the 300 km (200 miles) from Nairobi to Eldoret, far quicker than I had imagined. It was no more than a day's drive from Nairobi to Kampala if you wanted to rush. But we decided to spend the night at Eldoret Club, a place of quiet and tranquillity. By breaking our journey here we would arrive at the border early the following morning, refreshed to deal with whatever might lie in store for us there.

Eldoret is farming country. In the old days it was a stronghold for white farmers, among them the South African Boers, descendants of the Voortrekkers who had headed north to seek their fortune wherever they could find good country to tend their livestock and grow their crops – happiness measured by owning sufficient land to avoid seeing the smoke from a neighbour's wood fire when standing on your own front porch. But most of the whites had long since packed their bags and moved on, always searching for somewhere promising the old ways, somewhere to settle and call home – for a while, at least – until the next journey. Many who remained clung to the rituals of club and empire – caught in a time-warp of old reverences, tolerated as a harmless anachronism.

The grounds of the club were neatly trimmed, the cottages sparsely furnished with varnished wood and walls painted a dreary mustard yellow with counterpanes to match. The club was centred around an attractive golf course – wide fairways enclosed between stands of tall trees. Caddies hung around the car park, hungry for business. They could spot the 'punters' a mile off and ignored our arrival. That evening men in shorts and women in summery frocks gathered in the dimly lit reading room, perusing dog-eared copies of the British *Sunday Times* and *Guardian*. It was 'happy hour' and men of all races crowded at the bar, their backs turned to a large table crammed with metal food trays serving traditional curry, pepper steak, chicken wings and fruit salad.

Before going to bed I paused in the hallway to chat to the receptionist, who assured me not only that it was going to rain, but that this year the rains would be really heavy. The thought of Uganda in the mud brought little comfort. Nor would my conversation a day or so later with Professor Pomeroy at Makerere University in Kampala, who told me that unlike in Kenya there was no distinct rainy season in Uganda: 'Forget the big rains of April-May and the short ones of October. In Uganda it can rain at any time, that's why it is so green.' After that I stopped asking people about the weather and chanced to luck. '*Sharui ya Mungu*,' as they say in Swahili. 'It's God's business.'

In Africa you learn to dread border posts. Customs and Immigration officials in many countries can be surly and difficult to deal with, even when all your papers are in perfect order. *Chai* or *kito kidogo* – 'something small' – is the currency by which time is measured. It is not so much whether you will be allowed through as when. Sometimes their demands are outrageous. But either times are changing or God must have been looking over our shoulders when we arrived at Busia on the Kenya border. The officials were pleasant and efficient. No mention of *chai*, just a greeting, a smile, a joke, and we were on our way again.

*Uganda kob look rather similar to impala, but are more sturdily built. They spend almost all their time in open grassland not far from water. Only the males have horns.*

Malaba, on the Uganda side of the border, looked like the trucking capital of the world, with huge containers lining the roadside. Bringing what, I wondered? Food aid for Rwanda or Sudan seemed the most likely answer. Young touts in American jeans and snazzy Michael Jordan T-shirts hustled for business, fists full of money, offering twenty Uganda shillings for one Kenya shilling. 'You need money? You need help; you want easy way through customs?' Kids of eight or even younger lugged boxes full of cold drinks around the vehicles; one day they would graduate to being money changers. The Ugandan officials were as friendly and helpful as we had been told they would be, though the sounds of young voices from the cells behind the wooden counter reminded us of another world – poverty. Scrawny hands poked out from between the bars of the metal door; a child peered at us from the darkened floor. We walked back into the light and the noise and were gone.

Smiling with relief that our brush with officialdom was over, we brewed some tea on our gas cooker and treated ourselves to the first of the home-made cookies.

Everything I had heard about Uganda was true: it is the greenest place I have ever seen. As we drove past the low-lying marshy flats bordering Lake Victoria the grass and trees grew thickly right up to the road, dazzling us with their colour. At Jinja, on the shores of Lake Victoria, we passed the Ripon Falls which lie submerged beneath the Owen Falls dam, regarded now as the source of the legendary Nile, longest river in the world. On one side of the bridge the dammed-up water lies flat and calm; on the opposite side it swirls white and angry. Dense groves of banana trees and vast expanses of sugar cane flourished. The land spoke of recovery, of a new era unfolding.

*'In Uganda it can rain at any time, that's why it's so green.' These fields of tea, like the flourishing banana and sugar-cane plantations, bear witness to the country's rich soils and new-found prosperity.*

Resentment towards Europeans appeared non-existent – everywhere we went people smiled or waved, children reaching out their hands asking for sweets, as they do all over Africa. Uganda was never a colony – merely a British protectorate – and it shows. For centuries, Uganda was administered by a sophisticated form of self-government which the British were happy to leave unchanged. Now, officials adopt a low profile with travellers. Tourism is to be encouraged, foreign investment welcomed; all part of President Museveni's rehabilitation programme for his country. As often as not the checkpoints we passed were little more than a couple of policemen sheltering from the sun beneath a grove of trees at the roadside. And the roads were a revelation after the potholes and broken tarmac that are commonplace in Kenya and Tanzania. In many areas the roads were freshly tarmacked, courtesy of the sudden influx of aid money.

Never before had I seen so many people on bicycles. It was as if the Tour de France had arrived in Africa, with packs of riders slogging up and down the hills, thunderous

thighs pumping, at times competing against one another for the sheer joy of it. When they could endure the climb no longer they dismounted and pushed, leaning against their bikes, legs braced, heads and shoulders bent over the handlebars. Bicycle-repair shops did a thriving business, welding and reinforcing the brackets that held the back seat safely in place or mending spokes. Only the men rode bicycles, but there were no small bikes for the little boys – they struggled manfully with big ones. One child nearly ended up under our vehicle when he lost control and toppled to the ground.

Bicycles have found their calling in Uganda – as taxis. At first I thought how very polite: all those young men giving girlfriends, wives, mothers a helping hand with the shopping, the women perched elegantly side-saddle on the back of the bikes. It was only when I noticed whole stands of bicycles parked at a bus stop waiting for the next 'fare' that I realized that ferrying people around the countryside on bikes was big business. One sturdy-legged rider swept past us on the way down a hill, shouting, 'Come, I carry you to Kampala a lot quicker than that old car of yours!'

When there wasn't a passenger to transport, the cyclists struggled up and down the hillsides carrying impossible loads of plantains, the cooking bananas which are the staple diet of many Ugandans, hence the huge plantations that dominate much of the scenery. I couldn't help smiling at memories of my first introduction to these green bananas during my overland journey through Africa twenty-years ago. Being none the wiser I patiently waited for the bananas to ripen. It took me some time to realize that the only way to eat *matoke* is as a form of rather bland mashed potato or sliced up and fried in oil like potato chips.

The Buganda women dress in a style that I was to see again among the Himba of Namibia – colourful, wide-bottomed, Victorian-style dresses with high-pointed, padded shoulders. 'Don't be deceived,' I was told. 'Those voluminous dresses hide a multitude of shapes.'

Kampala, the capital of Uganda, is a city of decapitated sky-rises and rusted, tin-roofed shacks. Deep clefts in the land weave a tapestry of green among the buildings, where stands of bananas grow mid-city. I soon found out that the drivers of the local taxis or *matatus*, all packed with commuters, were just as impatient as those in Nairobi, beeping their horns the moment you slowed down. The rules of the road seemed to be 'Never give way, just keep going!'

During that first stormy night in the capital the lightning ripped across the darkened sky. Thunder crashed and roared all around as if Idi Amin's years of terror had returned to haunt us.

We awoke to a sultry grey sky, brightened only by the sounds of the city coming to life; the whistles of the matatu touts competing for business mingling with the incessant beeping of car horns. By 9 a.m. the sun had won a grudging victory with the clouds and it was time for us to depart.

Our first destination was Queen Elizabeth National Park, a six-hour drive from Kampala. The park lies astride the Equator in south-western Uganda and covers an

*Opposite: Sunrise over Kazinga Channel. When Kazinga National Park (later renamed Queen Elizabeth National Park) was first gazetted in 1952, a number of fishing villages were allowed to remain as enclaves within it. The Nile tilapia (Tilapia nilotica) is the most commercially important fish.*

*Pied kingfishers (Ceryle rudis) are very numerous among the swamps and reed-beds fringing the lakes and bordering the Kazinga Channel; they may be seen perching on overhanging shrubs and papyrus reeds or hovering above the water before plunging vertically downwards to catch fish.*

area of 1,978 square km (764 square miles). With the onset of the rains elsewhere in the country we were afforded a clear view of the snow-capped Ruwenzoris, the fabled 'Mountains of the Moon' which rise over 5,000 metres (16,400 ft) to the north-west of the park, looming out of the mist like ancient castles.

When Idi Amin came to power he renamed many of Uganda's famous national parks, scrapping all remnants of their European legacy. Recently the government decided to reinstate the original names to support the tourist industry, which remembers the time when the Ruwenzori National Park was better known as Queen Elizabeth National Park. Likewise, Kabalega Falls National Park has reverted to Murchison Falls National Park, Lake Idi Amin or Rutanzige is once again Lake Edward, and Lake Mobutu Sese Seke has relinquished its title to Lake Albert. The Ruwenzori Mountains have now assumed the title of Ruwenzori National Park.

The approach to Mweya Lodge in Queen Elizabeth National Park is breathtaking. A peninsula of high land juts out into Lake Edward, providing a spectacular view of both the lake and the Kazinga Channel, a 200 metre (650 ft) wide, 33 km (21 mile) long waterway linking Lake Edward with Lake George in the north-east. The lodge is situated on an 'island' at the end of the Mweya Peninsula.

I'm not sure what I had expected of the Kazinga Channel. The launch trip along it has always been one of the highlights of a safari to Queen Elizabeth National Park, a different way of viewing creatures such as hippo, buffalo and elephant, all of which at times gather in impressive numbers, even though their populations were drastically reduced during the war. There is something wonderfully relaxing about chugging along on the open water, guide book in hand to help identify the birds. There are 540 species of birds recorded here – more than in any other park in Africa – and the many waterbirds provided an added attraction to the river journey. I had never seen so many pied kingfishers. They were everywhere: perched at the edge of bushes overlooking the waterway, or flitting back and forth to their nest sites deep in tunnels in the sandy bank. I was used to seeing these distinctive black and white birds singly or in pairs, but here they gathered in extended families of four or five together at times. Over the years I had spent many hours trying to photograph these delightful little birds hovering over the water as they searched for fish and frogs: they are the only species of kingfishers that are true hoverers.

A three-hour trip on the park's launch costs US$145. When you divide this between the number of people choosing to travel it is not unreasonable: fourteen visitors arrived that first evening for a $10 ride. We were fortunate to be offered the use of one of the park's smaller boats so that we could take our time and make a thorough search of the area that we hoped to film.

As I stood outside Mweya Lodge waiting for the boatman to arrive I scanned a sizable colony of white pelicans and white-throated cormorants gathered on the far

*White pelicans (*Pelecanus onocrotalus*) are just one of many bird species to be seen on the launch trip along the Kazinga Channel. You might also expect to see cormorants, saddle-billed storks, African skimmers, grey-headed gulls and white-winged black terns.*

bank. Onen, our guide, assured us, 'This is just a few. You will see more than you can count further downstream. You won't believe your eyes.' The spot he referred to was a sandy bend in the river, favoured as a resting place by hippo and crammed with an assortment of birds: pelicans, cormorants, white-winged black terns, African skimmers, grey-headed gulls and saddle-billed storks. Overlooking the bank at the top of a rise was a fishing village. Each day the women and children came down to the river to collect water and to do their washing, ignoring the hippo and buffalo in their midst. The villagers had obviously learned over the years how to avoid confrontations with such potentially dangerous animals, proving the point that unless provoked most wild animals simply want to be left in peace.

One of the unexpected highlights of our visit to Queen Elizabeth National Park was the chance to see giant forest hog. Earlier in the year I had completed a *Safari Guide to East African Animals* – despite never having visited Uganda! I had wanted to include the giant forest hog, but had been unable to photograph it. Though sometimes shy and predominantly nocturnal, the hogs were for years relatively easy to observe in the Aberdares National Park in Kenya, a heavily forested region famous for its rare bongo, an antelope that inhabits the dense bamboo forests. In the evenings the hogs would invariably come to the waterholes at the world-famous 'tree-houses' of Tree Tops and the Ark, mingling with elephant, rhino and buffalo to eat the salt put down to attract the animals. But recently people have reported an alarming decline in the giant forest hog population, attributed to predation by lion which have been introduced into the park. It hadn't taken the lion long to realize that the saltlicks were ideal ambush sites. The bushbuck and giant forest hog proved particularly vulnerable to this form of predation, having never learned to fear attack by lion and being unable to defend themselves in the way buffalo or rhino can.

It is probably the relative scarcity of predators such as lion in Queen Elizabeth National Park that has lured the giant forest hogs into the open. We saw sounders with large numbers of young rooting around for shoots and tubers among the dry grass, bunching together and moving into the thickets when alarmed. Here too were bushbuck, exposing themselves in open ground to take advantage of the carpet of grass that had sprung up where seasonal fires had swept aside the old vegetation. But they were shyer than the giant forest hog and quickly ran for cover as soon as we stopped the vehicle. Warthog were also numerous, with good-sized litters; they seemed quite relaxed feeding alongside dense clumps of bush, which they would undoubtedly have avoided if there had been more predators. I listened for the sounds of lion roaring, but an eerie silence pervaded the night, broken only occasionally by the mournful whooping of a spotted hyaena – another predator that seemed surprisingly scarce for a park such as this. Wild dogs were absent altogether. The reasons are plain enough: predators have been shot and poisoned.

During our visit to Uganda, talks were taking place in Kampala between officials of the National Parks and the Game Department, over the merger of the two departments. Many of the wildlife reserves formerly under the control of the Game Department were now being taken over and declared National Parks. Senior Warden Abdullahi Latif told us that, even before the war, officials in the Game Department had allowed the administration of their duties to deteriorate seriously, even to the extent of selling off parcels of land to villagers to create banana plantations. It wasn't long before permanent dwellings appeared, followed by extended families and eventually villages. Even so, some people questioned the wisdom of amalgamating the two departments. Would there be sufficient money and trained staff to enable parks to do a better job? The debate continues. Certainly the current enforcement of law and order in Uganda's parks is laudable, and there is a heavy fine if you drive off the road or harass the animals. In Uganda the wardens are in charge – not the tour drivers.

Robin and I spent five nights at Mweya Lodge, rising each morning before dawn to get the best out of our visit. There was an abundance of waterbuck and Uganda cob. And on one occasion we were rewarded with a spectacular sunrise framed by silhouettes of the luxuriant euphorbia forest growing along the banks of the Kazinga Channel. Further down the road there were lovely views of fishermen in canoes setting out their nets. But our excursions by boat along the channel lacked drama. It was almost too gentle. Our emotions fluctuated daily – sometimes from minute to minute – between unbridled enthusiasm and a sense of despondency. One of our reasons for visiting Uganda was as an alternative to Zimbabwe, another country that offered us the chance of exploring wildlife from the water. Onen had certainly been right about the birds – there were plenty of those. But not enough for more than a few minutes of footage. Apart from some sizable concentrations of hippo, we had seen relatively few animals gathering along the water's edge. A handful of buffalo and a single bull elephant had come to drink. The cob 'lek' had been fascinating, with the added advantage of continuing throughout the year, so there was the possibility of picking up ten minutes' worth of filming with them. But nothing had really stood out. It would certainly make a lovely, relaxed holiday – we hardly saw another vehicle the whole trip. But Robin now had serious doubts about it making a *Dawn to Dusk*.

Perhaps we had missed something that could help us out of our dilemma. We went back to the notes our researcher Marguerite had prepared so meticulously and scoured the latest guide book for inspiration. People had mentioned the Ishasha Plains in the south of the park as being remarkably unspoiled and particularly beautiful. Ishasha is a savanna area, described to me as reminiscent of the Masai Mara, boasting large herds of topi and buffalo, as well as tree-climbing lion and that extraordinary ornithological rarity the shoe-bill stork, sometimes referred to as the whale-headed stork.

Much has been made of Ishasha's tree-climbing lion, just as it has about the lion in Lake Manyara National Park in Tanzania, which are also often to be found resting in the trees. All lions can climb trees and will do so if necessary or when the mood takes them. The fact that certain areas are renowned for this habit is probably due to a variety of reasons, such as a preponderance of biting insects which the lion wish to avoid or because (as is the case at Ishasha) the grass is often extremely long, making it easier to search for prey or to locate a pride mate. Sprawling among the luxuriant arms of an ancient fig in Ishasha or dozing in a flat-topped acacia in Lake Manyara must be a secure and pleasant way to spend a hot afternoon, safely out of reach of a herd of buffalo or a cantankerous cow elephant. The tree-climbing habit in these regions has become part of lion culture, passed down over the years by the older members of the pride to their offspring, becoming just another facet of being a lion.

The rains that a week ago had threatened to spoil our Uganda safari had failed to materialize, but both Robin and I agreed that it would be tempting fate to head south to Ishasha. The roads in that part of the park are over black cotton soil – a nightmare to drive through when wet, with the consistency of chewing gum.

Another suggestion had been to visit Kidepo National Park in the north. Here we were told we might find cheetah as well as zebra, though there were no wildebeest, and the black rhino had all been killed. We were warned that security in the area was tenuous. For years gangs of heavily armed Sudanese rebels had made driving in the area a risky business. In the end neither Ishasha nor Kidepo seemed to offer what we were looking for, and neither place could compare with similar savanna parks in Kenya or Tanzania.

That night we gathered on the veranda of Mweya Lodge for a beer. By chance Hans Klingel, 'Mr Hippo', was on one of his regular visits to the Institute of Ecology, which is based at Mweya. I had read about Hans's work on zebra in the late 1960s, when he and his wife had been based in the Serengeti. With his reputation established, he had chosen to focus on hippo. The park is one of the best places to study hippo, and prior to the culling scheme initiated in 1958 the hippo population had burgeoned to 15,000, with signs of severe overgrazing along the lake and channel. Areas near the lakes and wallows were trampled and overgrazed, causing soil erosion and leaving no alternative but to cull. By 1966, over 7,000 hippo had been shot using high-powered rifles at night when the animals emerged from the water to feed. The meat was given away to the surrounding villages as a goodwill gesture. Heavy poaching in the 1970s and '80s halved the remaining population, though it has already recovered to almost 8,000. Hans Klingel's fascination with these gigantic creatures sustained itself throughout the bad years, and a succession of students worked under his tutelage. Now he wanted to write a book and publish a definitive paper on the hippo, which despite its rather ponderous looks and slothful ways can run faster than a man and probably kills more people than either elephant or buffalo.

Until recently Queen Elizabeth National Park supported a greater density of large mammals – mainly elephant, hippopotamus, buffalo, kob and topi – than anywhere else on earth. The park offers a great diversity of habitat and during the last twenty-five years scientists from all over the world have conducted a variety of research here, covering such topics as fire ecology, termite colonies, the feeding habits of large herbivores such as elephant, the social behaviour of the banded mongoose and the

Uganda kob, and the population densities of various species of small grassland birds. Dr Eric Edroma, the current Director of National Parks, studied the vegetation here in 1971, the year before Onen, our guide, joined up as a park ranger.

Onen had stayed on during the war, though tourism slowed to a trickle and the revenue necessary to keep the parks alive was almost non-existent. Roads remained untended, and sometimes there was no money to pay staff salaries. The Ugandan army under the control of Idi Amin had free access to the parks and poaching was an everyday occurrence, a way of life. Elephant, hippo, buffalo and topi were the most commonly taken animals, and were killed in their thousands. The hippo were a particularly easy target, providing a mountain of food as well as fat to be rendered down as cooking oil. The pattern of killing was simple. The soldiers would shoot the hippo and sell the meat to the villagers. They taunted the park rangers, defying them to report them to higher authorities: 'Go ahead, report us if you like, but it will make no difference.' One day they came to Onen and forced him to take the head and neck of a freshly butchered hippo, pointedly telling him to eat it – they would be back. Onen knew that there was no way he could refuse their gruesome offer. Life was cheap in those days; he didn't want to die. Later the soldiers returned with a female kob, tender meat full of flavour, delicious eating. Soon everyone was living off the game – the army, the people and the rangers.

It wasn't only the meat. Poaching for ivory was rampant, reducing the number of elephants in the park from 2,500 to 250. There were tales of other kinds of atrocities: soldiers lobbing hand-grenades in among a pride of lions. Men can laugh in the face of a lion when they have the power of firearms to back up their bravado, exorcising their fear of predators, 'putting them in their place'. But it hadn't only been people doing the killing. Man-eating lions are known to have taken at least fifteen people over the years, mainly those walking or bicycling through the park at night, often too inebriated to know what was happening. One particular lioness was thought to have been responsible for eleven of the deaths. When she finally killed a woman the park authorities took action and shot her.

Despite the joys of liberation things weren't much better for the parks during the invasion of Uganda by the Tanzanian army. The soldiers were poorly paid and viewed the wild animals as an opportunity to recoup something for their efforts, shooting the game and selling it to the villagers. Over the years, eating wild animals has become entrenched in Ugandan culture, almost a right. Hippo meat is still sought after by people living adjacent to the park, though in general the fishing villages within the park refrain from poaching.

I still hadn't quite grown used to the sight of people from the villages riding bicycles through the park. It is an attractive thought – the indigenous human population co-existing with the wild animals, living off the land, cropping only sufficient game to feed themselves, fishing the rivers and lakes. But Onen was adamant that to allow people to continue killing animals for meat inside national parks would quickly create an impossible situation: 'If you don't protect the parks, the people will finish the animals. There is no doubt about that.' In certain places the villagers had broken up the concrete markers defining the park boundaries, and repositioned them to suit their needs, taking over the land. After the war many former soldiers brought weapons home to their villages. Every villager now knows how to use an AK47, a rather innocuous, stubby-looking weapon with an old ammunition case as a grip; deadly in the wrong hands, a killing machine for people and wildlife. It was as cheap to buy a gun as it was to take a life.

Everyone that we spoke to about our safari to Uganda said that we must visit Chambura Gorge, which marks the boundary between Queen Elizabeth National Park and the Chambura Game Reserve. Daniela de Luca had told us of the possibility of taking a canoe trip along the river at the bottom of the gorge, though she warned us that there were hippo in the narrow channel. In fact the boat she had travelled in had been attacked by a hippo and capsized. Not something that she would ever forget or want to repeat.

*Chambura* means lost or hidden and the gorge is a deep gash cut 60-90 metres

*Opposite: Chambura River Gorge marks the boundary between the Queen Elizabeth National Park and the Chambura Game Reserve, and is surrounded on either side by savanna. It is 10 km (6 miles) long and its steep sides are cloaked with thick forest, supporting many species of animals and birds, including chimpanzees, colobus, red-tailed monkeys, bats, black-and-white casqued hornbills, trogons and black bee-eaters. There are also hippo in the river flowing through the bottom of the gorge.*

(200-300 ft) into the surrounding savanna, only revealing itself when you are almost on top of it. It is cloaked with magnificent rain-forest trees, such as *Ficus mucoso* and *Cola gigantea*, which when fruiting provide a rich source of food for primates and forest birds, including a species unfamiliar to me, the black bee-eater. Our primary reason for visiting the gorge was to try and see wild chimpanzees, which we hoped might provide the highlight of our film and a fitting finale to the programme.

As we stared into the canopy of trees, black and white casqued hornbills brayed like donkeys from the tree-tops, gliding past the rim of the gorge with a noisy whooshing of their wings. The colourful Ross's turaco and Narina's trogon added to the ornithological spectacle, calling in distinctive song.

The chimpanzee habituation project was under the charge of Warden Seth Beres, a young Peace Corps worker who had been living at the ranger post for the past year. His job was to help habituate the chimpanzees so that they could be approached on foot, and to train the rangers for their role as tour guides. Seth had thoroughly enjoyed his stay in Uganda and still had another six months' tour of duty before returning to his home in America.

Our visit coincided with the final planning stage for the relocation of captive chimpanzees from Entebbe Zoo to a 400 metre (1,300 ft) long island in Lake Edward, opposite Mweya. It was certainly preferable to a miserable life incarcerated in a cage. Many of the chimps were six to ten years old and strong enough to be dangerous. A number of them had managed to escape in the past and the authorities worried that someone would be seriously injured. The older chimps had been sterilized so that they could not breed. They were due to arrive any day now.

I listened as the rangers ordered sacks of ground nuts over the radio. The vegetation on the island was unsuitable for the chimps to eat, so they would always have to be provided with food. Four keepers were to be assigned to the colony, with responsibility for feeding the chimps. Viewing platforms would be constructed so that visitors could take a boat trip to the island and watch the chimpanzees. The younger chimpanzees had already been interacting as a group and would act as a nucleus for introducing new animals into the Chambura population, where females mature at four years old, perhaps indicating that the population is capable of expanding. Certainly there are plenty of fruiting trees to support a larger colony. In Kibale, our next destination, where the population of chimpanzees is very dense, females don't start breeding until they are eight years old.

*Black and white colobus are diurnal and gregarious, and are found in forests from sea level up to 3,000 metres (10,000 ft). They differ from other monkeys in the absence of a thumb, which is reduced to a stump (the name Colobus comes from a Greek word meaning maimed or mutilated).*

While we chatted to one of our guides at the viewpoint overlooking the gorge, two of the rangers set off on foot to search for the chimps. An hour later we climbed into our vehicle and drove along the edge of the gorge, stopping every so often to listen for signs of the chimps, which are very noisy and can sometimes be heard from several kilometres away. We stopped to watch some colobus monkeys, their black, wizened faces and white beards making them look like the Father Christmases of the primate world. Small parties sat huddled together at the very tops of the trees or reclined along thick branches, soaking up the sun to thaw the night dampness from their bones. Every so often one of the territorial males would call, a wonderful harsh repetitive bark echoing back and forth along the gorge, helping to establish the position of each group before setting off for the patch of forest where they would feed for the day.

It was dark among the trees as we descended into the gorge. The air was cool and moist, the light piercing the thick canopy in places to illuminate the secret world within. We scoured the ground, searching for primate footprints in the mud. Fresh chimpanzee droppings are pale yellow, and those made the previous day were identifiable by the spitter-spatter of droplets of rain in the dung. The river running through the gorge was as brown as strong tea, barring our path ahead. The rangers felt sure that the chimps had already crossed, so we made our way to where a fallen tree bridged the river. I watched the rangers deftly tiptoe out on to the log, barely the width of a pair of feet. I faltered halfway, the weight of my backpack and the springiness of the log conspiring to try and throw me into the water. Unbearable thoughts of waterlogged cameras and ruined film flashed through my mind. I gritted my teeth and regained my composure – easy, easy does it.

I felt clumsy blundering through the forest. One of the rangers was tiny by comparison, moving nimbly through the undergrowth, his feet placed carefully on the ground, avoiding the twigs that would announce our presence to the forest's other inhabitants. I looked at his face, the olive-brown skin unmarked by exertion. He belonged here. I, meanwhile, tripped over the outstretched roots of fig trees and stumbled over rocks. My shirt was soaked, the sweat pouring down my face as we criss-crossed through the gorge, up and then down again, reassuring our guides that we were happy to continue in the hope of catching up with our quarry. It was 9.30 a.m., and we had been on the move for two hours.

The rangers shared our disappointment. This was our second visit to the gorge since arriving at Queen Elizabeth National Park. Though we had seen and heard a party of chimps feeding in one of the trees on our first outing, we had been unable to follow them. It was March, the end of the dry season, and food was scarce and scattered over a wide area. Under these circumstances a chimp might feed on a handful of fruit and then move on; there was nothing much to anchor them for any length of time – certainly not enough to allow us to approach for a longer, closer look. At this time of the year, when food was harder to find, the larger groups tended to split up into individual families of females and their young. Our guides kept telling us that it would all be 'no problem' if we returned in September.

But nothing is certain in nature. Suddenly the forest reverberated with the sound of drumming. It was the chimpanzees calling, beating a rapid tattoo on the flattened surface of one of the buttress roots. Perhaps the mother and child whose footprints we had been following had joined up with the rest of their group. Peals of excited whooping rang out. We tracked back, searching in vain for a glimpse of the apes. By now it was 10 a.m. and my rucksack was feeling heavier by the minute. Robin stared into the canopy, searching for a miracle, resting for a moment on the heavy tripod that he had been carrying for me. Neither of us spoke, but we both knew that nothing we had seen so far offered much hope for our chances of filming chimpanzees here in the gorge. Ideally we wanted to be able to observe them on the ground as well as in the trees. There was little cause for optimism. If the chimps were to be the finale to our programme, we would have to think again as to where else we might film them.

As if mocking our endeavours to locate them a big male chimpanzee emerged among the foliage at the top of a tree shortly after we had climbed out of the gorge. He peered at us with his dark brown eyes, reaching out with his hands to gather up the fruit. Having eaten he swung down through the branches, big and powerful, black and muscular, his easy, languorous movements belying his size. Then he sat, legs dangling, resting. A second, smaller chimp was just visible among the dark shadows. No wonder they were so difficult to find. They could move far quicker than the nimblest man, and if necessary sit so quietly that you might pass right by without seeing them.

This was not the end of our safari. Our next destination was Murchison Falls National Park, where we spent three days in the company of the dynamic warden, Max Linner, and where Shaun Mann, a young East African who was in the final stages of completing a guide book to the park, was happy to act as our guide. Most of the animals were to be found north of the river, which we crossed on the ferry. I had never seen so many oribi in my life, and there were parties of handsome Jackson's hartebeest, large herds of buffalo and Rothschild's giraffe. It was also an opportunity to try out the winch after we got stuck in the mud.

Through Shaun's perseverance and the knowledge of our boatman we managed to find our first shoe-bill stork. Shoe-bills are the size of a small person and look quite extraordinary with their massive shoe-shaped bills and ungainly appearance. The Arabs call them *Abu Markub* – father of the shoe. This bird had caused considerable excitement among Kenya's ornithological community by suddenly appearing at Musiara Marsh in the Masai Mara before continuing its migration to one of the swamps at Amboseli National Park in the shadow of Mount Kilimanjaro. It had never previously been recorded in Kenya and sent my friend Don Turner into overdrive just as he was putting the finishing touches to his illustrated tome *The Birds of Kenya and Northern Tanzania*.

Murchison Falls was both more and less than I expected. It may not be as wide an expanse of water or as tall as Victoria Falls, but it is nevertheless a sight to behold. We viewed the falls from above and below, staring spellbound at the sight of the Nile roaring through a gap no wider than 3 metres (10 ft) before exploding over the side of a rugged 30 metre (100 ft) high cliff. Plans were already being set in motion to offer canoe safaris along calmer stretches of the river above the falls, catering to the tastes of a new generation of travellers who want to combine wildlife watching with something a little more adventurous. From the park's boat we saw large herds of hippo and a number of huge crocodiles tending their nests on the sandy banks above the water. We paused at a spot where a brood of hatchlings had recently been deposited, carried in their mother's mouth to the river's edge, where they would be safest from predators among reeds sprouting in the shallows. The giant female kept a reptilian eye out for other crocodiles, and particularly for monitor lizards, which prey on eggs and young. I found the whole experience fascinating, and felt sure that this was to be the first of many visits that I would make to Uganda's parks. But by now Robin's thoughts were of Zimbabwe and how he could make the canoe safari there more interesting.

Neither of us was keen to admit it, but by the time we arrived at Kibale Forest to the south of Murchison Falls National Park, our hopes of filming chimpanzees in Uganda were flagging. It was the same old story: 'You should have been here yesterday when visitors saw a large group of chimps feeding on a windfall of fresh fruit.' We were joined by Adrian Treves, who was studying vigilance behaviour in red colobus and red-tailed monkeys, and spent a fascinating day in the forest, where we were able to see groups of blue monkeys, red-tailed colobus and red-tailed monkeys, a species that I had often watched in the Kichwa Tembo forest in the Masai Mara. Chimps hunt both the red and the black and white colobus, co-operating in a noisy, intimidating mob attack that terrifies most other monkey species. There are exceptions to this. Mangabeys often feed in the same trees as the chimps, and sometimes red-tailed monkeys dart in and out of the foliage to grab some food without being caught.

We did see one solitary chimpanzee at Kibale. It was the six-year-old female known as Nectar. She was immediately recognizable by her crippled left hand, the result of tearing herself free from a snare, embedding the wire noose deep into her wrist. Twenty per cent of the chimpanzees observed at Kibale suffer the loss of fingers or hands in snares set by meat poachers, hunting primarily bushbuck and duikers, though they will eat chimps too if they catch them. The villagers have mixed feeling about the chimps, which can be very destructive to crops and sometimes lie in wait until it is safe to raid the *shambas* (small cultivated pieces of land).

It was almost 6 p.m., and we were about to leave when Adrian spotted Nectar. It was time for her to start making the nest of leaves in which she would spend the night. She made a pathetic figure as she climbed 30 metres (100 ft) up to an old nest. Apparently females sometimes use old nests, while males build a new one each evening. Nectar avoided the other chimps, eating young leaves – second-rate foodstuff, as Adrian described it – and was gradually losing weight. It must have been a lonely existence for such a social animal. Nectar bent some of the nearby branches to reinforce her bed; it takes a healthy chimp only a matter of minutes to make a new nest, but with her withered arm the young female sought an old one whenever possible. All of the great apes sleep in trees at night; real sleep – not the catnapping indulged in by many mammals. Here they can rest, safely out of reach of most predators.

I hardly needed to wait for Robin's decision on where we would be filming this particular episode. Even though there were serious reservations about what Zimbabwe had to offer, Uganda was just too much of a gamble, given the limitations imposed by time. But I had seen enough of the chimps to spark my interest. When I got back to Nairobi I went in search of something readable on chimpanzees, and found just what I was looking for – a copy of Jane Goodall's latest book, *Through a Window*. Next I scoured the second-hand bookshops for more material, and picked out copies of *National Geographic*, which had supported Jane's work in Tanzania. A new and exciting journey was about to begin.

*At Murchison Falls the Nile funnels into a 3 metre (10 ft) wide gap in the rocks, then bursts out over a 30 metre (100 ft) high cliff. A launch trip will take you to the base of the falls, but it is only from the top that you truly appreciate the power and force of the water.*

# TANZANIA: MAN'S CLOSEST RELATIVES

*Opposite page: Ferdinand. Young chimpanzees are weaned at the age of three to five years. Males retain a strong bond with their mother into adulthood, while females leave their natal group and transfer to another group before beginning to breed. This long period of dependency allows young chimps to acquire and refine the social skills they need if they are to integrate successfully into the complex world of chimpanzee society.*

*There are many windows through which we can look out into the world, searching for meaning. There are those opened up by science, their panes polished by a succession of brilliant, penetrating minds. Through these we can see ever further, ever more clearly, into areas that once lay beyond human knowledge. Gazing through such a window I have, over the years, learned much about chimpanzee behaviour and their place in the nature of things. And this, in turn, has helped us to understand a little better some aspects of human behaviour, our own place in nature.*

*But there are other windows; windows that have been unshuttered by the logic of philosophers; windows through which the mystics seek their visions of the truth; windows from which the leaders of the great religions have peered as they searched for purpose not only in the wondrous beauty of the world, but also in its darkness and ugliness. Most of us, when we ponder on the mystery of our existence, peer through but one of these windows onto the world. And even that one is often misted over by the breath of our finite humanity. We clear a tiny peephole and stare through. No wonder we are confused by the tiny fraction of a whole that we see. It is, after all, like trying to comprehend the panorama of the desert or the sea through a rolled-up newspaper.*

*As I stood quietly in the pale sunshine, so much a part of the rain-washed forests and the creatures that lived there, I saw for a brief moment through another window and with other vision. It is an experience that comes, unbidden, to some of us who spend time alone in nature. The air was filled with a feathered symphony, the evensong of birds. I heard new frequencies in their music and, too, in the singing of insect voices, notes so high and sweet that I was amazed. I was intensely aware of the shape, the colour, of individual leaves, the varied patterns of the veins that made each one unique. Scents were clear, easily identifiable – fermenting, over-ripe fruit; water-logged earth; cold, wet bark; the damp odour of chimpanzee hair and, yes, my own too. And the aromatic scent of young, crushed leaves was almost overpowering. I sensed the presence of a bushbuck, then saw him, quietly browsing upwind, his spiralled horns dark with rain. And I was utterly filled with that peace 'which passeth all understanding'.*

**Jane Goodall *Through A Window***

In 1960, under the watchful eye of the famous anthropologist Louis Leakey, a young woman called Jane Goodall left her home in England to live among wild chimpanzees in what was then the Gombe Stream Game Reserve in Tanganyika. Thirty-five years later Jane Goodall's work is familiar to people the world over, and the field study she created is the longest continuous field project on record.

I too was captivated by the idea of living among wild animals, but not in order to study primates; Africa's great predators were what fascinated me most. It was only when Jane Goodall and her first husband, wildlife film-maker Hugo van Lawick, turned their attentions to the predators of the Ngorongoro Crater and the Serengeti that they really stirred my imagination. Their book *Innocent Killers* was a vivid and intimate portrayal of hyaenas, wild dogs and jackals – predators that had long been despised as ruthless killers, little short of vermin. Jane and Hugo chose to give some of the predators names – Bloody Mary, the hyaena matriarch; Solo, the wild dog puppy – something of which many scientists disapproved, dismissing it as anthropomorphic and lacking in objectivity. Animal subjects were to be thought of as objects of study rather than the living, breathing, flesh-and-blood creatures that they really are. But naming their study animals in no way prevented Jane and Hugo from producing a fascinating pictorial account illuminated with words on the lives of these animals. Not only were there new findings on how these creatures behaved, but there was also an empathy with them that touched the hearts of the general public and helped win support for creatures that have often been ridiculed or persecuted by man.

Jane and Hugo divorced a few years later, and while Jane returned to her beloved Gombe and later married Derek Bryceson, Hugo continued his own love affair with the Serengeti. I well remember the excitement I felt when I walked into a bookshop in Nairobi in 1978 and picked up a copy of his latest book, *Savage Paradise*. I had only recently arrived in Kenya and here, captured in all their magnificence, were the lions and leopards that I hoped to follow in the Masai Mara: intimate portraits of the big cats, hyaenas, jackals and the elusive wild dogs jumped from the book's pages. Hugo is the master of back light, and the drama of the landscape was here too, depicted in all its varied faces. The fact that someone had even managed to *see* the sights depicted in *Savage Paradise*, let alone capture them with a camera, left me gasping in admiration. If this was what the Mara might have in store for me I was blessed indeed.

Hugo stills spends much of his time based at Ndutu, just south of the boundary dividing the Serengeti from the Ngorongoro Conservation Area. His tented camp is known to friends as 'Hugo's Hilton' – and there are many who drop by to mull over old times with a glass of brandy and a dish of chocolate mousse the like of which I have never tasted. Now in his late fifties and dogged by emphysema, Hugo still indulges his penchant for endless cups of black coffee and strong cigarettes. He laughs, charming as ever, at the concern of his friends. After thirty years of recording the day-to-day existence of the Serengeti and its denizens, Hugo shows little sign of living or working anywhere else.

It had troubled me for some while, my sidelining of the primates. I suppose it was just that I found the big cats and wild dogs more fascinating and intriguing to study than either primates or people. There never seemed to be time to visit the gorillas or chimpanzees – and still keep track of the lions and leopards that I had come to know as individuals. Every so often I would read an article on Jane Goodall's work or watch a television programme featuring the chimpanzees at Gombe, often including old footage taken by Hugo, who had first met Jane when he was sent by *National Geographic* to film her work. Though I always found the material interesting, twenty years had now passed and still I hadn't seen the chimps for myself. But hopefully that was about to change.

Towards the end of 1995, we were becoming increasingly desperate to finalize a location for our sixth programme. After our lack of success in Uganda, we had hoped that the Mahale Mountains on the shores of Lake Tanganyika might provide sufficient footage for a programme on chimpanzees. Mahale is a beautiful place, with mountains rising steeply from the wide sandy lake-shore beach to a height of 2,591 metres (8,500 ft). The chimps at Mahale have been studied by students from Kyoto University in Japan for the last thirty years; they number approximately a hundred individuals, the largest known chimp community anywhere. The dominant or alpha male, Ntologi, who had reigned supreme for the last ten years, had recently been challenged by another male called Saba and the harmony within the community was disrupted. But after our experience in Uganda trying to locate filmable chimps, Robin Hellier was naturally cautious about the prospects of finding sufficient material to fill a thirty-minute programme. The key consideration was whether we could capture enough film of me with the chimps within a mere two weeks. Our priorities were quite the reverse of what is generally considered the way to make a wildlife documentary, a process usually taking many months – even years – of painstaking observation.

The only other location where we could film chimpanzees was Gombe National Park, to the north of Mahale. But Alistair Fothergill, the head of the BBC Natural History Unit, was worried that Gombe had become too familiar to wildlife viewers over the years, and that the clearing around the feeding station, with its neatly trimmed grass, would look unnatural. The feeding station was often chosen as an easy option to grab some chimp footage. Here the chimps were occasionally fed bananas to help to keep them habituated; they could also be weighed as they clambered on to the scales to reach the fruit.

Then Robin Hellier phoned me to say that there was now some doubt as to whether there would be a sixth programme at all. The logistics of filming at both Mahale and Gombe were proving difficult. Time was running short and unless an alternative location could be found within the next week or so the series would be cut to five programmes. One possibility was an underwater show in Mozambique. I had always hoped that we might be able to feature places that had hitherto received relatively little publicity – countries that had disappeared from public view because of their

inaccessibility or the effects of years of war and civil disorder, abandoned as areas of recreation or as places where conservation still had a part to play. Mozambique would certainly have fitted that category, but again there were logistical problems that could not be sorted out in the time available.

Much as I respected Robin's judgement I naturally felt disappointed at the prospect of the series being cut back. I had gradually warmed to the idea of featuring primates – particularly if it were to be chimpanzees. Since returning from Uganda I had buried myself in Jane Goodall's book. Little had I realized what a treat lay in store for me.

Not only did *Through a Window* help to fill a gap in my understanding of the natural world, it awoke a latent interest in another area of science that I had long neglected – the study of early man. Louis Leakey was the catalyst for some of the most exciting field work ever undertaken on Africa's wild animals. It was he who encouraged and helped to find the funding for Dian Fossey, Jane Goodall and Beruite Geldikas to devote the best part of their lives to the study of the great apes: gorillas, chimpanzees and orang-utans respectively. Leakey hoped that his three protégées would provide him with insights into the behaviour of our earliest ancestors – into what made us human.

In the final analysis Louis Leakey's trio of field workers accomplished more than he could ever have dreamed – his 'ape ladies', as they became known, opened our eyes to the extraordinarily complex world of these highly intelligent creatures, prompting a wave of interest in the plight of the great apes and the whole basis upon which man has removed himself from his rightful place alongside his closest living relatives. We now know that the biological differences between modern man and apes are very small. Though chimpanzees are undoubtedly not humans, the physical differences are not much more marked than those between the different breeds of dog. At the molecular level the differences are minute, as witnessed by the fact that of the several hundred amino acids in the haemoglobin of man and the gorilla, only one is different. Human beings and chimpanzees share 99 per cent of the same genetic material. The chimpanzee is more closely related to human beings than the fox is to the dog; about the same difference as that between a zebra and a horse. Knowing that should surely change our outlook on life – all life.

Finally, and with a sense of great relief, I was told that we would be going to Gombe in early January 1996. My co-host would be Charlotte Uhlenbroek, a young Englishwoman who had initially been helping Jane Goodall to conduct a census of a chimpanzee population that roamed near a local settlement in Burundi. Charlotte had then spent two years at Gombe habituating the Matumba chimpanzee community in the north of the park, to try to lessen the impact of tourism on the most habituated chimpanzees at Gombe, the Kasakela community. After a further two years studying chimpanzee vocalizations for her Phd, Charlotte returned to England, to Bristol University, where she had taken her first degree in zoology. That was two years ago and, having just completed her Phd, she was delighted to have the opportunity to return to Gombe for our programme. She would arrive a day or so before us.

I joined the rest of the crew at Nairobi Airport on 8 January 1996 to fly to Lake Tanganyika in Tanzania. A trouble-free flight took us to Mwanza on the shores of Lake Victoria, where we cleared customs and immigration. Onward then to Kigoma Airport, a sleepy transit point where we stopped for lunch while our equipment was loaded on to the boat that would take us to Gombe National Park.

When Robin Hellier began planning the Gombe film it quickly became apparent that we would need a special team of people to be able to work in the kind of terrain that the chimpanzees favour. Like Mahale, Gombe is characterized by deep valleys and steep ridges, with *korongos* or drainage lines running west from the Rift Valley escarpment (1,700 metres/5,577 ft) down to the shores of Lake Tanganyika (772 metres/ 2,532 ft). Climbing hundreds of metres up and then down again in search of the chimps might be easy for creatures adept at slipping between the vines and under branches on all fours or 'crutch' walking downhill by swinging their hind legs forwards between their arms. For humans to do the same requires considerable energy and enthusiasm and a dogged determination to succeed. The key participants were the documentary cameraman Chris Openshaw and his assistant Andrew Thompson, and soundman Adrian Bell. All three immediately proved to be more than up to the task – particularly as they had recently returned from filming at the base camp (4,725 metres/15,500 ft) on K2, the world's second highest peak, rated by climbers as the most difficult climb there is. They soon found that they were in good company, as Charlotte had herself climbed to 5,500 metres (18,000 ft) on Everest in 1979 when she was twelve years old.

Our specialist cameraman, Bill Wallauer, lived at Gombe and had just returned from a visit to his home in North America. Muscular and bearded with a lively twinkle in his eye, Bill was transformed the moment his feet touched dry land at Gombe; from being a rather shy, conservatively dressed thirty-year-old he turned into a whirlwind of activity. Bill's heart was here with the chimpanzees. For my part, I had always relished a physical challenge and looked forward to some real exercise after being cooped up in my Landcruiser for days at a time photographing cheetah in the Masai Mara.

Low, thatched shelters dotted the shoreline, nestled high up on the beach, temporarily abandoned by the fishermen and their families during the full moon, which made fishing difficult. During our twelve-day visit we would see them reappear – lines of canoes strung out across the water, the lights of their paraffin lanterns bobbing along. Everywhere the shoreline was dotted with dugout canoes, the fishermen's nets lying idle on the beach. A man stood on a rock in the shallows with rod and line, casting into the clear, pale blue waters of the lake. Children laughed and played, skipping through the water, and clusters of baboons gathered to pick over the vegetation and search for scraps of food in the clearings made by the villagers, totally unconcerned by the people walking among them.

After an hour and a half's boat ride we landed along a narrow strip of pebble beach, swathed by a backdrop of intensely green vegetation, growing thickly on the steep slopes. I had seen so many photographs and watched so many hours of film footage on Gombe that I felt a strange sense of familiarity. A series of steep-sided valleys cloaked in emerald green rose from the shore, cut deep into the round-topped hills with their grass-covered peaks. In the distance I could see fires.

The beach at Gombe disappears so sharply around a corner that you feel as if you have been cast ashore on a tropical island. Robinson Crusoe would have been happy to have been washed up here. As we landed we were welcomed by Anthony Collins, the senior member of staff from the Jane Goodall Institute at Gombe, which has been his home for most of the past twenty years. Anton, as everyone calls him, is a gentle, quiet man and one of the world's authorities on the olive baboon. He hoped in the coming years to be able to get back to research work rather than administration, and was involved with the analysis of long-term data with Craig Packer, co-ordinator of the Serengeti Lion Research Project. Though baboons are less 'intellectual' than chimpanzees, they are more adaptable and are found virtually all over Africa. Anton had a soft spot for baboons, which he considered thoroughly entertaining, more so than chimpanzees on a minute-to-minute basis, providing lots of laughs to brighten up the rainiest day.

That evening we swam in the lake – at 1,435 metres (4,708 ft) the deepest in Africa and second deepest in the world. The water was the perfect temperature for swimming, clear as a bell, clean and fresh-tasting. As I swam back to shore, a chorus of whoops and grunts drifted down from the thick canopy of forest. Bill Wallauer suddenly appeared, a red and white bandanna tied round his head, sweat streaming down his face. 'Virtually the whole of the Kasakela chimpanzee community are here. Fifi and Sandy are both in oestrus, so there is a lot of activity – males displaying all over the place.' The alpha male Freud and his younger brother Frodo were there, too – all the big males. It was incredible luck to have found them so soon.

We celebrated our arrival with cold beer and freshly caught fish and rice, with a banana and coffee to finish. Inevitably the talk was of the chimps, particularly of old Fifi – now thirty-eight and still producing babies as regularly as clockwork. Everybody smiled as details of the chimps' sexual habits were discussed – as I was later to find out, the description 'pink bottoms' was something of an understatement for the outlandish genital swellings of females in oestrus.

After supper I walked down to the lake. Silvery moonlight glistened across its calm waters and I could just make out the mainland of Zaire, almost 60 km (40 miles) away to the west. To the north lay the tiny mountain state of Burundi, whose people are still caught up in the endless cycle of tribal violence which they share with their neighbours in Rwanda. In fact the local people living in the Gombe region are the Waha, kinsmen of the Hutu of Burundi.

The bloody disturbances in Rwanda and Burundi have virtually killed off tourism to Gombe. Only one other person from overseas, a young German, visited the park during our stay, while a group of Asians made a day trip from Kigoma to see the chimps.

Ironically, in recent times the authorities had begun to feel that too many people were visiting the chimps, so park fees were increased in an attempt to reduce the number of visitors while maintaining the revenue. Overseas visitors now pay US$100 per day, and you must either camp or pay an additional US$25 per night to stay at the hostel, a bare-boned brick building with corrugated-iron roof.

To reach Gombe from the nearest departure point at Kigoma, you either join the throng of people crowded into one of the 'water taxis' that ply the shores of the lake, or travel with your own group by hiring a boat from Sunset Tours for US$120 one way. You have to bring all your food with you (unless you hire the services of a safari operator), and there is access to a kitchen of sorts. Near the hostel is the rest house, previously used by Jane Goodall, which has wire mesh enclosing the dining area to prevent the baboons from helping themselves to the food. The rest house now serves as a base for film crews such as ours or for VIPs from the National Parks Department.

We divided ourselves between the two buildings to sleep, and ate together at the rest house. Accommodation was basic but comfortable – a metal-frame bed in a bare room illuminated by a paraffin lamp. The toilets were of the 'long-drop' variety, and our bath was the lake. But we enjoyed the simplicity of it all, and Joseph our cook produced delicious food for us each evening, greatly appreciated by hearty appetites stimulated by the rigours of steep climbs. His repertoire included rice and fish cooked in coconut and tomato sauce, chicken masala and tomato salad – even chips. Lunch was chocolate bars, peanuts, raisins and water – quite sufficient for our needs and light to carry.

As I walked back to the hostel that first evening, the pebbles crunching under my feet, I saw a shadowy figure with an automatic rifle standing motionless beneath a clump of trees, keeping watch over our rooms. He was a reminder of the nightmarish evening in May 1975 when forty armed men from Zaire crossed the lake and kidnapped four of the Gombe students. Anton, who came to Gombe in 1972, was fortunate to have left for Ruaha that same day. The students were eventually released unharmed, but only after a ransom had been paid by the father of one of them, and the incident proved highly sensitive politically, involving as it did Tanzania, Zaire and the United States. Though the kidnapping put paid to any further research at Gombe by overseas students, the Tanzanian field staff continued to collect data on a day-to-day basis, charting the movements of the chimps, which individuals associated with whom, and what they were eating. With Jane Goodall's encouragement the staff were able to work on their own and gather increasingly sophisticated information on the chimps. Before long they knew as much about the chimps' habits as any expert. When Charlotte Uhlenbroek began her study four years ago, she became the first overseas student to work for her Phd at Gombe since the kidnapping.

I gulped down a couple of bitter-tasting anti-malarial tablets, put the paraffin light outside my door and crawled under the mosquito net. We had been warned that the mosquitoes could be a real plague, and that malaria was rife in the area. But I was too tired to care. The air was damp and musty and smelt of mildew, but the bed was comfortable and I lay listening to the sing-song voices of the fishermen on the lake and dreamed a little about my first encounter with the chimpanzees.

Whatever I might have expected, my first glimpse of the chimps was just as exciting as everybody had predicted it would be. It was an hour or more since we had started to hike up the steep valley, and my shirt was sodden from the exertion. As we topped the rise we found ourselves at the edge of a clearing in the *miombo* woodland. Charlotte pointed ahead of her to where Freud lay watching our approach.

Freud is Fifi's eldest son; now twenty-five years old, he is currently the alpha male of the Kasakela community. He lay totally relaxed, with one foot crossed over his leg and one arm cupped behind his head. It was uncanny. But perhaps the most startling revelation came when I looked into his eyes. It was like meeting the gaze of another human being – questioning, expressive, inquiring. When you look into the eyes of a buffalo or an antelope there is little sense of inquiry or recognition, no feeling that they see in the way we do. But a chimpanzee looks to see what you are doing. Freud's

*Freud about to display. Freud is now in his second year as alpha male, and achieved the top-ranking position through the help of Goblin, himself a former alpha male. Freud is a very relaxed and calm leader, only intervening in disputes when absolutely necessary; he does not terrorize community members in the way that Goblin used to.*

eyes were the colour of hazel-nuts and glistened with a familiar knowingness. They were quite different from the eyes of any other animal I had ever seen.

I had only just started to get over the excitement of seeing Freud, when Fifi appeared, accompanied by her two youngest offspring, Faustino and Ferdinand, and followed by one of her daughters and another infant. Fifi stopped to let Ferdinand climb off her back and lay down in the grass next to Freud, who began to groom her. Suddenly little Ferdinand walked towards me and grabbed me by the hand, tugging at it. I have always tried to distance myself from the idea of wild animals as pets, much as I love the companionship of my own domestic cats and dogs. But that moment of unsolicited contact between myself and the young chimp totally entranced me – not because the chimpanzees seemed almost human in many of the things they did, but simply because it underlined for me that we humans are just as much a part of the natural world as they are.

Charlotte explained to me that chimpanzees live in what are described by scientists as fission-fusion societies, in which males usually remain within their natal home range and young females emigrate. Each community is composed of twenty to a hundred individuals, all of whom interact with one another on a relatively friendly basis and share a common home range, though members of a community do not always travel together. The males in a community are often closely related and band together to defend the females. Gombe, which is 52 square km (20 square miles) in area, provides a sanctuary for three communities of chimpanzees, approximately 120 animals in total: the Mitumba community in the north with twenty to thirty individuals, which Charlotte had helped to habituate when she first came to Gombe; the Kasakela community, of which Fifi and her family are a part; and the Nyasanga community in the south, which has never been studied. The best known and most habituated chimps are the Kasakela community, which currently numbers forty-six and occupies a home range of 15-20 square km (6-8 square miles).

I couldn't believe how lucky we had been to encounter such a large group of chimpanzees so quickly, and to find them in relatively open habitat. By the end of that first day, I had watched the chimps grooming, feeding, playing, mating and displaying. The fact that we had good light to film in had been the icing on the cake. But we all knew how suddenly things could change, and so for the first few days we tried to spend as much time as possible with the chimps, locating them early in the morning and keeping track of their whereabouts until nightfall. Sunrise was often shrouded by cloud cover and it was usually only later in the morning that the sun emerged. After a quick wash in the lake, a slice of pawpaw and a plate of fried eggs, it was time to pack the equipment into rucksacks and share them out among ourselves and the porters. Fortunately I had been kitted out with a pair of hockey shoes intended for use on astroturf. The soles looked like a multi-studded monster or rubberized caterpillar, but whoever designed them certainly knew what it took to keep someone from slipping on wet surfaces.

Fortunately we could rely on the help of the Tanzanian field assistants to find the chimps. Working in pairs, they went out first thing each morning to the place where the chimpanzees had nested the previous night. We communicated with them by radio, and with Bill and Charlotte to guide us through the forest it was relatively easy to track them down. Relatively easy it may have been, but it was still exhausting.

Of all the animals featured in this series, the chimpanzees' activity cycle most closely mirrored our theme of 'from dawn to dusk'. Their daily routine begins with an early rise just before first light, followed by bouts of displaying by the males and periods of grooming. Sometimes individuals wander off in search of food immediately after they have left their nests. The middle of the day is siesta time and is often relatively quiet with the chimps resting up in trees – some sitting, others reclining along branches with the youngsters suckling or playing with one another. For a while, sometimes an hour or more, an air of peace prevails, increasingly punctuated by the occasional outburst of pant-hoots and displays as the chimps decide to move on again. On occasion members of the community move off on their own, but during our stay there were often twenty or thirty chimps within a few metres of each other. This was due in part to Fifi and Sandy's being in oestrus and in part to the crop of fruiting vines that were currently their preferred food source. The relaxed pattern of intermittent grooming and feeding continued until well into the evening; then some time between 7 and 8 p.m. they all climbed into the trees and made their nests.

Being with the chimps was as unique and moving an experience as spending time with Randall Moore's elephants had been; more so in many ways because the chimps were truly wild and did not depend on humans for either their food or their protection. It also provided us with the best possible filming opportunities, allowing Charlotte and me to position ourselves close to the chimpanzees without affecting their behaviour or disturbing their routine. In fact the chimps simply ignored us. Most of them had grown up with human beings; they were watched almost daily and did not feel threatened by our presence. Some of the females were shyer and less relaxed with people around, in many cases because they had immigrated from other communities that were less well habituated to human company.

We soon found that chimpanzees are highly mobile and can travel widely in their search for suitable sources of food, and when patrolling the borders of their home range. They are primarily frugivorous or fruit-eaters, though they also feed seasonally on young leaves, which are rich in protein, and the flowers of certain species of plants, as well as killing and eating monkeys, young bushpig and bushbuck, and insects.

The complex mosaic of plant life at Gombe means that there are always some species of trees bearing fruit for the chimps to feed on throughout the year. The sides of the valleys are cloaked with forest dominated by species such as *Newtonia* spp., *Pseudospondias microcarpa* and *Trichilia* spp., flanked by vine tangles and woodland thickets. The forests are rich in nutritious fruiting trees with at least sixteen species of fig, and many evergreen vines such as *Saba florida* and *Landolphia lucida* (called in

Swahili *Mabungo makubwa* and *Mabungo madogo* respectively) flourishing on the upper slopes. During our visit the Mabungo madogo vines were laden with round yellow and red fruits varying in size between a grape and a lime. Charlotte and Bill were addicted to the fruits, and I soon learned that when you are thirsty and your mouth is dry, breaking open a Mabungo fruit is the perfect solution. The seeds are covered with soft succulent tissue and taste rather tart. The chimps also eat the pith of the vines and chew the fibrous oily orange parts of the fruit of the oil palm nut, which is available year-round. But they are unable to crack the 'nut' itself. Olive baboons manage to do this by using their immensely powerful canines, especially if the nuts have fallen to the ground and dried out a little. In Guinea-Bissau in West Africa, chimpanzees crack open the oil palm nuts using a stone and anvil, but here at Gombe the chimps haven't learned this particular use of a tool.

Ever since I began to take an interest in chimpanzee behaviour, I have been fascinated by the discovery that chimps have the ability to make and use simple tools. But I never for a moment expected to have the chance to witness such behaviour for myself or that we might be able to film it. However, one morning as we followed a group of chimps along a path through the dense vine tangles, the males suddenly started to display, hair bristling, flailing their arms about them and pulling on the willowy saplings. As one of them raced up a tree, screaming loudly, Freud came charging into view, hair erect and making him look larger than ever. Everyone – the females in particular – pant-hooted in appeasement as he continued to display in front of them.

Charlotte looked puzzled as she tried to make some sense of their behaviour. Then through the bushes I caught sight of two or three chimps sitting with their backs to me on a termite mound at the base of a dead tree. At first I couldn't make out what they were doing. But as we moved closer, I saw that they were 'fishing' for termites, breaking off a slender branch from a bush and then stripping off the leaves with their lips before dipping the twig into one of the holes in the mound and carefully withdrawing it again. Some of the chimps had perfected the technique and gently twirled the twig around and around inside the hole, collecting up as many termites as possible before withdrawing up to a dozen of them at a time and carefully holding the twig across their forearm to catch any that fell off.

Even the youngest chimps attempted to eat the termites -with varying degrees of success, according to their age and experience. Some simply picked the termites up in their fingers or bent forwards and tried to lap or suck them up, bottom lip extended to prise them from the earth. One young chimp -Faustino, I think – picked up someone else's discarded twig and fished for himself, though he was generally too impatient to let the termites climb on to the twig or allowed them to drop off before he could get them to his mouth. Soon there were chimps 'fishing' at nearly every hole. Some arrived having already prepared their 'tool', and this is the remarkable thing – the chimps were not only *using* a tool, they were making one for a specific task.

It was during her first year at Gombe, 1960, that Jane Goodall discovered that

*One of the Kasakela community fishing for termites. Jane Goodall's discovery that chimps were capable of fashioning tools prompted Louis Leakey to respond, 'Now we must redefine tool, redefine Man, or accept chimpanzees as humans.'*

chimps were capable of fashioning a tool. She watched in disbelief as David Greybeard, the first chimp to accept her presence, trimmed a wide grass blade and poked it into a termite nest, withdrawing it again laden with termites. The discovery sent shock waves through the scientific community. Up until then one of the defining characteristics of 'Man', setting him apart from all other animals in his inventiveness, was the ability and intelligence needed to make a tool. Suddenly people were forced to accept the fact that chimpanzees too were capable of reasoning and insight. That same year Jane was amazed to see David Greybeard eating a bushpig, confounding the long-held belief that chimpanzees where purely vegetarian. When she wrote to Louis Leakey to tell him that she had observed one of the Gombe chimps not only using bits of straw to fish for termites but actually stripping leaves from a stem so making tools, he replied by telegram: 'Now we must redefine *tool*, redefine *Man*, or accept chimpanzees as humans.' It was later apparent that tool-using traditions were capable of being passed from one generation to the next through observation, imitation and practice, and that each population might be expected to have its own tool-making culture.

*An adult male chimpanzee displays his powerful teeth. Chimpanzees have thirty-two teeth (which are larger than those of humans) and the males are armed with powerful conical canines, twice as long as their incisors, which can inflict terrible wounds. Males sometimes gang up and kill or seriously injure individuals from communities bordering their territory, though it is more usual for neighbours to pant-hoot and demonstrate without attacking one another.*

Charlotte was surprised to find the chimps feeding on termites at this time of the year. Termite season is normally at a peak around November and continues intermittently into December. It had rained the previous night, prompting the release of alates or winged termites, which emerge during the rains to search for suitable sites to form new colonies. Their translucent, lace-like wings littered the base of the mound. These future kings and queens were laden with rich sources of energy, full of fat, protein and carbohydrate. But the chimps didn't need to fish for the alates, simply scooping them up in handfuls and stuffing them into their mouths.

Each day at Gombe was a revelation. I was totally hooked on chimp-watching. Individuality is so well defined in chimpanzees that it was like following a soap opera, as entertaining as any that humans have thought up. With Charlotte to guide me I soon learned who was who, and once I could recognize individuals I could begin to understand the relationships between members of the Kasakela community; I could watch and comprehend as alliances were reinforced or weakened in the constant jostling for power and status.

Charlotte proved to be the ideal choice as co-host for the chimpanzee programme. She had the perfect combination of good looks and a pleasant voice, coupled with the ability to communicate her love of the forest and its inhabitants with enthusiasm. Her scientific background did not prevent her from expressing her knowledge succinctly, without ever losing the sense of joy that she obviously felt in living and working among the chimps. Friendly and forthright in her manner, Charlotte spoke fluent Swahili and was obviously popular with all the staff and residents at Gombe. She constantly reminded us just how important the contribution of the Tanzanian field staff was to life there. Without the Tanzanians to assist her, Charlotte's study would have taken far longer.

The forest is an enchanted, secret world, a mysterious land in which you hear but often do not see. Butterflies flitted in and out of the shadows, illuminated in the windows of light. Streams coursed like blood vessels through the valleys, and in one hidden corner a waterfall tumbled 25 metres (82 ft) over sheer rock, caught by the eye for a moment in time like fragments of ice sparkling with life. There were memories here of one of my favourite children's books, *The Secret Garden* – a place of gentle spirits, hobgoblins, ghosts. A green lush world, scented with wild flowers. Ross's turacos and robin chats called but remained unseen among the canopy. The heavy wing-beat of a pair of trumpeter hornbills sounded overhead and from somewhere in the dark interior a male Narina's trogon must have been displaying, for I heard it call. On occasion the almost incessant whine of the cicadas drowned out the quieter sounds, but when they paused we heard tree frogs and crickets.

In places the vegetation grew so thickly that you could hardly see a way through; elsewhere it opened out like a magnificent cathedral, palm fronds arching skyward, filtering the light. As you climbed towards the blue, the land opened out, windows of green spear grass reaching out above the valleys. Far below, the blue waters of Lake Tanganyika beckoned, an inviting half-moon of sand and pebble beach 300 metres (1,000 ft) below us. There must have been a time when elephant roamed these valleys, and names such as Sleeping Buffalo Ridge were a reminder that stumbling over a buffalo in this type of country was something to be avoided. But the last of the buffalo disappeared fifteen years ago, poached for their meat.

The forests of Gombe and Mahale are remnants of more extensive highland forests that once stretched from Lake Kivu and north-eastern Zaire along the shores of Lake Tanganyika. Now they have retreated under the influence of climatic change and human development. Each morning in this unfamiliar world there were signs of other denizens, creatures of the dark. Freshly torn soil marked the places where bushpig had rummaged for roots and tubers, bulbs and seedlings, carrion and insects, leaving piles of dung which would help to fertilize the thin soils that they had so diligently worked. The dainty tracks of bushbuck criss-crossed the pathways, stopping every so often to browse on the leaves and flowers – but we never saw them. Overhead I could hear the 'krroop-krroop' of parties of Eurasian bee-eaters, stifled suddenly as a raucous, yelping cry echoed from the forest's edge. At first I thought it must surely be the call of the African fish eagle. But Anton told me that fish eagles are rarely seen at Gombe, and that what I had heard was the palm-nut vulture, sometimes known as the vulturine fish eagle. They are common along the shores of Lake Tanganyika, with their distinctive white heads and bodies, taking fish from the surface of the lake, feeding and breeding in the oil palms and commonly calling in flight. Once we saw the silhouette of a huge bird of prey, almost hawk-like in appearance, with a rufous tinge to its tail and white wing-patches. It was a crowned eagle, riding the thermals, climbing quickly.

Pursuing the chimps was like training for a cross-country run. Each day I was getting stronger and fitter, but each morning as we started up the slopes once again my legs felt stiff and tired. Weary as we all were at times, there was consolation in raising our spirits to meet the challenge. We certainly weren't the first to feel the effects of trying to keep up with Fifi and Co. Heartbreak Ridge seemed to go on for ever, its name perfectly describing the effect the terrain had on me: one foot plodding wearily in front of the next, trying not to let the side down, determined to keep up with the pace set by Bill or Charlotte. I longed for the flat traverses, then it was up again, the summit retreating each time I thought that this was it. But knowing that we were seeing the chimps again made it worthwhile. My head was full of questions. I found myself wanting to know how they all were and what they were doing – how was Freud's injured foot, was Fifi still in oestrus, and what might Frodo have in store for us today?

Frodo, Fifi's second son, is twenty years old and becoming something of a legend. Although Freud is the dominant male, Frodo is the largest of the community and a bit of a bully – particularly where people are concerned. Yet big as he is, Frodo seems to lack the ability to make the alliances with other males which he would need if he were really to impose himself, and when challenged by Freud or a former alpha male such as Goblin, he tends to capitulate quickly. Most of the staff at Gombe thought it unlikely that Frodo would ever become the alpha male.

Frodo is huge. Weighing in at 54 kg (120 lb), standing 1.5 metres (almost 5 ft) tall when up on his hind legs, and with biceps and shoulders befitting an all-in wrestler, he is about as impressive a chimpanzee as you could hope to meet. He is instantly recognizable not only by his size but by the brownish tint to the hair on his back and shoulders. He exudes power and has taken to throwing his weight around with the people who come to watch the Kasakela community, be they researchers, film crews or tourists. Charlotte and Bill had warned us about Frodo and his antics, which they felt were in the main conducted with a touch of humour – if Frodo had really wanted to hurt someone he would have no trouble in doing so. A friend of mine who used to work in a zoo in Sweden told me years ago about a keeper in charge of the chimps who had his nose bitten off and lost both hands due to infection after being bitten while trying to intervene in a dispute between some of the chimps. Fortunately Frodo was a 'thumper' rather than a 'biter'.

Frodo's favourite trick was to launch a display from the blind side, suddenly appearing on one of the pathways with his hair bristling. Sometimes he walked; at other times he was already running by the time you noticed him. Robin Hellier was the first to tangle with him, having his feet pulled out from under him with a lightning grab at his ankle. But it wasn't just Frodo that we had to keep watch for.

One morning as Charlotte and I were watching a group of adult males quietly grooming, the chimps suddenly stood up and started to pant-hoot with excitement. At first we couldn't understand what was happening. Only when we turned around did we realize that the reason for their exuberance was my rucksack, which I had left

*Opposite: Frodo, aged twenty, is one of the biggest chimpanzees ever recorded at Gombe National Park, weighing around 55 kg (120 lb). He is one of Fifi's sons and the younger brother of Freud, the alpha male. Frodo delights in throwing his weight around, particularly with humans, sometimes sending the field assistants and visitors sprawling. Chimpanzees are said to be four times stronger than a man, but fortunately Frodo doesn't bite – just thumps, trips and pushes.*

unattended by the path while we filmed. Within seconds a dozen chimps had gathered around it, sucking and licking the straps and back of my bag, which were saturated with salty sweat. I was dismayed, knowing that thousands of pounds' worth of cameras were stashed inside the bag, especially when Frodo sank his teeth into one of the straps and pulled. Every so often the scrum broke apart with a chorus of wild pant-hoots as each individual vied for a better position around the rucksack. At one point when the novelty of it all had begun to wane and Freud had moved away – just when I began to think that I might retrieve my possessions unharmed – Frodo grabbed the bag from Fifi and swung himself into the tree, flailing the bag around his head and thumping it against the trunk.

There was absolutely nothing we could do except wait for the chimps to lose interest – trying to snatch the bag back would have been like putting your hand in a fire; the chimps would almost certainly have resisted aggressively any attempt to rescue it. Eventually, once they had sucked and licked all the sweat off the  bag, they did lose interest and I was able to rescue my precious cameras.

That same afternoon we were forced to wait an hour and a half after the chimps stole Chris Openshaw's lens bag with his 200mm lens in it. And that wasn't all they took. Fifi managed to grab a prized roll of film that Bill Wallauer had just shot of the chimps grooming and Freud displaying. Also missing were an empty 'bum bag' and a meter bag – all of which were eventually retrieved, chewed and soaked through with chimp saliva. Luckily, although the chimps gave everything a thorough working over, they did not rip and bite as baboons would have done, with the youngsters determined to get into everything.

Before long we all had a healthy respect for Frodo and constantly kept an eye out for him and our equipment. At one point while Marguerite, our researcher, and I were photographing Gremlin and her young daughter Gaia grooming each other in a low bush, Frodo emerged from the undergrowth. Gremlin started to scream in fear as Frodo moved in her direction. As he swaggered past me he grabbed at my ankle, then stood up to thump Marguerite in the back. Running now, he directed his attention to Adrian, first shoving him and then returning to flatten him as he struggled to hold on to his sound equipment and keep his balance. 'Drive-by shootings', Bill described them as. Later, as we waited in single file on one of the narrow pathways that crisscross the steep slopes, I spotted one of the chimps sauntering towards us. 'Here comes a chimp,' I said to Charlotte. 'Who is it?' In the same instant I realized it was Frodo. He barged past, giving me a thump in the back for good measure. I grabbed for the nearest tree, spinning round it like a child on a maypole from the force of Frodo's shove. Gaining speed as he continued downhill, Frodo grabbed Andy Thompson by the ankle, yanking him to the ground and dragging him for a metre or so before letting go. The whole performance seemed prompted by the sight of all of us standing there – we had become part of his display.

But Charlotte and Bill were both quick to point out that Frodo was definitely not some psychotic chimp, bordering on the savage, who should be viewed as inherently dangerous. He simply liked showing off and had done so ever since he was much younger. Jane Goodall was genuinely frightened of Frodo, having become the focus of his displays whenever they met and having been jumped on and kicked on a number of occasions. When I spoke to a veterinary surgeon about Frodo's behaviour he said that a short, sharp shock from a cattle prod might help to break the habit, without endangering either the chimp or humans.

Each male displays differently; his performance is like an individual's signature, an imprint of his character. Sometimes these charging displays are short and fade as quickly as they started; at other times they go on for minutes at a time. They are incredible noisy: the males crash around, throwing rocks, stomping, tearing off saplings and branches – all intended to impress and intimidate a rival and other members of his community. Only males display like this; the females vocalize in acknowledgement of the males' power, sometimes with genuine fear, teeth bared in a 'fear grin'. But the chimps that we were watching looked remarkably unscarred and it is rare to see them carrying serious injuries. And this is the point. The aggressive war dances are ritualized so as to avoid harming members of the group as each male strives to achieve a higher position in the hierarchy. It is a non-damaging performance with a forceful message: 'Look at me, see how strong and powerful I am, take note.'

Studies at Gombe have proved just how important it is to form alliances: it is not so much who you are as who you know. Building strong bonds with other individuals is one way to gain added status and this applies to the weakest and the strongest members of the group. One of the most successful alpha males at Gombe was Figan, who reigned for almost ten years from 1973. But part of the reason for his success was the help that he received from his older brother Faben, who aided and abetted Figan in his quest for alpha status. When Faben eventually disappeared, Figan had to fight hard to ward off the inevitable challenges from the other males. The benefits to the provider of support can be considerable. An alpha male will often allow an ally to share a food source or mate with an oestrus female without running the risk of becoming the target of aggression.

Serious fights do sometimes occur between members of different communities, in which individual animals are injured – even killed. In fact in 1974 a period known as the Four Year War began, revealing to Jane Goodall that chimpanzees, like their human cousins, are capable of the ultimate act of warfare. A split had occurred in the community that Jane had been studying, giving rise to two separate sub-groups, the Kasakela community and the smaller Kahama community, which occupied the southern part of the original range. The 'war' was instigated by male chimps from the Kasakela community in a series of brutal attacks on their former companions. Groups of Kasakela males would creep through the forests in single file, hair bristling with fear and excitement, moving with the utmost caution to avoid alerting their enemies. There was no doubting their intentions – to attack and to murder; they would stamp

and pummel their victims, holding them down and then biting and tearing at their flesh as they do when killing and eating a colobus monkey. By the time the war ended in late 1977, the Kahama community had been annihilated; seven Kahama males and three females had died.

Though the war was over, another more insidious evil now revealed itself. In 1975, one of the Kasakela females, Passion, killed Otta, the infant offspring of another member of the community, Gilka, sharing the flesh with her daughter Pom and son Prof. I remember reading about this incident in Jane's book and looking at a black and white photograph of Passion. Some human killers show little sign of their murderous nature; they may be outwardly impassive, even angelic in their demeanour. Others look wild, demented, half-crazed. Passion, I remember thinking, had that look of derangement. The killings lasted for two years, during which time Passion and Pom, who had become a willing participant in her mother's cannibalistic ways, are known to have killed three Kasakela infants and almost certainly another seven that inexplicably disappeared. Only Fifi among all the females in the core of the Kasakela range managed to raise any offspring during this period, and the chimp community was shadowed by fear. Whenever possible, mothers sought protection from the males, desperately trying to avoid contact with Passion and Pom. But inevitably a moment came when there was nobody around to help defend them from the killer females and their infants were snatched from their grasp and eaten. Only when both Passion and Pom became pregnant did the killings finally stop.

Evenings were glorious at Gombe. After returning from the chimps, exhausted and desperate for a drink and a swim, we would grab our swimming costumes and sink into the waters of Lake Tanganyika. Before we arrived, none of us had given a thought to the soothing and reviving effects that the lake might provide. We would soak our clothes and leave them to dry on the pebble beach, before swimming 500 metres (⅓ mile) north along the shore to a rocky buff, where cormorants sometimes perched and spread their wings in the sun. The lake is an aquatic paradise, so clear that you could see shoals of fish skitting about near the bottom – just a few of the ninety-five species endemic to the lake.

The combination of wearying days and desert island scenery at sundown was enchanting. The sound of waves breaking over the pebble beach was music to the senses, and now that the moon had waned, I would lie awake listening to the voices of the fishermen drifting back across the water. They would fish throughout the night, dozing at times while they waited for their prey to gather in the circles of light cast by pressure lanterns resting on a wooden frame across the bow of the boat. Working in groups, the boats would move towards the shore, dropping their nets only when they were 100 metres (330 ft) or so from land, throwing the lines to their comrades on shore to help pull the nets in with their catch in tow. The reward for their labours was hundreds of *Stolothrissa* or *dagaa* as they are known in Swahili, finger-length fish resembling sardines which the fishermen lay out on the beach to dry during the day. This is a commercial operation – once dried, the fish are sent to Dar es Salaam on the coast for sale to the city-dwellers.

Our visit to Gombe coincided with a lull in the rainy season, which usually begins in November and continues until late May with a spell of drier weather in January and February. There is very little rain during the rest of the year. But the weather is as fickle here as anywhere else in Africa – periods of drought or stormy skies can arrive and depart without warning. On this occasion we were blessed – the weather behaved impeccably for most of our stay. Even when clouds billowed into the sky, they invariably passed over again quickly, revealing windows of blue and speckling the forest with rays of soft sunlight. It was often damp and humid in the forest, causing sweat to stream down our faces, relieved occasionally by a faint breeze emerging from deep within the green heart of the forest, whispering like the sighing of an ancient spirit.

Then the day before we were due to finish filming the heavens finally opened in a dramatic thunderstorm typical of the height of the rainy season. The cloudburst lasted most of the morning, then stopped abruptly. Until now we had been able to film the chimps playing and feeding, displaying and grooming, in open country or on pathways in the forest with windows of light to illuminate them. How different things would have been if we had been trying to film them during the rains. The steep terrain would quickly have become a nightmare of slick, muddy pathways and it would have been almost impossible to have kept our footing and to film.

Even with good weather there were many occasions when the chimps disappeared into a dense tangle of vines and undergrowth, leaving us stranded with our heavy, bulky equipment and forcing us to make lengthy detours in an effort to meet up with them again. We soon learned that it was far better to back up than to try to bulldoze a way past the vines. Even the most slender tangles could hold you fast, trip you up and send both you and your equipment crashing to the ground.

One of the most extraordinary and rather eerie moments with the chimps was watching them build their nests prior to settling down for the night. Before the last of the light had drained from the sky they would select the tree where they would spend the night. Often a female wanders off on her own with only her immediate offspring as companions. But during our stay at Gombe a dozen or more chimps frequently nested in the same grove of trees. Quickly and with the utmost dexterity each animal selects a suitable site among the branches, bending the smaller limbs into a leafy lattice-work that acts as a mattress. Infants sleep with their mothers, and it was spellbinding to watch the younger chimps making tiny nests for themselves, though Charlotte told us that at first light she often found that recently weaned youngsters had crept into bed with their mother during the night. Since our first day at Gombe we had hoped that we might be able to film a sunset sequence with the chimps nesting in trees overlooking the lake. Fifi and Sandy were still in oestrus, so the majority of the community continued to travel in a tightly focused group. But as often as not the chimps chose a site well out of view of the lake or the sun slipped beneath the horizon hidden from view by clouds. Then the evening before we were due to finish filming, Fifi led the way towards a grove of trees (*Annona senegalensis*, or *Umotope* in Swahili) on a steep slope overlooking the lake. Bill was already busily filming some of the females preparing their nests as we hurried to join him. Some of the chimps had built nests barely 2 metres (6½ ft) from the ground, others were high in the trees. There was little to fear from predators; leopards were rarely seen and there were no records of them killing chimps at Gombe, although a leopard recently killed a chimp in the Tai Forest community in the Ivory Coast. Charlotte and I scrambled down the bank to where one of the males – Wilkie – was adding the finishing touches to his nest. He lay back on the bed of leaves, a look of utter peace and contentment on his face. I wondered what he was thinking, whether there was any semblance of understanding of the ways of his world – and mine?

The following morning we returned to the spot where the chimps had nested. I climbed into the tree which Wilkie had chosen and lay back on the bed of leaves. The branches easily supported my weight and the mattress of leaves was as comfortable as any cushion. I resolved that if I ever found myself stranded or lost at night in the bush, I would try to be as inventive as the chimps and build myself a nest – though preferably not in a thorn tree.

Having spent years watching wild animals from the confines of my vehicle, following the chimpanzees on foot at Gombe was the ultimate safari experience. Sitting among them, watching them quietly feeding, the youngsters endlessly playing, the males indulging in outrageously flamboyant bouts of display – it all had an immediacy that is hard to describe.

Leaving the forest and the chimps was tinged with sadness – the same sense of emptiness that one feels when saying goodbye to friends. I had expected nothing from the chimps, but still I felt a sense of connection from simply sharing time with them. They were them and I was me, but our meeting had moved me in ways that I had not expected; had given me a clearer understanding of our place among our fellow creatures on this planet.

During that last afternoon we struggled to tie up all the loose ends to complete our programme. The chimps had climbed high up on the slopes and when we reached the place where they had been resting they quickly moved on again. We eventually found a spot where Charlotte and I could discuss her work on male vocalizations within view of some of the chimps. That evening the sunset spread red and gold along the horizon. Bands of light blossomed higher and higher into the sky as the sun sank further.

It was a like a gift from the gods. I rushed back and forth like a madman, frantically changing cameras and lenses in an attempt to record its every mood. Eventually I just sat at the edge of the lake and watched, abandoning my cameras and half submerging myself in the water. Scenes such as these are so intense that you keep trying to record and describe them, needing to share the experience with others. Being able to marvel at the world around us and to communicate our thoughts through language is a gift that we share with no other species. Charlotte, and Jane Goodall before her, have begun to unravel and transcribe the meaning of chimp vocalizations, which to my undiscerning ears had sounded initially like the screams and cries from a madhouse. But even though chimpanzees communicate with a non-verbal language there are subtleties that we are only just beginning to understand.

Twenty-five years ago chimpanzees at Gombe were seen 'dancing' at the sight of water cascading over the rocks at a waterfall deep within one of the valleys, expressing in their own inimitable way a sense of great excitement and heightened emotion equivalent to what Jane Goodall has described as awe – the same awe that I now felt as I looked across Lake Tanganyika as the sun set, wishing that things were different in our world, where beauty and sadness, joy and cruelty too often merge. Jane believes that such expressions of awe on the part of the chimps may resemble the emotions that sparked religious beliefs in early humans.

Everywhere in Africa there is a great thirst for land. Land to cultivate, to clear, to settle. As we sailed for Kigoma, I stared back at the forested slopes of Gombe. They were a deep green, luxuriant beyond description, layer after layer of foliage blanketing the valleys. The vistas beyond the park were bare by comparison, the semi-deciduous forest having been replaced by open woodland as the land has been repeatedly cleared and burned. In places the trees had all but vanished from the landscape and the thin soils had given way, eroded by man's destructive ways.

The great forested regions where chimps once flourished will not last forever. Earlier this century there were hundreds of thousands of chimpanzees in twenty-five African nations. Today substantial populations remain only in Zaire, Gabon, Cameroon and the Congo – the areas with the largest undisturbed tracts of forests. Chimpanzees are still killed for food in parts of Africa or captured and sold to collectors for the pet trade or as entertainment or for medical research – though this does not happen in Tanzania. The future looks bleak. If we do not heed the words of people like Jane Goodall, then the last of the great apes will increasingly be confined to small forest reserves, imprisoned in a genetic cul-de-sac where the effects of inbreeding will hasten their road to extinction: 'And unless we act soon, our closest relatives may soon exist only in captivity, condemned, as a species, to human bondage.'

# NAMIBIA: AFRICA'S LAST WILDERNESS

*The desert people themselves show an indifference towards the Almighty that is decidedly cavalier. 'We will go up to God and salute him,' said Bedu to Palgrave in the 1860s, 'and if he proves hospitable, we will stay with him: if otherwise, we will mount our horses and ride off.'*

**Bruce Chatwin,** *Songlines*

Namibia is a revelation: a country full of surprises, its landscape painted in shades of earth brown and purple. It is a desert country, the vegetation sparse and hardy, with one of the lowest population densities in the world. In places it is difficult to believe that you are in Africa. A century ago during colonial days German surveyors first discovered its glittering treasures and diamond prospectors scoured the desert for gems in what was then South-West Africa. This is the home of the Kung bushmen, last of the hunter-gatherers, who have lived here for generation upon generation, recording their passing with delicate oxide-rich paintings and engravings etched on rock.

A few bands of bushmen still cling to the old ways as nomadic hunters in the Kalahari Desert, where for thousands of years they were the only human beings in this part of the world.

All living things – elephants and rhino not excepted – appear tiny in the vast landscape, much of which remains untouched and unexplored. It is a harsh land where wild animals were often perceived as a menace by the farmers and ranchers who preside over the large-scale cattle and sheep ranches that cover the country's grazing land. Since farming began here, they have battled with the wilderness, fencing it off. Lions and leopards were shot or poisoned, and even today the endangered cheetah is still classed as vermin – predator turned calf-killer. Some of the more enlightened farmers hire the services of professional game-catchers to trap the cheetah for translocation to areas still harbouring their natural prey. Others shoot them on sight.

Amidst all the dryness, like an oasis of life some 160 km (100 miles) inland, is Etosha National Park, one of the largest and most famous parks in the world, which in times of rain becomes a shallow, 6,000 square km (2,300 square mile) lake, a photographer's paradise teeming with wildlife. I was naturally delighted when I heard that a safari to Namibia was to be included in the series.

A friend of ours, David Coulson, had spent years photographing in Namibia and had fallen in love with the dune country known by the Nama and Bushmen people as the Namib – meaning endless space – covering an area of some 260,000 square km (100,000 square miles). I called in to see David before departing for Namibia and was regaled with tales of wild horses and of 'star dunes' at Sossusvlei towering up to 350 metres (1,200 ft) high, of a country guarded by 1,600 km (1,000 miles) of the most treacherous coastline on earth. I flicked through his book *Namib*: visions of towering sand dunes competed for space with the wastelands of the Skeleton Coast, where shipwrecks and bleached whale bones create an atmosphere of unreality quite unlike that of any other land.

Namibia was certainly going be very different from our other locations. We wanted to capture the vastness of the land and to highlight the extraordinary diversity of both the wildlife and the landscape. Instead of selecting a single species or trying to film in just one area, we chose three or four places of interest to visit and decided to fly between them.

To heighten the sense of adventure we had hoped to use microlights to fly across the desert interior. The idea was to borrow machines used by fellow wildlife cinematographers Des and Jen Bartlett. But before anything could be finalized we heard that Des had narrowly escaped death when one of the machines lost its engine and plummeted to the ground, burying its nose in the mud. Des had been accompanied by Mary Plage, widow of wildlife cameraman Dieter Plage, who himself had been killed in an airborne accident, falling from an airship in the Philippines. Fortunately Jen Bartlett was piloting the other microlight at the time and was able to radio for help. Des emerged with a badly smashed ankle and Mary suffered spinal injuries, though both are now back on their feet.

The Bartletts spent many years in East Africa as part of a highly successful partnership with Armand Denis – creator and host, with his wife Michaela, of the television series *On Safari*, which provided a huge stimulus to my early interest in Africa's wildlife. The Bartletts had been based in Namibia since the late 1970s and had spent the first six years at Etosha National Park. They had become obsessed with filming the desert-dwelling elephant, making month-long camping trips into the desert from their base at Mowe Bay, exploring the ephemeral Hoanib and Hoarusib Rivers which remain dry for most of the year. Much of what I knew of Namibia and its wildlife had come through watching their films and reading their beautifully illustrated articles in *National Geographic*, though to this day I have yet to meet them.

When producer Mike Gunton met me in London to discuss Namibia the first thing he told me was that a three-day-old beard and far less neat and tidy appearance would be in order. Namibia, for all its beauty, was a hot and thirsty land – somewhere you could easily get lost with little hope of being found. My appearance should reflect that fact. I did my best, but in the end my 'beard' became something of a liability as far as continuity was concerned.

By now our production deadlines for completing the programmes and the book were very tight indeed. Namibia and Zimbabwe were filmed back to back, due to considerations of the changing seasons and the busy schedules of both our camera crews and our hosts. I toyed with the idea of travelling to Namibia a week before the crew arrived, to try to ensure that I could spend some time taking photographs and familiarizing myself with the area. But in the end time did not permit me to do this. A lot of the writing for the book had to be completed on location. Whenever there was a break in filming I would reach for my notebook, trying to capture a sense of the place, the people, the mood.

Fortunately Robin Hellier and the other producers were sympathetic to my need to snatch as many pictures of the animals as I could. Because my role as a presenter was being what I am – a wildlife photographer – it was often possible for me to be filmed taking a photograph. But in many instances sound was running even when I wasn't needed on camera, and I would sit desperately wanting to take a picture, knowing that the click of my camera would spoil the sound take. Agony! I would have loved the luxury of spending weeks at a time taking stills, as I do in the Masai Mara.

Just before I left Nairobi, my wife Angela spotted a footnote on Namibia in the travel section of a magazine, mentioning an old acquaintance of mine, Jan Oelofse. Jan is one of the most colourful characters I have ever met in Africa, a former park ranger, animal catcher extraordinaire and currently a professional hunter and entrepreneur. In the old days catching wild animals invariably meant risking life and limb chasing them across the bush in a battered old Toyota. The animal would be caught

*The Namib's dune fields form neat parallel fingers of sand which extend north and south for hundreds of kilometres. The sands become progressively redder the further inland you go, with those to the east in the Kalahari being the reddest of all.*

with a noose of rope secured to the end of a pole or simply grabbed by the tail or horns and wrestled to a standstill. The work was hard on everyone – people, vehicles and the quarry, which was sometimes so exhausted by the chase that it subsequently died. Nowadays things are far more sophisticated, with modern drugs available to immobilize the animal using a dart gun. In fact, while Jan was a ranger in South Africa he helped to perfect an innovative method of capturing hoofed animals known as the 'boma technique'.

During his many years with the Natal Parks Board, Jan and his fellow rangers patrolled the wilderness on horseback. In those days it was necessary to shoot surplus animals from the herds of wildebeest and zebra to prevent overgrazing. Jan felt frustrated by this seemingly wasteful approach to game management and pioneered the boma technique for capturing animals rather than shooting them. By erecting and concealing hundreds of metres of plastic sheeting among the bushes to form a funnel it was possible to herd the animals towards a capture pen. As the animals moved further into the funnel, men would pull a curtain of plastic across behind them to prevent them from escaping and then chase them forwards into the pen. A helicopter eventually replaced horses as the means of rounding up the animals, and by the time I met Jan the operation had been refined to a very professional means of capturing and translocating wildlife.

Jan sports a goatee beard and has piercing steely blue eyes that can intimidate you as easily as they can smile with genuine warmth. He is always in the thick of things, cool as a cucumber, trademark black cowboy hat covering his bald head. He is known for his hardness, and has a temper to match. As he remarked in warning to one person, 'I don't want to have to embarrass you in front of your friends.' He carries a handgun on his hip and can cut leaves from a bush with a bull whip, yet those same strong hands have sculpted beautiful animal studies in bronze. Jan is an enigma, a contradiction; he hunts animals, yet loves the wilderness.

Jan is very much a believer in 'use it or lose it' as far as wild animals are concerned. In this respect he shares the views of many southern African conservationists who engage in consumptive use of wildlife as well as promoting tourism. Trophy hunting and game ranching in Namibia, Zimbabwe and South Africa have for many years generated an income for private landowners while helping to preserve habitat – wildlife is paying its way, which on private land is its only hope of survival. In 1967 the government of the then South-West Africa granted farmers an ownership in the wildlife living on their land, and before long wildlife utilization had become a multi-million-dollar business. Wild animals are far more efficient than livestock at producing protein from the natural habitat, though there is considerable resistance to the idea of replacing cattle with game; cattle have traditionally been viewed as both a symbol of wealth and a source of profit. Jan believes that 'if we can make money from game, cattle pastures will be converted to game ranches and wildlife habitats may be reclaimed.' There are 3,000 animals of forty-two species on his 16,000 hectare (40,000 acre) game ranch.

With trophy hunting prospering in Namibia, the government is able to auction off surplus wild animals to the hunting concessions. Professional hunters can charge hefty trophy fees: US$8,000 for an elephant, $3,500 for a lion, $2,000 for a cheetah or leopard, $1,000 for a giraffe. Small cats, jackals and baboons are free of charge. Such ideas are now gaining favour in East Africa, too. Kenya, where all wildlife is the property of the government and where trophy hunting and all forms of wildlife utilization were banned in 1977, will soon start to licence a limited amount of hunting on private land as well as game ranching for meat and hides. This will in effect give the people a greater say in what happens to wildlife on their land. But the worry, as always, is whether or not a strict quota system will be adhered to, or will corruption and abuse of the system once again become rampant as was the case before the ban.

I worked with Jan in 1984 as the presenter for two wildlife programmes filmed at his game ranch in Kalkfeld. Both films were action-packed and featured Jan's expertise as an animal catcher. Most of the animals we filmed had already been sold to other ranches who wished to add to their herds or to introduce new species. We captured white rhino, giraffe, zebra, hartebeest and oryx – for the last of which I soon developed a healthy respect after seeing a cow oryx pierce a sturdy metal barrier with one swipe of her spear-like horns. The giraffe were destined for the newly created game sanctuary in Bophuthatswana (then a homeland in South Africa) where Randall Moore had eventually found a home for his elephants Orwalla and Durga. Though catching game is incredibly exciting it can also be highly dangerous, even for the most experienced professionals. One member of the capture team was almost decapitated when a young giraffe lashed out with a plate-sized hoof as it entered the transport vehicle. Those weeks spent at Jan's game ranch, Mount Etjo, certainly provided me with an exciting introduction to Namibia.

I leafed through the itinerary sent to me by production manager Diana Richards, giving details of the people we would be meeting. There were names and places here that I had read about, notably that of Mary Seeley, Executive Director of the Desert Research Foundation of Namibia, who had dedicated the last thirty years of her life to arid-land research, and the application of this research to national environmental issues through education and training. Mary's work at the Gobabeb Desert Research Station in the central Namib has helped to illuminate how desert animals adapt to a wilderness of sand, where daytime temperatures often reach 54°C (130°F) and the moisture comes from the head-on collision of warm air with the cold Benguela Current, producing dense, moisture-laden fog that billows across the immense dunes from the Skeleton Coast. The desert is surprisingly rich in wildlife, proof of nature's adaptability: trap-door spiders which lie in wait for unsuspecting ants and beetles, toktokkie beetles with their own inimitable way of collecting moisture; the insectivorous

golden mole with the sand-adapted coat and super-sensitive ears that lead it to prey. Many of the animals are nocturnal in their habits: night-time reveals owls, geckos, dune crickets, shovel-nosed lizards and side-winding adders.

I was excited to see that our first destination would be Halifax Island, just off the Diamond Coast near the old German town of Luderitz, where we were due to film a jackass penguin colony. Mention penguins to most people and the last place they are likely to think of is Africa, even though jackass penguins are commonly seen in zoos and marine parks around the world. To me it seemed a far cry from the more familiar icy wastelands of the Antarctic peninsula.

In fact, seals and penguins are ideally suited to life in these icy South Atlantic waters, which are rich in plankton and fish. The source of this profusion of marine life is the Benguela Current, born thousands of kilometres away in the Antarctic Ocean and flowing northwards until it is deflected around the west coast of Africa, before merging with the South Equatorial Current at a latitude of 15° South, off Angola. The Benguela carries a rich store of nutrients which, combined with the cold temperatures, allows the plankton and fish to flourish, which in turn feeds thousands upon thousands of sea-birds and seals.

Having spent the night in the Namibian capital, Windhoek, and feasted on low-cholesterol ostrich steak, we flew south to Luderitz. The weather was perfect, providing us with good visibility and allowing us the chance to marvel at the landscape. The predominant colour was that of rust-red sand, speckled with knots of stunted vegetation, growing close to the ground. A ripple of hills like sharks' teeth pierced the distant horizon, rising jagged into a vivid blue sky. The ground looked as if it had been ravaged by a great inferno, the dry river-beds begging for rain. In places I could see a web of vehicle tracks forming spidery patterns across the land. Tracks leading where, I wondered? If ever a country spelled out exploration, fortitude, a Spartan existence, this was it.

Luderitz is an old German mining town and seaport hidden among the rocky fjords separating the Atlantic Ocean and the Namib Desert. The town looks as if it has been caught in a time-warp and has certainly seen better days. My first impression was of being on a film set: neatly structured timber pre-fab houses lined the streets. But it was strangely quiet, as if no one actually lived here. The town is named after the German merchant Adolf Luderitz who, with Chancellor Bismarck's blessing and the promise of protection, sought his fortune here at the turn of the century. The port attracted diamond prospectors and fishermen who plied the waters for rock lobster.

Diamonds were discovered at Luderitz in 1908, precipitating a frenzy of activity in the area. Weathered from numerous volcanic pipes dating back 100 million years or more deep within the southern African interior, Namibia's diamonds owe their existence to the Orange River, which 70 million years ago cut a path through the eastern coastal escarpment, finally reaching the Atlantic Ocean. Over millions of years seasonal floodwaters have transported their precious load, washing the ancient gravels

*Namibia is guarded to the west by 1,600 km (1,000 miles) of the most treacherous and desolate coastline on earth, where shipwrecks and whale bones create an atmosphere of ghostly unreality. The coast is often shrouded in mist which blows inland across the desert interior, bringing life to a unique and complex array of animals and plants.*

and diamonds into the sea. Some of the diamonds have been carried hundreds of kilometres northwards along the coast, both by the current and by the strong south-westerly winds, a process known as long-shore drift. Some were deposited in layers on beaches which today lie up to 3,500 metres (over 2 miles) from the shoreline.

The reason for the rich deposits of diamonds near Luderitz is the lie of the land: sand and diamonds reaching the coast at Elizabeth Bay were funnelled north into a series of narrow, windswept valleys leading to Kolmanskop, the first station out of Luderitz. This area is part of the *Sperrgebiet* or 'forbidden region', created originally during colonial times by the German administration to restrict prospecting and mining (and preserve their own interests), and it has remained in the hands of those who have governed the country ever since. Abandoned mining sites litter the 54,861 square km (21,182 square miles) Restricted Diamond Area, a vast museum of rusted machinery and decrepit buildings, home of the shy and solitary brown hyaena, the 'strandwolf' of myth and folklore, wanderer of the night, which scavenges among the Cape fur seal rookeries, taking whatever the sea washes up.

Over time the profile of the coastline has changed, as witnessed by the ancient raised beaches such as those at Oranjemund, the only diamond-mining site currently in operation in Namibia, near the mouth of the Orange River on the border with South Africa.

A church, starkly beautiful in its simplicity, brightened the corner of the street above our hotel. Wispy white clouds radiated into the deep blue sky above it, like winged angels in a biblical motif. I looked for signs of life, for faces at the windows, listened for the noise of dogs barking or children laughing. Where was everyone? The past loomed large among the faceless modern buildings, memories of colonial opulence and splendour – mansions styled on nineteenth-century German architecture. One extraordinary dwelling place known as 'the blue house' towered impressively above the other buildings. It was built into the base rock and was surrounded by an extravagant flower garden. It demanded chamber music, men in top hats and spats, ladies in voluminous skirts bearing fans.

People used to say that it never rained in Luderitz – at least only once in every seven years; the average annual rainfall is only 50 mm (2 in). But this year it had rained heavily on four occasions in the three weeks prior to our visit. As someone remarked, 'Luderitz may even turn green!'

With the arrival of independence, Luderitz is buoyed by hopes that its resources can be developed and the town can begin to live again. There are plans for improved harbour facilities and a rail link to Aranos and nearby Botswana to provide an export centre for rich coal deposits.

I paused at the top of the main street and looked back towards the harbour. Men

*Opposite: Lappet-faced vultures are the largest of Africa's vultures. They feed on carrion and occasionally kill small prey such as young antelope for themselves. Unlike the more numerous griffon vultures they live in pairs and defend a territory year round.*

were busy offloading crates from the first of a line of brightly coloured fishing boats waiting to deliver their cargo. Marooned in the ink-black water a yacht named *Sedina* rocked gently back and forth. She was the property of Manfred and Gabi Wedell, a German seafaring couple who had sailed round the world on a three-year voyage of exploration, shunning the wealth of modern electronic equipment that is the norm on most vessels and relying instead on the time-honoured methods of navigation employed by the Portuguese mariners who landed here five centuries ago. As Manfred said, 'If you know how to navigate with a sextant you won't run into trouble.'

Manfred looked the part of the intrepid seafarer with his heavy beard and large square face topped by a navy blue woollen beret. His was the face of the sea, weather-beaten skin and sharp blue eyes scanning the horizon. Manfred and Gabi earned their living by chartering their boat out to day trippers – mainly Germans.

The weather along the coast was usually grey and cloudy, sometimes raining, often cold. But mugs of hot coffee helped to keep the chill air at bay as the *Sedina* set sail, the heavy slap and rustle of the sails catching the wind. It was a glorious sight to see her fully rigged, a fitting reminder of those early explorers from Europe who sought fame and fortune manoeuvring their tall ships along Namibia's rugged coastline. Many failed to navigate these treacherous waters successfully, and their remains are still to be seen along stretches of the coast.

We decided to charter the *Sedina* to sail to Halifax Island, where the jackass penguin colony was nesting. My guide for this first part of the journey was Jean-Paul Roux, a French biologist from the Department of Fisheries and Marine Resources. Jean-Paul sported long black ringlets and the stubble of a permanently half-grown beard. He had a rather taciturn manner enlivened by a dry Gallic wit. He had been conducting research in Namibia for the past eight years and his great love was marine birds and mammals. Manfred anchored the *Sedina* in the shallows and ferried us ashore in a tiny rubber dinghy.

Halifax Island is tiny, only about 800 metres (2,600 ft) across. It is low-lying and rather featureless, a desolate place, windswept and wave-lashed, with the rugged profile of a sub-Antarctic island. As we waded ashore our feet crunched over the thickly piled shells, as colourful as gems, reflecting the richness of the ocean. A mummified seal carcass grinned up at us, preserved by the cold, its sharp fish-catching teeth bared in a ghoulish grin. One of our crew nearly stumbled on a penguin burrow concealed beneath a small bush. Penguins peered out at us from their darkened dwelling places, turning their heads this way and that, reptile-like, curiosity fixed in their dark beady eyes.

How easy it must have been to kill these strangely fashioned flightless birds. Penguins show little fear of humans and you can walk right up to within a couple of metres of them if you tread slowly and carefully. But it is vitally important not to disturb them when they are nesting for fear of endangering their brood. The moment the penguins expose their eggs or young chicks to view, the gulls and crows swoop down

*Opposite: Jackass penguins* (Spheniscus demersus) *normally nest in burrows, but if conditions are not ideal for burrowing they will lay their eggs on the bare ground. On Halifax Island I found that some penguins had adopted a derelict building as a nesting site and a refuge from the elements: one pair had established itself in the old metal oven.*

from the sky to try and pick them off, provoking a chorus of donkey-like braying cries – hence the name 'jackass' penguins.

As Jean-Paul guided me around the colony, a fine drizzle began to fall, the droplets coalescing and glistening on the penguins' snow-white chest feathers. Abandoned, ramshackle huts scattered the foreshore with the old stationmaster's house providing a shelter for some of the penguins. One pair had chosen an old iron oven as their nesting site, others huddled in the corners or waddled to the entrance of the hut and stood on the step as if in welcome, before hopping in single file to the ground. There are between 1,000 and 1,300 birds on the island with the main breeding colony numbering 330 pairs. The breeding birds huddled in the open in a dense mob, clustered in their pairs within pecking distance, giving that distinctive braying call.

For thousands of years coastal regions such as Halifax Island have been the home of sea-birds. There were once a million or more jackass penguins along the coast of southern Africa, but the population has dropped to 150,000 in the last twenty-five years. They are still found between Port Elizabeth, along the southern tip of South Africa as far north as Mercury Island, halfway between Luderitz and Swakopmund on the coast of Namibia. The population has changed dramatically in the last twenty years, with an increase in numbers along the southern part of the coast and a decrease along the Atlantic coast, though most of the penguin populations are protected now. Jean-Paul showed me some of the records for Namibia as a whole and for Halifax Island, both of which underscored the sharp decline in the population.

**Namibia:**
1950s   70,500 penguins with approximately 50,000 breeding pairs
1970s   12,000 nests
1980s   5,000 nests

**Halifax Island:**
1950s   8,689 penguins
1970s   1,750 nests
1980s   334 nests

Two factors seem to be responsible for the drop in numbers – a reduction in food supply and the harmful effect of oil pollution. In the late 1960s there was a huge increase in purse seine fishing, which relies on a large net towed by two boats that encloses a school of fish and is then closed at the bottom by means of a line – just like closing a purse. This practice led to a collapse in pilchard and anchovy stocks in the early 1970s. Industrial fishing involving the so-called 'factory ships' resulted in huge offtakes – 1.5 million tonnes of pilchards in one season during the early '70s. Jackass penguins feed on small pelagic fish which form dense shoals close to the surface and close to shore, making them difficult to catch by trawling but easy to detect by the sonar used by the larger vessels. The penguins particularly favour small pilchards (which formerly made up half of their diet) and anchovies as well as a variety of non-commercial species.

Oil pollution first hit the penguins' breeding and feeding areas in 1967. That was the year the Suez Canal was closed and many tankers were diverted around southern Africa, leading to the inevitable oil spills. The tankers' practice of cleaning out the 'bilges' into the ocean is still a constant source of pollution in the waters north of Cape Town. Even very small oil patches are a potential disaster for penguins swimming through them. Being flightless they cannot fly over the oil, and once their feathers become contaminated the 'waterproofing' is lost and they cannot clean themselves. If penguins swallow even very small quantities of oil the results can be disastrous: either they do not breed, or their eggs do not hatch, or their chicks do not survive.

But at least now an attempt is being made to deal with the problem. In the wake of the 1994 *Apollo Sea* oil spill off the west coast of the Cape, one of the world's largest sea-bird rescue operations was mounted and 10,000 jackass penguins from two breeding colonies on Dassen and Robben Islands were captured for cleaning. Unfortunately half of the birds died either during capture or transport, or within twenty-four hours of arrival at the sea-bird cleaning station at Tableview, probably as a result of stress, the toxic effects of oil they had swallowed or suffocation due to inadequate ventilation while in transit. A further 1,000 birds died at the cleaning station. Of the 4,000 penguins that appeared healthy enough to be released, 2,000 returned to their breeding colonies and a high proportion of them bred within a year of being released.

Although jackass penguins feed in the cool Benguela Current, they breed on dry land under the hot African sun. They normally nest in burrows, excavating shallow holes in the earth, which not only helps protect them from the sun but allows them to defend their nests more easily from predators – particularly kelp gulls which steal eggs and young chicks – and man.

Vast numbers of these birds existed when European settlers first arrived in Namibia. By the late 1700s English and American whalers and sealers were operating from what is now Luderitz and Walvis (Whale) Bay, and the penguins provided them with an easy source of meat and eggs. It was a cold and drab existence – the stench of the whale carcasses and the seals, a shortage of fresh water; but the money was good and the ocean must have seemed like an inexhaustible provider.

Millions of eggs were collected for human consumption from the early 1900s to the 1950s. I was reminded of a comment about penguin eggs in Tony Chater's book on the Falkland Islands: 'When cooked, the white remains transparent while the bright red yolk stares back up from the frying pan like a bloodshot eye.' The penguins themselves could be eaten fresh or salted down and dried for consumption later. While the settlers were exploiting the eggs it was discovered that penguin meat was also good as bait for catching crayfish or rock lobster.

But it wasn't just as a source of food that penguins were sought. The numerous off-shore islands along the Namibian coast provide ideal nesting sites for gannets and cormorants, as well as the penguins, all of which produce excretory products known as guano, which accumulates over time as a thick, nitrate-rich deposit, once referred to as 'white gold'. The high nitrate content of guano make it an excellent non-polluting agricultural fertilizer.

The first published record of guano was in 1828, when Captain Benjamin Morrell, an American, described seeing islands covered in guano 8 metres (25 ft) thick. But not until the late 1830s, when Peru began sending shipments of guano to Europe, did people realize the value of the deposits along the Benguela Coast. The 'Great Guano Rush' of 1843 was not unlike the unseemly and sometimes violent scramble for gold and diamonds. At the height of it, Ichaboe Island, 50 km (30 miles) north of Luderitz and barely 300 metres (1,000 ft) long had 5,000 people collecting guano with twenty tall ships waiting off shore to transport it away. Between 1844 and 1845 guano worth £2,000,000 was removed and by 1855 the rape of the islands was virtually complete. In more recent times the government farmed out private concessions to guano hunters, who built houses on the islands and managed the resource to optimize production of guano and protect it from unauthorized removal.

Man's depredations have had a dramatic influence on the ecology of these islands. In undisturbed habitat jackass penguins make their nest burrows in the guano area; gannets nest in colonies on flat sections among the steep rocky promontories on the higher ground, leaving the fur seals to dominate the foreshore. But by scraping the guano down to the bare rock the guano hunters prevented the penguins from burrowing, forcing them to nest on the ground and leaving them vulnerable to predation from kelp gulls and pied and black crows. The removal of guano led to an increase in the cormorant population, which does not require guano for nest-building and prefers to nest on the scraped areas. The fur seals took over the old nest sites as breeding grounds of their own, displacing the penguins. Gannets produce better quality guano because they do not burrow, which means that their excrement does not get soiled with sand and earth. Some of the leaseholders built stone walls to try and prevent the penguins from coming ashore, though they were allowed to nest on certain areas so that their eggs could be harvested. For this reason, today the commercial value of guano provides an economic incentive to protect bird populations.

The following evening we flew from Luderitz to the Desert Ecological Research Station at Gobabeb in the Central Namib. We took off directly into the sun, rising quickly into a clear blue sky. The landscape suddenly took on shape and form, as if we were looking out across a giant relief map of the coast and beyond. Sand dunes that had appeared flat and lifeless became sculptured sand-castles, stretching in sinuous lines as far as the eye could see, fashioned anew by the light. This was the 600 km (400 mile) long Diamond Coast, named by the early prospectors who scoured the beaches

*Along the 600 km (400 mile) Diamond Coast the great dunes reach the sea. Just like the diamonds, the sands of the Namib have been swept, grain by grain, out of the heart of Africa.*

for the glint of precious stones. In places the great dunes reached the sea, sway-bellied like beached whales, the sun dipping low, casting long shadows down their lustrous flanks. Waves rose up to pound the rock faces, crashing spumes of white water against the dark craggy buffs.

I craned my neck as the second plane caught up with us, a giant white eagle nosing closer, closer. I could feel the adrenaline pumping through my body. We all felt exhilarated as the plane edged towards us, now almost wing-tip to wing-tip, the pilots holding their positions while Brian McDairmant's camera whirred away silently through the open door space. I looked back at Mike Carling, the assistant cameraman, who had taken on the appearance of a polar explorer, the wind slapping straight into his face, a reflector wrapped around him to try and keep out the chill. Suddenly the other plane turned belly up and seared down and away from us. I held my breath – it was like seeing a giant bird plummet after prey, growing smaller and smaller before levelling out. It helped to create a sense of perspective amid the grandeur of the scenery – a tiny white bird dwarfed by the vastness of the land.

We headed onwards, marvelling at the extraordinary variety of shapes and colours of the dunes, from mustard brown to brick red, elliptical and hump-backed. Then we saw the fog – the source of life itself to the hardy inhabitants of the dry interior – evolving like a cotton-wool blanket at the interface between land and water, rolling inland, with its bounty of moisture pressing down across the dunes. We descended through the grey, the light fading fast, the sun a golden orange hemisphere dropping through the mist.

The plane lost itself in the clouds, and when land reappeared a spread of spectacular rusty-brown dunes snaked away beneath us. I could see Gobabeb's space-style water-tower rising from a flat clearing at the edge of the dunes, located next to the ephemeral Kuiseb river-bed – marked by an oasis of deep-rooted acacia trees and ground-hugging bushes. The trees mark the boundary between sand and rock, the junction of desert dunes and gravel plains. The greenness of the vegetation was startling – but where was the water to support it?

We were warmly welcomed by my guide for the visit, Juliane Zeidler, and other members of the staff from the research station, who provided us with comfortable living quarters and the best of home cooking.

For all its eminent work Gobabeb Research Station is low-key and unobtrusive in style. A scattering of flat green roofs marks the buildings which are maintained by the Ministry for Wildlife Conservation and Tourism. The centre is equipped with a library, laboratory facilities and several computers; it acts as a base for field research, attracting scientists and students like Juliane from all over the world.

The following morning we rose at five. The sky was clear and starlit. We sat among ancient rock monuments waiting for the sun to emerge before heading into the dunes. Juliane drove the four-wheel-drive vehicle with the skill gained during three years working in the desert. She had visited Gobabeb in 1991, as a first-year biology student and volunteer for the Ministry of Wildlife Conservation and Tourism. After spending three weeks counting 25,000 !Nara seeds for Kew Gardens Seedbank (the ! denotes the 'click' characteristic of Khoisan languages), she returned on a six-month volunteer internship with the Desert Research Foundation of Namibia (DRFN), assisting with fieldwork at Gobabeb and helping with the herbarium and the library.

Juliane had recently completed her MSc, on tick ecology in the Kuiseb River, under the auspices of the Johann Wolfgang Goethe University in Frankfurt, and would begin her PhD, on aspects of soil microfauna, in 1996. She was definitely not a stuffy academic. She not only loved her work but she had fun doing it – just the right temperament to cope with the rigours of long, hot days collecting data in the desert. As she herself said, 'I did not know much about the field of applied biology. What I brought with me was lots of enthusiasm and curiosity, the love for nature and some travelling experience in Africa.' It proved more than enough.

Accompanying Juliane was field-research assistant Snake Vilho Mtuleni, whose duties included monitoring pit-traps – all 150 of them – at Khomabes, one of the long-term study sites in the dunes. At first glance pit-traps look like discarded white plastic pots. Every second month they are opened for five consecutive days and any animals falling into them are identified, counted, recorded and then released. This painstaking business has been going on for more than twenty years, along with the monitoring of dune movement and plant-growth studies. There are pit-trap sites on the gravel plains, the inter-dune valleys, one of the dune slopes and slipface, and the stretch of river next to Gobabeb. Between 1976 and 1994 the traps at Quartz Hill alone yielded 365,230 tenebrionid beetles (81 per cent of the catch) and 86,622 other crawling insects, spiders and scorpions. Add to this the collection of meteorological data and research at four automatic weather stations and a picture begins to emerge of how natural systems respond to environmental change in hyper-arid and semi-arid Namibia. This painstaking work, the legacy of Dr Mary Seeley, aims to provide scientific data to enable the country to manage its arid lands and protect natural ecosystems; the foundation is also pioneering community education in an attempt to inspire the local people with a respect and a sense of responsibility for Namibia's natural resources.

We passed a small Nama village with crudely fashioned shelters of acacia bark, pieces of old wooden packing cases and odd bits of scrap metal; a patchwork quilt of shapes held together with branches and strands of wire. Thank goodness it hardly ever rained – the occupants would have been soaked in the first storm.

Water is a precious commodity here. The intermittent flooding of the ephemeral Kuiseb River holds out hope to the people, bringing life. Their goats and donkeys forage along the river-banks for leaves and flowers, consuming whatever they can find, and when the !Nara melons ripen among the dunes the villagers harvest them, scooping out the sweet-tasting pulp which is cooked into a pancake, while the seeds are eaten by their livestock or sold to dealers who export them as a delicacy.

During the 1960s and '70s the Kuiseb River flooded virtually every year, swollen by rains to the east. But from 1979 to 1985 it remained dry, until brief annual floods returned again. The reduced flow is probably aggravated by dropping ground-water levels caused by the digging of wells and sinking of boreholes, activities which now threaten the health of the large acacia trees. Arid and semi-arid lands constitute 97 per cent of Namibia's land surface, so good rains are like gold to Namibians. The only perennial rivers are the Orange, Kunene, Zambezi and Okavango, all of which must be shared with neighbouring countries. The Okavango starts its life in Angola, flowing through Namibia into Botswana, where it merges with the Kalahari sands to give birth to the spectacular Okavango Delta. It is hoped that by working with the other countries Namibia can utilize the Okavango to help to solve its major water problems. Each year there are more people needing food and water, and the inevitable drift to the urban areas means that the demand for water is increasing all the time.

It is one thing to marvel at the sea of dunes from the air. A totally different kind of awe settles over you when you are on foot and see them towering above you. As soon as the vehicle could go no further (and Juliane had wisely positioned it facing down the slope) I hurried to the top to savour the view, feet squidging into the sand – three steps up, one step down. In places the sparkling face of the dune had 'slipped' to create the most exquisitely patterned etchings, like abstract art. I stood mesmerized as a trickle of sand, like salt running through an egg-timer, eroded the knife-edge of one of the dunes. Further on I could see a miniature dust storm raging along the crest of a dune, the grains of sand forever moving, constantly changing the shape of the desert. The sands become progressively redder the further inland you go, with those to the east in the Kalahari being the reddest of all. Just like the diamonds, the red sands of the Namib have been swept, grain by grain, out of the heart of Africa by the Orange River on Namibia's southern border, then borne ever so slowly northwards on the ocean currents, piled up on the shore and blown inland, forming neat parallel fingers of sand which extend north and south for hundreds of kilometres.

Namibia's southern dune fields are probably no more than 10 million years old. But buried beneath them lie ancient fossilized sands, an older Namib that dates back between 40 and 80 million years, making it the oldest desert in the world. The dunes, the life-giving fog and food-bearing easterly winds are all to be found elsewhere in the world. But the magnitude of geological time helps to explain the unique array of fauna and flora inhabiting this region. The Namib is unique among deserts, a sea of dunes surrounded by arid plains, supporting species found nowhere else which have evolved in response to millions of years of stability and isolation, the grist on which natural selection works. This is why the golden moles, legless lizards and many of the beetles that can be found here today also inhabited the fossil deserts.

Juliane explained how life had adapted to these arid lands. Rainfall counts for very little most of the time: it may be months, even years, before the next rains, with an average of just 50 mm (2 in) of rainfall a year, insufficient to allow plants from further inland to bridge the gap and take seed. The only regular form of precipitation to slake the desert's thirst comes in the form of the blanket of fog that we had seen the previous evening along the coast. Every few days the fog drifts inland for up to 100 km (60 miles) as far as Gobabeb, carried along on the north-westerly winds, bringing a chill veil of mist which nourishes everything from beetles to elephants with droplets of moisture. These precipitate on the sand, on plants and the animals themselves. Unlike in the Sahara, the dryness and heat are modified by the fog, protecting the desert from the sun. Some mornings the tussocks of rank grasses are laden with dew, watery diamonds clustering on the quill-like stems. To reproduce as a plant you have to be able to produce and release your seeds at just the right moment – quickly – or simply keep up a bombardment of reproductive products to increase your chances of success.

Adaptability is the only way to survive in the Namib, which has spawned a treasure-trove of species bearing witness to nature's flexibility. Juliane reached into her basket and pulled out a jam-jar containing a collection of large black beetles. Gobabeb is 'beetle city', with eighty-two different species of tenebrionid beetles so far recorded. One of the most unusual is *Onymacris unguicularis*, which is the size of a thumbnail and has developed the most bizarre way yet devised of trapping water from the moisture-laden fog. This is the fog-basking or 'handstand' beetle that I had heard so much about. Instead of drinking the drops of fog and dew, *Onymacris* elevates itself into the wind in a handstand on the crest of a dune, allowing moisture to condense on its hind legs. The water then runs down a groove in the beetle's back, delivering a life-giving droplet directly to its mouth. Having performed its gymnastics *Onymacris* disappears from view, swallowed up again by the sand. We had hoped to film *Onymacris*, and Juliane had collected a number of specimens the day before we arrived, careful to keep them cool so that they didn't immediately run off and bury themselves in the sand. The idea was to squirt a fine spray of moisture at them to imitate the effect of the fog, but, alas, they refused to perform.

Many of the tenebrionid beetles look like miniature spacecraft or dune buggies, raising their bodies above the hot sand on long, spidery legs. Having sheltered from the sun for much of the day, they emerge again as it begins to cool, feeding on leaves, seeds and plant detritus carried into the desert on the winds and accumulated at the base of the leeward slipface of the dunes.

Most days there is no fog to bring moisture to Gobabeb, only a hot, dry wind blowing in from the east, sending temperatures soaring. But it is life-giving nonetheless, carrying particles of organic matter and seeds for the creatures to feed on, depositing them over the inter-dune valleys. The food chain is driven by these cyclical events of intermittent moisture – plant matter and detritus are dispersed by the wind to feed the primary consumers, who in turn provide food for the predators. Of these jackal are the most commonly seen, along with the occasional hyaena.

Juliane pointed out a grapefruit-sized fruit covered with sharp spines which was lying on the sand: 'That is the fruit of the !Nara plant, which is endemic to Namibia. Ants suck the moisture accumulated at the base of the stem, or lick it from each other's bodies. You see jackals running off with a !Nara melon stuffed in their mouth, and hyaenas, elephants, even ostriches feed on them for the moist pulp and seeds. So do people.'

Giraffe, darkly patterned and merging with the earth-brown colours of the terrain, are sometimes to be seen browsing along the ephemeral Kuiseb river-bed, feeding on the fog-moistened leaves of the acacia trees. They never drink in these dry regions, conserving water by concentrating their urine to a trickle and producing droppings no bigger than a walnut. Of all the large animals sometimes seen wandering across the dunes, the gemsbok or oryx – a magnificent, lance-horned antelope – is the best adapted to the desert, often feeding at night or in the early morning when the vegetation contains the maximum amount of moisture. Oryx simply absorb the heat, allowing their body temperature to rise from its normal 35.7°C (96.3°F) to 45°C (113°F) – storing heat rather than reducing it by panting, which would mean losing water. As the temperature drops during the night the stored heat is gradually dissipated.

Next to emerge from Juliane's basket was a beautiful *Peringueyi* adder. You have to be a very special kind of snake to survive in the desert, and whether in the Gobi, the Baja or here in the Namib they have all adapted to the problem in the same way, by adopting a mode of locomotion known as 'side-winding' to minimize the amount of time the body is in contact with the hot sand and to gain purchase on the loosely compacted surface, giving maximum traction and minimum body contact. There is no cover behind which to hide in order to ambush prey, only the camouflage of your skin. To catch its prey – mainly lizards – the side-winding adder buries itself in the sand so that only its eyes, set high on its head, look out – and even its eyes are the colour of sand. It obtains moisture by sucking it from its scales.

There is no shortage of prey for the side-winding adder to feed on as there are numerous lizards and geckos living among the desert sands. Among them is the *Aporosura* lizard, which performs an outrageous piece of ballet – an extraordinary dune dance to ward off the heat of the day. Unlike many of the lizards, snakes and beetles, which burrow 30-50 cm (12-20 in) below the surface, where temperatures vary little throughout the year, *Aporosura* thermo-regulates by balancing first on one leg then on the other, eventually standing statuesque on opposite back and fore legs with tail held high. Meanwhile we humans can only keep our hats on, wear total sunblock and carry plenty of water to escape the breathless, brain-numbing heat of the middle of the day.

The rains are a rare event at Gobabeb and life has adapted in different ways to take advantage of it. It not uncommon for no rain to fall, but in the late summer of 1976 and again in 1978 over 100 mm (4 in) of rain was recorded and the desert was instantly transformed – grasses sprang up almost overnight, releasing their feathery seed-heads into the wind. The sudden availability of such a profusion of moisture created a hive of reproductive activity among many beetle species. During the next few years some of these species disappeared completely, leaving their dormant eggs to await the next rainy period. Other populations survived longer, feeding on detritus and the moisture from the fog. Over time it has become apparent that some beetles do not respond to summer rains as their cue to breed, preferring the winter rains which fall every few years, even though they do not yield any grass. The sand is cooler during the winter, so it is able to store the water for longer, providing a moist environment more suited to vulnerable larvae. The micro-environment is so complex that the beetles, gerbils, lizards, plants and insects inhabiting the windward dune slopes differ from those of the slipface.

One of the Namib's most important residents could easily be overlooked, passing much of the time unnoticed beneath the ground. But according to Mary Seeley harvester termites account for 80 per cent of the grass consumed on the Namib Plains, outcompeting all the larger herbivores and providing a rich source of nutrition for the myriad life forms that feast on them: birds, lizards, scorpions, meerkats and jackals.

But can the beetles, ants, lizards and snakes of the Namib provide the kinds of answers that scientists such as Mary Seeley and Juliane are looking for? Is this just research for the sake of it – where does it lead to, other than to a Phd? Juliane was quick to reply that it helps to broaden our understanding of how the interaction of climate with the desert surface influences animal populations. This may allow scientists to make predictions about some effects of global climate changes, particularly which

*Opposite: Péringuey's adder or side-winding adder (*Bitis peringueyi*): a small adder 20-25 cm (8-10 in) in length, with eyes situated on top of its head, allowing it to bury itself in the sand while keeping watch for prey. It moves in a side-winding motion, undulating in lateral curves and thereby lifting most of its body clear of the surface, which enables it to move swiftly over hot, loose sand.*

factors allow animal populations to sustain themselves during prolonged droughts. And that may prove vital in helping humans and livestock to eke out an existence in such a harsh environment without damaging it unduly.

The Namib Desert had cast its spell, inspiring feelings that still linger, a desire to return, to explore the dunes and learn more about how life has evolved here. Our stay at Gobabeb had been all too short.

*Cape fur seal at Cape Cross. Fur seals belong to the same family, Otariidae, as sea-lions. They differ from seals (family Phocidae) in having large fore-flippers which they use to row themselves through the water, small ear-flaps and hind flippers which can be turned beneath the body to enable them to walk on land – they can run as fast as a human.*

It was time now to rejoin Jean-Paul Roux from the Department of Fisheries and Marine Resources for a visit to Cape Cross to film the Cape fur seal colony. These waters are home to a variety of marine mammals in addition to the seals – dusky dolphins, bottle-nosed dolphins, heaviside dolphins, killer whales, southern right whales and sperm whales.

Namibia is the custodian of the majority of the world's Cape fur seals, with a population of 800,000. During the eighteenth and nineteenth centuries there were no legal controls regulating the sealing industry – it was simply a free-for-all. Rookeries were invaded even during the breeding season, and by the end of the nineteenth century

numbers were very low. Since 1900 controlled 'harvesting' has taken place at certain colonies almost every year. The most valuable seal product has always been the skin of seven- to ten-month-old pups, with the bulk of harvesting taking place between 1 August and 15 November. The carcasses are transported in trucks to the processing factories, where they are boiled down for oil and as 'carcass' meal, which is rich in protein – equivalent to fish meal – and used as cattle food. The 45 cm (18 in) penises of the adult bulls are dried and sold as aphrodisiacs in the Far East – a pathetic reflection on the fact that bulls show considerable sexual stamina, herding females into harems and mating with as many of them as possible.

Killing is never pretty. Pictures of men walking among the colonies wielding clubs and bludgeoning seal pups to death have resulted in a storm of protest from the international community. Sealing is not even a particularly profitable activity for the Namibian government. Only sixty people find full- or even part-time employment in the industry and for each seal killed the government gets 50 cents, which in 1994 added up to a total of 26,508 rand – not much more than US$7,000 – for the year's cull. At that price it would hardly seem worth all the adverse publicity that the killing generates. But no government likes to be dictated to and old ways die hard.

During 1994 at least 120,000 seal pups (perhaps as many as 200,000) and an unknown number of adults died, due to what rangers at first thought might be a respiratory disease. In fact the explanation was far simpler than that. The seals had died from lack of fish – starving to death due to a combination of overfishing by commercial fisheries and a phenomenon referred to by Jean-Paul as a 'warm event'.

The ocean waters along the Namibian coast are normally cold as a result of upwelling from deep below by the Benguela Current. But 'warm events' in 1993 and again at the beginning of 1995 caused the productivity of the sea to diminish, with warmer, nutrient-poor water replacing the colder water. This in turn precipitated a 'red tide', which occurs when temperature and nutrient levels trigger a population explosion in a type of plankton known as dinoflagellates. When the dinoflagellates decay, oxygen levels plummet, killing large numbers of fish and having the inevitable knock-on effect on the seal population. The 'red tide' earns its name from the natural red pigments in dinoflagellates which at high levels colour the water crimson.

It is hard to argue against the culling of seals if it can be done on a sustainable basis; indeed the right to cull is enshrined in the Namibian constitution: 'The State shall actively promote the welfare of the people by adopting...policies aimed at...the maintenance of ecosystems, essential ecological processes and biological diversity of Namibia and utilization of living natural resources on a sustainable basis for the benefit of all Namibians both present and future.' But any killing should be done in as humane a manner as possible, and with such a massive decline in the seal population, albeit due to a natural disaster, it hardly seems to be adhering to the principle of 'sustainable' utilization to insist on killing 12,000 bulls and clubbing the greatly reduced number of pups. Far better, surely, to have a moratorium on killing until the impact of the die-off can be assessed. But to do that might put the sealers out of business. Fishermen, too, vigorously support seal culling, although the seals' impact on fishing is more disruptive than anything else – following the fishing boats and scattering the shoals before the fishermen can set their nets. However, when people's livelihoods are concerned the animals invariably come off second best.

Seal colonies have a particularly pungent and somewhat unpleasant odour. With animals crowded together in breeding colonies, the combination of oily skins, accumulated faeces and decaying carcasses from seals that have died natural deaths can be almost overpowering. But this shouldn't be used by officials as part of their justification for culling seals. It all harks back to the days when southern Africa viewed all predators as vermin. Times have changed and public opinion in South Africa has been a major factor in persuading the government there to end sealing. Whether or not it has the same effect in Namibia remains to be seen.

It was a cold, grey afternoon at Cape Cross, where a quarter of a million seals were recorded in 1993 before the die-off occurred. The rocky shoreline looked miserably bleak and I found it hard to believe that this was Africa, clad as I was in long trousers, warm jersey and anorak. The strangely mournful cries of the seals evoked thoughts of the sea – of the mariners who had risked their lives to land along this treacherous coast with its fog and jutting rocks. Even the seals sometimes perish in the foam and the spray, bruised and battered by the pounding waters, which some years take a heavy toll on the pups.

Visitors are permitted to photograph the seal colony at Cape Cross from behind a low stone wall. The seals are so used to the presence of people that they lie up in piles on the shore, often right against the wall. Unlike true seals, fur seals and sea-lions possess external, clearly visible ears, and hind flippers that can be turned beneath their bodies to enable them to walk on land. In fact they are surprisingly fast and can outrun a human.

It was still early in the breeding season when we visited the colony, and most of the bulls that had come ashore were youngsters, not yet old enough to breed. This did not deter them from defending a territory, refining their skills, rushing around, snapping and growling at potential rivals. It looked impressive enough to me, but Jean-Paul assured me that this was nothing compared to the scene when the mature bulls or 'beachmasters' came ashore. Then it was like witnessing the massed herds of wildebeest on the Serengeti Plains, with animals so close together that they looked like a single amorphous entity.

During the breeding season each beachmaster stakes out a tiny patch of shoreline, defending it against other bulls and driving the younger males back into the sea. The cows arrive several weeks later to give birth, and each beachmaster establishes a harem of several cows, with which he mates within five or six days of the pups being born. It is not uncommon for the young pups – who need milk for up to ten months – to be injured or killed as a result of being squashed by the rampaging bulls. Before long many of the bulls bear the scars of battle, sporting gaping wounds on their heads, necks and flippers. I knew from my visits to South Georgia how aggressive beachmasters could be. Each of us carried a long pole with a hook to keep them at bay. Some were content to sit with their noses pointed up in the air, growling their strange growl at us as we beat a path up through the tussock grass to reach the site of a wandering albatross-breeding colony. Others ran to confront us, reluctant to give way, snapping and snuffling. Males are twice the size of females and during the summer can swell up from their normal 190 kg (420 lb) to 300 kg (660 lb).

Once the pups are born they are preyed on by black-backed jackals and the secretive brown hyaena or strandwolf. We saw a number of jackals trotting to and fro among the colony, searching for afterbirths and the chance to feed on the carcass of a young pup or to snatch a live one. They looked mangy; one had lost the hair on its tail, another kept stopping to scratch itself endlessly.

While people argue over the justification of culling seals, a far more endangered species was the focus of the last stage of our safari – the desert rhino. To try and find them we would have to continue north, flying from Swakopmund to a bush strip at Sesfontein, in the North West Region, where we would rendezvous with our guides, Blythe and Rudi Loutit.

Flying is the only way truly to appreciate Namibia. I have never seen such a dry land. Whichever way you look, whether flying or driving, there is no escape – just the heat, the sand, the bare rocks. That life survives at all is a miracle of ingenuity and adaptation. The sun sucks the moisture from your body – it is so dry that you don't even realize it is happening, that the water is going. You just want to keep drinking – litre after litre of fluids.

From the air, the countryside looked as if it has been scraped over by an enormous grader, scoured and torn free of all life. Trees and bushes are a rarity, and only occasionally were there signs that man had penetrated this far – a cluster of stark buildings, a splash of green cultivation. It reminded me in places of other deserts. A mixture of the sandy oceans of the Sahara and the weathered outcrops rising starkly from the land in Arizona or New Mexico – a lunar landscape, with images that fool the human eye, a lost world of rock architecture mimicking the enormous stone buildings of an ancient civilization.

Blythe and Rudi were there to welcome us, their dust-covered vehicles fit to burst with supplies for our safari into the desert. They had lived for many years in the Skeleton Coast National Park, where Rudi had been the Senior Warden since its inception in 1971, overseeing the whole of Damaraland. The park protects a 40 km (25 mile) wide strip of wilderness. The wildlife roams far and wide, wandering east beyond the protection of the park, and many animals have been shot by poachers and herdsmen.

The combination of remoteness, utter wilderness and solitude among wild animals proved irresistible to the Loutits. Blythe had always loved horses and in the early days in the park they used to ride everywhere. While Rudi dealt with the day-to-day administration of the area Blythe studied the brown hyaena. Little was known of their habits in those days and Blythe would lie out on the shore to observe them as they ambled about looking for food. In between writing an occasional column for the *Cape Times* and investigating the diet of the area's black rhino (with the help of Mary Seeley), Blythe painted. Then the poaching started.

Up until 1978 Damaraland and Kaokoland were Bantustans – ethnic homelands. To control and police these areas the authorities – themselves an extension of the South African government – restricted entry, except for officials. During the 'war' between the South African government and the Namibian independence movement, the local people were issued with .303 rifles to protect themselves against 'terrorists'. With a gun in their hands many of the Damara and Herero villagers turned to poaching, shooting animals instead. But abuse of the system went far deeper than that. It is common knowledge that high-ranking officials and even the South African president of the time used the area as a private hunting concession. And members of the South African Defence Force (SADF) committed a catalogue of atrocities in the area, shooting the wild animals for meat, for trophies and sometimes just for the hell of it. Army helicopters were used to make the hunting of elephants even easier; their heads were sliced through with chain saws to remove the tusks.

There were thought to be some 300 elephant in the western Kaokoveld in 1970, but by 1981 poaching and legal trophy hunting had reduced the population to seventy. In two years alone, between 1980 and 1982, 152 elephant carcasses were found in the Kaokoveld. Counts made in 1992 established that the whole of north-western Namibia had only 250 elephant, including those on the edge of Etosha National Park. The good news is that Rudi has evidence that elephant are tentatively moving north into Kaokoland again.

The drive to the Hoanib river-bed was long and dusty, clouds of fine powdery soil churning around us, filling the cars and covering everything with a layer of dust. We stopped to wash our faces at a stream of clear water, and shortly afterwards saw our first elephant – a magnificent bull standing tall on the raised embankment, browsing on a flush of green.

When we arrived in camp Rudi showed me a huge map of Namibia's ephemeral rivers. He traced the route that we had taken to our campsite at the edge of the Hoanib River. The Hoanib is dry for most of the year, and is the only river that fans into a broad flood-plain with multiple channels to the east of the sand dunes. Earlier in the year it had been transformed into a raging torrent. The wet season – when there is one – is December to April, and this year rains from the east brought the blessing of 300 mm (12 in) of rain during April, with virtually all of it falling in a single week – three days even – just after the Easter weekend. Because the catchment area is very narrow,

it collects all the run-off. The transformation could not have been more dramatic. Rudi shook his head: 'It is almost unheard of for a desert area – or shall we say a semi-arid area – such as this to receive 300 mm rainfall. It was unbelievable. You could hear the thunder and see the lightning for miles around – it just went on and on. The river flowed for some 70 km (45 miles), breaking through 30 km (20 miles) of dunes along the Skeleton Coast, carving out a canyon just north of Terrace Bay, and pushing right into the sea, taking the main road with it.' The Hoanib spread out downhill from the dunes in a big fan some 300 metres (1,000 ft) wide, pushing silt for a kilometre (over half a mile) into the sea. Rudi pointed to the base of the larger trees in the dry river-bed which were gift-wrapped with branches and dry vegetation that had been swept downstream by the river.

A damp mist moved into the valley during the night, cloaking the land with a ghostly aura. We rose at 6 a.m. and headed back up the Hoanib River to search for elephants. Gradually the curtain of mist lifted, dissolving in the heat of the desert. A solitary bull elephant – a different one from yesterday – walked up the river-bed ahead of us, unconcerned by the sound of our vehicles. The bull paused beneath each *Acacia albida* (sometimes called *Faidherbia*) tree to gather up ripe seed pods the length of a man's finger. The pods change from green to deep red, eventually ripening to a purple hue. The seeds pass unharmed through the elephant's gut, their outer wall softened by digestive juices and dispersed in their droppings, germinating wherever they are deposited; tests have shown that acacia seeds have an almost 50 per cent better chance of germinating if they have first been digested by an elephant. Elephant also feed on palm nuts, mopane, wild tamarisk and river green thorn. Because of the high nutritional value of desert plants, large animals such as elephant and rhino are able to survive on surprisingly little vegetation in these arid areas.

A few kilometres further on we came upon another big bull heading towards a small group of cows with three calves, one of which was barely a year old. The bull was in musth, with temporin secretions oozing down the sides of his face. He stopped behind the first cow and reached between her hind legs with his trunk, touching her vulva, scenting to see if she was in oestrus. Then he wheeled around and charged towards the other bull, chasing him off.

Ephemeral rivers such as the Hoanib create linear oases or 'hot spots' of animal activity, attracting wildlife to the lush vegetation. These areas provide a rich setting for viewing wildlife: gemsbok (oryx), springbok, giraffe, rhino, elephants, ostriches – all are to be found here. There used to be lots of lions, too, but the Skeleton Coast Park is so narrow that it does not provide them with the food or the space they need if they are to stay there all year round. The lions hunt seals, oryx, ostrich, giraffe; when prey becomes scarce during the dry season they are forced to move east along the ephemeral river-courses for up to 100 km (60 miles) in search of food. Under these circumstances it is inevitable that at times they come into contact with herdsmen bringing livestock to drink at springs and wells. Sometimes the lions kill livestock, occasionally

*Opposite: A bull elephant feeding on lush vegetation along the top of a bank of the ephemeral Hoanib River. Though desert-dwelling elephants are the same species as savanna elephants, they have adapted to these harsh conditions, trekking up to 70 km (45 miles) a day in search of food and water, forced at times to go for three or four days without drinking. They know the position of every waterhole within their range. Their water intake during lean times is thought to be as little as one tenth that of elephants in well-watered habitats, and they can exist on less food thanks to the high nutrient content of the vegetation. Consequently, even in the harshest droughts few adult elephants die, though calves do, and the birth rate declines.*

humans, and inevitably the farmers shoot them – which by law they are entitled to do when protecting their lives and livelihood. But the same lion that the farmer views as a menace is a valuable asset to tourism, which is increasing every year. As Rudi says: 'If some of the revenue from tourism can reach the local people and be ploughed back into their own areas, then there may a chance of protecting predators.'

We stayed with the elephant for most of the day. Sometimes weeks can pass without an elephant passing through this area, but we had been lucky, seeing twenty in all. One of the bulls stood out, instantly recognizable by his small body and enormous head, a 'middle weight' among elephant, short and stocky. Another wore an identification collar around his neck. Twenty elephant had been collared in the Huab region by the authorities to put some 'presence' on them, as Rudi put it. They had lost a lot

*Black rhino keep their young calves hidden during the first few weeks as a way of avoiding predators such as lion and hyaena. Rhino have been known to kill lion with a single swipe from their horn, and when fully grown are virtually immune to these predators – but not to man.*

of bulls to poachers in 1989, and sixteen elephant and five rhino had been killed. People estimate that there are 5,000 elephant in Namibia today. Before the killing started there were 800 in Kaokoland alone, but by 1900 there were only a few hundred in the whole country.

Though desert-dwelling elephant are the same species as the bush elephant, they do seem to have developed certain adaptations to their harsh environment. They may well be the world's tallest elephant – one bull known to Rudi and Blythe is perhaps the tallest of all. Their oversized feet and long legs are thought to be an adaptation to the long treks that they must make if they are to find sufficient food and water to sustain themselves, though some people argue that the long legs are not long at all – just thinned during extended periods of drought, making them look longer. During the dry season the elephant may be forced to go for three to four days without drinking and they know the position of waterholes within their range intimately – even ones they have not drunk at for years, sometimes as much as 80 km (50 miles) away. Their ability to dig deep below the ground for water is often their saviour, and it is possible that in lean times they are able to survive on only a tenth of the water consumed by savanna elephants. Even during the harshest droughts – such as that lasting from 1977 to 1982 in Kaokoveld, which claimed as many as 80 per cent of the other desert-adapted animals such as mountain zebra, kudu, gemsbok and springbok – not one adult elephant succumbed. But calf survival was poor and birth rates always decline under such extreme conditions as a natural way of regulating numbers. It isn't drought that has crippled Namibia's elephant population. Man has always been their greatest enemy.

Now it was time to drive to our final camp, at Hunkab Springs, where Blythe hoped to show us the desert rhino that have become the focus of her life these past ten years. We left the Hoanib and headed southwards into the Mudorib. Gradually the knot-headed hills evaporated, giving way to yellow plains speckled with small herds of springbok, racing away with the startling white flash of long hairs erect from halfway down their backs to their rumps. Springbok are known to form vast herds, but only at the time of the rains when the grass flourishes. A group of five gemsbok swept nimbly up the stony hillside, nervous in the open, while a chicken-like bird, the Damara korhan, scuttled beneath a patch of bush as we passed. Further on a pair of ostriches, starkly profiled – the male black, the female brown – hurried their two-month-old chicks over the cobbled plain. The previous day we had seen a cock and two hens racing ahead of us with 150 chicks in tow, speckled brown earth-colours as camouflage against the veld. Rock buttresses towered above the narrow track, stacks of squared-off slate balanced precariously like a pack of cards. A rock kestrel, its rufous mantle speckled with black spots and with slate-grey tips to its wings, hovered overhead. It swooped down and larks that had remained perfectly camouflaged on the ash-col-oured ground suddenly revealed themselves among the stones and pebbles, rising into the air. They landed again – all except one clasped in the talons of the predator.

I asked Blythe what it had been like during the bad years, when poaching threat-ened to destroy Namibia's elephant and rhino. The black rhino population inhabiting communal land in Kunene Province (previously Kaokoland and Damaraland) had been particularly hard hit, she said. Those in Kaokoland were reduced to only ten ani-mals, with fifty to sixty in Damaraland.

The turning point for Blythe had come in 1985 when a friend showed her the car-casses of seven black rhino which had been ambushed and killed at a waterhole. Horrified by what she had seen, Blythe determined to try and do something to stop the slaughter, and founded the Save the Rhino Trust (SRT). But stopping the poach-ers was never going to be easy. A further seven rhino were killed in 1989, and wildlife officials, with the logistic and moral support of SRT, decided to tranquillize the remaining rhino in two of the most vulnerable areas and remove their horns – the first time this had been tried anywhere in the world. One of the areas chosen was where Blythe was working. The results speak for themselves. In 1990 they lost one; in 1991 a six-month-old male calf was stoned to death by local boys who were later caught. In 1994 a small sub-adult was killed by locals and possibly one other has been lost. At the time of writing there are nearly 600 black rhino in Namibia, 114 of them in the Kunene region – thirty-eight males, forty-three females, five of unknown sex and the rest calves.

Like the ivory trade, the killing of rhino in Africa is a dirty business, ruthlessly con-trolled by wealthy middlemen and corrupt officials and fuelled by the demands of those who believe in the medicinal powers of powdered rhino horn. Rhino horn has been one of the mainstays of traditional medicine in the Far East for at least 2,000 years, mainly to treat fever, flu and convulsions. In recent years much of Africa's rhino horn has gone to the Northern Yemen, where it is used to make handles for *jambas* – traditional J-shaped daggers which are worn as a symbol of manhood.

The rhino's story is one of appalling butchery. Some 60,000 of these ancient crea-tures have been killed in the last thirty years in Africa. Today there are perhaps 2,500 surviving – most of them in some form of protection – fenced in, guarded day and night by rangers in situations more akin to a military operation than anything else. In some countries, including Zimbabwe and Kenya, the government approved a shoot-to-kill policy to try and stop the slaughter – but it was of little use for as long as the price of rhino horn rivalled gold ounce for ounce. The Zambezi Valley – once the ref-uge of 3,000 black rhino – soon succumbed to the gangs of heavily armed poachers, from both Zambia and Zimbabwe, until only a hundred animals remained. These too were eventually removed to safety behind fences elsewhere in the country.

Dehorning is a controversial procedure, as rhino use their horns to dig for water and to defend themselves and their calves against predators. But Blythe and Rudi are convinced that dehorning has not compromised the rhino, and refute the recent contention that cow rhino in the region have lost calves to predators (which are rare here) as a direct result of dehorning; they cite drought as the most likely cause of any deaths. Even with horns it is not always possible for a rhino to thwart a determined attack by lions or hyaenas, and I know of instances in East Africa when these predators have killed or injured rhino calves, despite the presence of their mother. The best form of defence is for a cow to seek the shelter of thick bush for her calf, and in many instances an animal of this size can deter all but the most persistent predators – with or without its horn.

Unfortunately dehorning has not always prevented the poachers from killing rhino. In the Zambezi Valley, poachers deliberately killed dehorned rhino when they had gone to the trouble of tracking them down and found them without horns. But in Namibia's desert regions dehorning has certainly proved successful.

Many a good idea has foundered on an overdose of emotion and a sheer lack of practicality. That has not been the case with Save the Rhino. Their success is based on the solid foundation of support from the local community, a good investigative network, constant patrolling of the area and the full co-operation of the Ministry of Wildlife, Conservation and Tourism. Goodwill is essential and Blythe has done a lot to help local communities deal with the problems of elephant damage – mainly by assisting them to protect their pumps, reservoirs and underground water troughs, and providing the wild animals with alternative waterholes.

Twice each year Blythe and her team undertake a complete census of rhino in the area. Four patrol units operate in the field year-round, but for the purposes of the census a fifth team is included. Monitoring such a large area sounded impossible for a small field force, yet it is highly effective in its operation. Blythe employs local men to police a road barrier, noting the movements of all vehicles using the sparse network of tracks leading into the rocky desert – just in case. Date of entry, vehicle registration, number of passengers, purpose of visit are all recorded to help create a presence in the area. The scouts follow up the tracks of people considered dubious.

So how do you find rhino in an area such as this? It is hard enough at times in the Masai Mara, where the animals are used to being viewed. Our chances of seeing rhino here on such a short visit appeared slim. But Blythe was in buoyant spirits, and so were the trackers. To find a rhino you must learn to think like one. You must be able to read the signs left by their wanderings. Rhino frequent waterholes, usually drinking every other day. They are very active at night, particularly in the desert, because this helps them to avoid heat stress and reduces their dependency on water. For this reason the tracking teams drive out towards waterholes in the early morning in the hope of picking up fresh rhino spoor.

When searching waterholes for rhino you look for territorial markings, signs of browsing, evidence of rolling, dung middens and 'rubbing stones'. In the old days geologists and surveyors working in such regions always avoided camping near waterholes, as there were rhino everywhere. One man counted sixteen coming to just one waterhole, implying a total population of approximately 500 rhino, 75 per cent more than today!

Each time rhino tracks are discovered they are measured to help estimate age and sex. Some of Blythe's trackers can identify an individual rhino just by looking at its spoor. Over the years a wealth of information has been collected on each of the rhino in the area. I thumbed through a file as thick as an encyclopedia; here were details of the age, health, movements, range size and history of each individual known to the trust. A series of photographs had been pasted on to the sheets – there were cows with tiny calves, bulls with tattered ears and massive thick horns, rhino caught in the act of charging forward to investigate, or blundering off, tasselled tails cocked ramrod straight in the air.

Whenever a rhino has had to be immobilized – whether for dehorning or to be treated for some ailment – a distinctive notch is cut into its ear to make identification at a distance easier. The focus of activity for each tracking team varies by the day and might involve monitoring the condition of a sick rhino, locating a new calf or searching for the carcass of an individual that had disappeared and might have been poached. A ministry scout armed with a high-powered rifle accompanies each patrol and is responsible for law enforcement; some have proved to be excellent investigators, and nearly every poaching incident is solved.

With only two days in which to find and film a rhino we were relying on Blythe and her trackers' expertise – and on a fair measure of luck. We rose at 5.30 a.m., crowding around the dying embers of the campfire. There was an air of excitement and expectation prompted by the fact that the previous evening, one of our cameramen, Kim Wolhuter, had filmed a male rhino feeding on euphorbia bushes, marking its home range by defecating and scraping with its hind feet.

We soon found fresh spoor – plate-sized footprints in the dusty soil. Simpson, one of the trackers, stopped and measured them – 22 cm (9 in) across.

'Van Gogh or the Mudorib bull,' he proclaimed, a twinkle in his eyes.

Van Gogh was the one with the missing ear, while the Mudorib bull was a stroppy character with tattered ears and a ragged temper to match. Either would be ideal for filming. The trackers jumped from the side of the vehicle and disappeared over the rise at the double, galvanized by the sight of a patch of bush freshly doused with urine and tracks pointing to where the bull had stopped to drink. By now Simpson had joined the rest of the trackers and Blythe was driving. Not long afterwards, Simpson came running up to the car, gleaming with pleasure, a ball of fresh dung held triumphantly in his fist.

Minutes ticked by, then hours, the heat beating down, dry and merciless. The crew were getting tired, the momentum beginning to fade. Some slept, covering their heads with their jackets, faces ghostly white with sun block. Two o'clock – no canopy to shield the car, we had left it back at base. Should we go back to camp and wait for

*More than 60,000 black rhino have been killed during the last thirty years, making it one of Africa's most endangered species. Today there are perhaps 2,500 surviving, mostly in heavily protected, fenced sanctuaries, guarded by armed rangers. Namibia has more than 500 black rhino and has experimented with dehorning in an attempt to combat poaching.*

the trackers to find the rhino while we sought the shade? But what if we missed the rhino? In the end we stayed where we were.

A pair of pied crows followed our tracks, chuckling overhead as if taunting us. Perhaps they could see what we were searching for so anxiously on the ground.

Finally, at 3.30 p.m., ten hours after leaving camp, hot and dusty, the backs of our throats like sandpaper, heads thumping, the words that we had all been hoping to hear came crackling over the radio: 'We have a rhino.' It was neither Van Gogh nor the

Mudorib bull, but another fine male resting in the shade of a bush. Blythe drove as close as she could up the valley, the wispy white grass backlit against the sun. Ahead I could just make out three men perched high on the top of a rocky outcrop. To one side a lone figure sat looking into the valley where the rhino was sleeping. We jumped from the car and hiked up the hill a kilometre (over half a mile) away, cameraman Brian McDairmant leading the way, all of us suddenly finding reserves of energy that only minutes before had appeared to have evaporated in the heat. One of the trackers waved his arms wildly in the air to keep us well to one side of the rhino, for fear of him hearing us or catching our scent.

Cresting the rise I stared down into the valley and there, its dusty grey hindquarters massively visible in the lee of a patch of euphorbia, was the rhino. Blythe had already warned us about the euphorbia bushes which dotted the hillside. The milky latex of this particular species of euphorbia, *E. damarana*, is a severe irritant to the skin and can even poison you if you inhale the smoke from burning its wood as a fire. Rhino eat the long tendrils with great gusto, apparently becoming almost addicted to it; the latex drooling from the corners of their mouths, reddening the skin. But its sap is so poisonous that only the black rhino eat it, though greater kudu nibble the flowers.

There were hurried discussions as to how best to position ourselves for filming. Blythe and I would be with Simpson, who needed to take pictures of the rhino to help identify it and add to the rhino file. Kim crossed the valley and positioned himself with the trackers, their heads peering across at the rhino from behind another euphorbia bush. But just as Blythe and I crossed back to a platform of rocks where we could wait for the rhino to wake up, he twitched his tail a couple of times and then rose to his feet – suddenly and quickly, up and alert, partially concealed from us by the bush. Unfortunately Brian McDairmant and producer Brian Leith had paused to put a 300 mm lens on the camera for a close-up of the rhino resting. Now both were stranded directly opposite the rhino, with no cover except for the flat rocks and feathery grass stems – hardly what they would need to hide behind if the rhino charged.

The bull wheeled round the bush and stared up at us. He was surrounded on four sides by people, all of them on foot. The great beast stared up at us with his short-sighted eyes, ears the size of saucers trying to pinpoint our position, nostrils flared on his wrinkled snout, sniffing the air for clues as to exactly what he was confronting. Blythe, Simpson and I held our position on the rocks. Simpson clicked the shutter of his camera and the rhino jumped as if he had been hit by a bullet. I thought how easy it must be to slaughter these prehistoric creatures, virtually unchanged in form or function for 40 million years. The bull trotted uphill towards us. Uncertain whether to charge, he stopped before continuing up the rocky ground, then turned and ran back up the valley towards the trackers, coming within 10 metres (30 ft) of them. He hesitated, head held high, tail cocked. The trackers stared back at him; nobody moved, hearts pounding, the youngest of the trackers facing a rhino for the first time. After what must have seemed an eternity the rhino trotted off, leaving the trackers barely able to control the somewhat hysterical giggles that come all too easily when you have escaped unharmed from danger.

This was perilous work, yet the tracker teams seemed to relish the challenge of finding the rhino, inspired by the very human desire to succeed in their task; they hated to fail. Three years ago one of the trackers had been gored in the armpit by a bull rhino. The animal had charged from behind, unseen, knocking the tracker to the ground and then standing over him, spittle drooling from his mouth, soaking the man's shirt, making him think it was his own blood coursing down his back. The other trackers rushed to their colleague's aid, distracting the rhino, which eventually moved off. The tracker recovered and had recently reapplied for his old job. Simpson summed it all up: 'Anytime fresh tracks are found we must eventually find the rhino.' And when they do, a bonus of 30 Namibian dollars is paid for identifying it, providing a tangible incentive for their efforts. Save the Rhino also pays a reward of $5,000 for information leading to the conviction of a person who shoots rhino or deals in rhino horn. The local people are proud of their achievements in promoting conservation and regard poaching as a crime that can no longer be tolerated.

What Blythe and her dedicated team of rangers were doing was holding out hope in one of the last places where black rhino can still survive in the wild, protected by the very harshness of this land where people rarely venture. Their success has been possible thanks to a three-way union between the Ministry of Wildlife, the goodwill of the local communities and the resources of non-government organizations such as Save the Rhino Trust. The achievements in Kaokoland and Damaraland, where numbers are increasing despite poaching, would not have been feasible without involving local people in conservation so that they benefit from wildlife. And by helping to protect the rhino they ensure that the other wildlife of the area is also conserved.

Our last evening before flying back to Windhoek was spent at a small tourist facility called Palmwag Lodge, close to Blythe's base camp. Sitting at the bar sipping a cold beer I looked out over a waterhole often visited by herds of elephant. In the distance I could see rugged hilltops which looked as if they had been hand-carved in stone. Palm trees rustled in the breeze. I went to my room and took a shower, washing away the dust and the grime. When I emerged again, cut off from the world around me on a vacant part of the lodge, I caught my breath. The sunset was one of the most glorious I had ever seen. Too late now for photography, I was compelled to enjoy it with my own eyes rather than through the lens of my camera. There is nowhere else in Africa quite like Namibia. I would be coming back.

# ZIMBABWE: THE GREAT ZAMBEZI

*When I returned to Zimbabwe after that long absence, I expected all kinds of changes, but there was one change I had not thought to expect. The game had mostly gone. The bush was nearly silent. Once the dawn chorus hurt the ears... the shrilling, clamouring, exulting of the birds as the sun appeared was so loud the ears seemed to curl up and complain before – there was nothing else for it – we leaped up into the early morning, to become part of all that tumult and activity. But by the 1980s the dawn chorus had become a feeble thing. Once, everywhere, moving through the bush, you saw duiker, bush buck, wild pig, wild cats, porcupines, anteaters; koodoo stood on the antheaps turning their proud horns to examine you before bounding off; eland went about in groups, like cattle. Being in the bush was to be with animals, one of them.*

**Doris Lessing,** *African Laughter*

Rhodesia, 1974: Up until now our afternoon game drive through Wankie (now Hwange) National Park had been rather quiet. We had seen a multitude of impala and zebra, buffalo and elephant, even a brief glimpse of a serval. But like all visitors on safari in Africa I had hoped that we might be lucky enough to see something of the big cats. It was the end of the rainy season and with the grass growing taller by the day lions, leopards and cheetahs were hard to find. Then, an hour before dusk, just as the light was at its most beautiful, we spied a solitary lioness sprawled in the open close to the road. She looked magnificent lying there, head raised above the blond grass, nose into the wind. Perhaps she was looking for other members of her pride or would soon be setting off to hunt. Though we could only stay with her for a few minutes I felt it was enough just to have found her.

We hurried back towards our tented camp, the sun setting at our backs. My thoughts had turned to the hot shower and cold beer that would wash away the dust; then we rounded a corner and came upon a sight that is as clear in my mind today as it was then, twenty years ago. In an open glade at the edge of thick bush two male sable antelope were fighting furiously, their black coats contrasting starkly with the brilliant white of their bellies. They were down on their knees, heads flung forward, sabre-like horns locked together. They reminded me of knights jousting at a medieval court. Nothing could disturb the contest; they were oblivious to the world around them. If the solitary lioness had seen them I felt sure that she would have begun to stalk and that one of the bulls would have found itself fighting for its life. But the lioness was far away, and the bulls continued to battle for another five minutes – it seemed like an hour. Finally they broke apart, nostrils flared, sucking in air, lungs bursting from their exertions. They snorted in alarm, startled now by our presence. One of the bulls bolted and was immediately pursued by the other. Normally I would have been busily taking photographs, but I had smashed my camera the previous day, knocking it from the bonnet of the car. Perhaps that is why the memory is so vivid – I was forced to watch rather than relying on my photographs to remind me of what had happened.

Over the years I had travelled to Zimbabwe on a number of occasions, and had visited most of the national parks. The people were warm and friendly, the country somewhat dated: I still remember how old-fashioned and rather quaint everything had looked when I first passed through in 1974. Ten years later I was asked

*Paddling a canoe along the great Zambezi, dominated by the Zambian Escarpment, is one of the most tranquil and relaxing ways of experiencing a safari in Africa. Hunkered down in a lightweight fibre-glass canoe, a paddle in your hands, the combination of exercise and game-watching is irresistible.*

to present three programmes for an American television series. We netted lions, wrestled with ostriches and made a film about crocodile farming, using traps and noose poles to catch adult crocs – exciting fare. But I had seen nothing that could compare with East Africa's wildlife areas.

Although Zimbabwe was included in our plans for the series from its inception, of all the countries that we were due to visit it seemed to have the least to offer as far as wildlife was concerned. In fact the only reason it had been given the go-ahead was that Uganda had failed to provide a suitable alternative. One of the reservations about Zimbabwe was whether the scenery along the Zambezi and in the Mana Pools National Park would be sufficiently interesting for our film. In fact the Zambian Escarpment with its steep profile and purple hues provided the perfect backdrop to the river, and the mere mention of John Stevens's name drew accolades from all who knew him or had been on safari with him. John has an encyclopedic knowledge of all aspects of Zimbabwe's wildlife, and he would be my guide for the walking and canoeing parts of our safari. But would viewers find it exciting enough to hear him expounding on how to identify the scat of a civet or revealing details of the social life of a termite colony – rivetting stuff if you are actually there?

We all agreed that the great Zambezi River held the key to our plans. Some

2,575 km (1,609 miles) in length and flowing from north-western Zambia through Mozambique to the Indian Ocean, with a wide delta near Chinde, the Zambezi is full of character. As we talked about the opportunities for filming on the river, I realized that perhaps I had been too quick in my dismissal of Zimbabwe as a tourist destination. Here was the chance for me – and our viewers – to experience adventure of a different kind. The combination of white-water rafting below Victoria Falls – which boast the best Grade 5 rapids in the world – canoeing in calmer waters within a few kilometres of Mana Pools, and a walking safari with John Stevens couldn't fail to be exciting. We decided to start the film at Victoria Falls. It would make a dramatic opening and then allow us to travel further downstream to more tranquil stretches of the river in order to enjoy watching some of the wildlife.

Victoria Falls are, of course, inextricably linked in many people's minds with the great Scottish missionary and explorer David Livingstone, the first white man to see them. I had often stared up in awe to meet Livingstone's implacable gaze outside the Royal Geographical Society in Kensington Gore in London. The bronze sculpture seems to capture his indomitable spirit perfectly. I have nothing but admiration for Livingstone's incredible fortitude during those long years of exploration in equatorial Africa. As Charles Miller wrote in *The Lunatic Express*:

> *Considering the climate alone, this could have been tantamount to a death sentence. In the pre-atabrine, pre-antibiotic nineteenth century, five years was generally considered an excessive tour of duty for any European in the tropics. Nearly a full decade of vindictive heat, unremitting attacks of fever, constant personal risk and overwork had left an indelible mark on Mackay.*

Alexander Mackay, pioneering missionary in Uganda, died of fever in 1890 at the age of forty-one.

I well remember my own visit to the Hospital for Tropical Diseases in London to be treated for malaria. I was told by one of the doctors that perhaps it was time I thought about leaving Africa – 'white man's grave, you know'. The sight of other diseases with which I might have been afflicted was far worse than the malaria; fortunately the quinine made me deaf for most of my stay in hospital, so I was spared the more gruesome accounts: most of the patients had worms or bugs of some sort burrowing into just about every conceivable part of their anatomy.

*Overleaf: 'The smoke that thunders'. As Livingstone wrote, 'Scenes so lovely must have been gazed upon by angels in their flight.'*

Livingstone arrived in Africa in 1844, reaching Lake Ngami in 1849 before travelling along the Zambezi in 1851. He always maintained that his pilgrimages were journeys of faith, carrying the word of God to the people of Africa. He never explored for geographical rewards – or so he said – though he tended to try and discredit the feats of

his rivals in an attempt to consolidate his reputation of being the first white man to set foot in an area. Though Livingstone had heard stories of Moise-oa-tunya or the 'smoke that thunders' (as the falls were referred to by the local people), he did not travel to see them until 1855. By then he had cast his eyes on many memorable sights, but he had seen nothing quite like this. The approach to the falls from upstream is an extraordinarily beautiful tapestry of islands and rapid waterways. Livingstone was stunned and amazed by the wide expanse of white water cascading 120 metres (400 ft) into a narrow gorge only 30 metres (100 ft) wide on what is today the border separating Zimbabwe and Zambia. The Zambezi Valley is a vast, fractured bed of volcanic rock into which the river has found its way through a series of fault lines – water alone could never have created the 100 km (60 mile) long Batoka Gorge.

When Livingstone saw the falls he realized that his dream of harnessing the Zambezi as a commercial highway leading deep into the heart of Africa was an impossibility. Perhaps the paddle-steamers he had envisaged bringing cargo could be dismantled and transported round the falls, he mused. Certainly his estimate of the height of the falls was considerably less than the true figure – a deliberate miscalculation, some would later say, to cover his disappointment. But despite the setback to his plans, Livingstone was so moved by the sight of the falls that he named them in tribute to his queen, Victoria.

We arrived in Zimbabwe to find the country firmly in the grip of the drought that had held its people hostage for the past four years. Erratic rainfall and water shortages have for years caused failed harvests, chronic food deficiencies and the spread of disease. In some parts of the countryside starvation and misery are the currency of life. According to the experts, Zimbabwe is destined – with the rest of southern Africa – to a future bedevilled by increasing aridity due to the effects of global warming.

We could see the clouds of mist from kilometres away. Our pilot pulled the aeroplane round in a tight turn, revealing the full expanse of the Victoria Falls. In places, the rain forest grew lush and thick, and I could see people clustered at a series of viewing points close to the edge of the falls. They were mere specks by comparison to the size and power of the Zambezi. Despite the lack of water it was an impressive sight, although the sheer drop of bare rocks made poor fare for photographers whose expectations had been fed by pictures of the river in full spate. The falls had all but evaporated and the Zambian section was almost dry. We landed and drove to the Victoria Falls Hotel, where a representative from Shearwater, the white-water rafting company which was to organize our safari over the rapids, was waiting to meet us.

Trevor was big. He looked like a rugby player and wore training shorts and a T-shirt with the words 'Shearwater – the adrenaline company' emblazoned on the back. I later found out that he had boxed professionally in the United States. Now he was the manager of Shearwater, the most successful white-water rafting operation in Zimbabwe. Trevor was a salesman par excellence, and had a quick answer for everything. He was trading in adventure and excitement – white-water rafting was within the grasp of anyone who cared to don a life-jacket and a crash-helmet. You didn't need to be big and tough, or even lean and fit – that was immediately apparent from a quick look around the crowd of people who had gathered that morning to prepare themselves for their adventure. There were boys in their teens and women in their sixties, young adults whose muscular bodies spoke of years of exercise and middle-aged physiques that had seen too much steak and beer.

As I listened to the briefing that Trevor had obviously given a hundred times before, my mind began to wander, filled with questions. Just how dangerous *was* white-water rafting?

'We pride ourselves on never having lost anyone....' I suddenly became aware of Trevor's words. 'Never having lost anyone!' Was this going to be more than I had bargained for? Though I hadn't lost any sleep over my participation and was excited about the prospect of encountering the rapids, I couldn't help wondering what lay ahead. Shearwater's boast is true – no one has died on one of their trips down the Zambezi, though people have been killed rafting on the river. But all the companies – and their number seems to be growing by the day – have had their share of accidents, be it broken bones, cuts or just bruises. But by now Trevor had hooked us with the hype – anyone who walked away at this point would have given in to their fears. Nobody seemed in a hurry to leave. After all, Trevor had finished by reminding everyone about the hike back up the steep gorge after we had safely completed the rapids. That, he assured us, would test our endurance much more severely than the water.

We decided that I would join the boats when they stopped for lunch. By that time the participants would have navigated their way through rapids 1 to 10. I climbed aboard a minibus taking some of the staff to the lunch site, and was joined by a young Englishman who was holidaying in Zimbabwe, earning his keep as a safety kayaker. A number of kayakers are employed to run the rapids ahead of the rafts and then wait in the calmer water to assist anyone who flips out and needs help to get to safety.

We descended the steep wall of the gorge to where the Shearwater staff were busy preparing lunch. As the boats arrived I sat and watched the people get out – no obvious signs of bumps and bruises, though one lady told me that perhaps she would give the afternoon rapids a miss: it had been as rough as she felt comfortable about handling. I don't know whether the lunch fortified her (it was delicious), but I noticed that the same lady got back into the raft when time was called, as if she had never given a thought to quitting.

My raft was in the confident hands of Gary, a Swiss oarsman with years of experience navigating white-water rapids in Europe. He was joined by some of the other Shearwater oarsmen to make up numbers. 'Should be fun' was their opinion. My only previous experience of white-water rafting had been taking a small zodiac inflatable

*The Zambezi is classed as Grade 5 white-water rapids, the highest grade commercial rapids in the world. Rapid 18 is known as 'Oblivion', and for many it is the ultimate in white-water excitement. At its most ferocious when the water is low, it provides thrills with little risk of injury, even when the raft flips over and dispatches its passengers into the drink!*

down a relatively quiet stretch of the Mara River. On that occasion I soon learned that you don't kneel on the floor of a raft unless you want to face the hard knocks that come with hitting the rocks. Far more worrying than the rocks were the hippo. The Mara River is narrow and tortuous, twisting and turning to reveal herds of hippo congregating on the sandy banks at every corner. And if you happen to fall into the brown waters there are some huge crocodiles to welcome you. It had all been relatively calm and peaceful until we met our first bull hippo, standing half-submerged mid-stream with the look of someone who was prepared to fight for his territory. Reluctantly we pulled into the side – and that was it.

Hippo and crocodiles would not be much bother on the Zambezi, I thought. They tend to avoid fast-flowing sections of any river, and it was only in the white-water stretches of the Zambezi that you were likely to take a bath. You might be unlucky, I suppose, and find yourself still floating downstream by the time you reached the calmer sections; then you ran the risk of being taken by a crocodile, but the chances of that happening were too slim to worry about. The real dangers here were the power of the undercurrents and sink holes, the back waves and sheer force of the water. That was why the kayakers were always positioned to help the 'swimmers'. Trevor had explained to us that there were two sorts of 'swimmers': 'short' swimmers, who go overboard but manage to hang on to the ropes and can easily be hauled back on board again; and 'long' swimmers, who end up separated from the raft, in which case the oarsman throws them a bag containing a rope and hauls them alongside, or they simply hang on to a ring attached to the front of a kayak and are towed back to the raft. The most important thing to remember if you are a 'swimmer' is to keep your legs up and always to face downstream – that way you can fend off the rocks with your feet. Trevor had warned us never to try and stand up in fast-flowing water 'in case you snag a leg between the rocks and end up being swept forward by the power of the water and break something'.

With the first half-a-dozen rapids under my belt I was beginning to think that the mighty Zambezi wasn't going to live up to its reputation. The rapids all have names and 'Overland Truck Muncher' and 'Creamy White Buttocks' ('has a tendency to rip your shorts off!') had been exciting enough, but nothing too serious. Then we came to rapid number 18 – 'Oblivion'. I had heard a lot about 'Oblivion' since arriving at Victoria Falls and the previous evening Robin Hellier and I had watched a video of the highlights from earlier rafting trips. In one of the clips the boat pitched straight up in the air and remained suspended for a moment at ninety degrees to the water, with people falling all over the place before the raft flipped over. It looked totally crazy, like riding the Big Dipper at a funfair and having the wheels come off.

'Oblivion' is meant to be at its most ferocious when the water is low – and it was. It comes at you in three waves. As we drifted downstream towards this last rapid I heard Gary rather nonchalantly telling the others that 'we are almost certain to flip if we go straight down the middle of the rapid, but that is definitely the most spectacular approach. It should look great for the film crew.' By this stage I was thinking more of self-preservation than what it was going to look like on film, and told Gary that it wasn't absolutely essential that we flipped. He smiled knowingly. We watched as the first raft went over the edge and saw it re-emerge a few moments later, people's arms raised in triumph, their shouts of exhilaration drowned by the noise of the water. Then the second boat disappeared from view – and didn't reappear. 'They must be surfing on the top of the wave, held there by the back wave,' said Gary. Suddenly the raft floated into view, upside down, with the passengers' blue helmets bobbing about like corks in the water, kayakers paddling through the spray to the rescue. We were boat number three.

Just before we went over the edge, I asked the man next to me what I was supposed to do. 'When we flip, just hang on to one of the loops of rope attached to the side of the raft, don't let go.' We dropped head first into the churning water. The noise was deafening; it was like putting your head in a washing machine, all spinning and tumbling. Now I understood what everybody had being talking about. This was it.

*Hippo spend much of the day resting on sand banks in the river. Though they have a thick hide, the epidermis of their skin is thin and they do not have sweat glands, which means that they lose water at several times the rate of other mammals. If they stay out of the water in hot weather they are liable to dehydrate and overheat. This African pied wagtail (*Motacilla aguimp*) is searching for flies attracted to the hippo's skin.*

The raft popped up, a wave of water lifting us on to the next section. Again we surfaced, but by now I had lost my bearings and had no idea what was happening. Water was crashing everywhere, blocking out the sky. Suddenly the raft began to vibrate, locked in a vice-like grip, surfing on top of the wave. Next moment we flipped over with such violence that people were thrown in every direction. I hung on as if my life depended on it. There was total darkness before I popped out from under the boat – or was it just from under the water? I saw panic on the faces of the oarsmen as it became apparent that the young girl who had joined us from another raft to make up numbers for this rapid was missing. 'There she is,' someone shouted, as they spotted her bobbing along near the bank. She looked frightened and a little confused, but was uninjured, as was the lady I had spoken to at lunch who had changed her mind and continued rafting through the afternoon. I wondered how she was feeling now that she had survived the worst – despite becoming a 'long swimmer' like most of the rest of us. I didn't have to ask.

Back in Nairobi some weeks later a friend told me that he had been white-water rafting on the Zambezi for the third time earlier in the year. The first two occasions had been everything that he had hoped for – thrills without mishaps. But the third trip ended with my friend taking a 'swim' at 'Oblivion'. That was quite enough excitement for him, he said. There was no point in stacking the odds any further. On the other hand, for some the rush of adrenaline is so addictive that they go back again and again. I certainly will. But what about bungee jumping at Victoria Falls? There is even one lunatic who makes the leap into the unknown backwards. Now that is something I would never do.

Our Zimbabwe safari coincided with the descent towards what is known locally as suicide month. The heat and humidity of November leave everyone jaded. Tempers are short, feelings almost literally suicidal. The slightest exertion can turn beads of perspiration into rivers of sweat. The sun beats down remorselessly – clouds of dust obscure the landscape. Grass fires burn, filling the sky with acrid smoke as villagers prepare to welcome the blessing of rain – if it comes at all. There are times when it just keeps promising, never to deliver. The villagers are resigned to all this, and a perverse optimism prevails for much of the time, replaced when necessary by acceptance that ill fortune is just a part of living.

We flew from Harare to a bush strip two hours' drive from Ruckomechi Camp, the launch site for our canoe safari with John Stevens. The land was bare; in places the trees were devastated by elephants, creating a graveyard of fallen limbs. Impala added a splash of colour; baboons sauntered through the clearings, plump and heathy-looking despite the seeming lack of anything edible for them to feast on. I couldn't help thinking that the game-viewing from the land was going to look pretty sparse.

It was swelteringly hot at Ruckomechi the evening we arrived, though I was told that it had been even hotter the previous night. I lay with the bedclothes flung to one side, spread-eagled on the mattress like a sick bird. I felt sure that come the early hours I would be reaching for the blanket, but I never did. The heat was remorseless: it radiated back from the roof, trapped by the mosquito net. The 'mozzies' buzzed about for most of the night and by the morning they had made a pretty mess of my feet. The next evening I sealed the gaping holes in the mosquito net with camera tape.

John Stevens was not in the least what I had expected. I had imagined one of those young bucks in a singlet and shorts, full of tall stories of adventures in the bush. By contrast John proved to be one of the most unassuming and modest men I had ever met – shy, even reticent at times. No fuss, no boasting, no conceit. Always a ready smile, always the first to help – whether carrying someone's equipment or enquiring after their well-being. The young Zimbabweans running the camp seemed genuinely in awe of him. They admired his fitness and respected his knowledge: he knew the river better than anyone and 'You should see him without his shirt on,' they said. To John physical fitness and mental toughness went hand in hand: 'You have to respect yourself, to have pride.' He chuckled at the antics of some of the younger men, who were desperate to cling on to the dying embers of a dream that John had made his life.

John is one of only a handful of Grade A trackers in Zimbabwe and holds a professional hunter's licence. He is on the board of examiners of the Professional Guides and Hunters Association, which rightly prides itself on the standards of excellence it expects from its members. It only takes one incident, one moment of poor judgement or incompetence for things to go horribly wrong.

To become a professional safari guide you must serve a year's apprenticeship as a learner guide, during which time you are not allowed to conduct walking safaris, though you can take visitors on game drives. In your second year you work towards your professional guide's licence, and must prove yourself able to shoot both elephant and buffalo so as to help ensure that you are competent to safeguard the lives of your clients when on foot. You must also know how to set up a fully equipped safari camp and be able to maintain a four-wheel-drive vehicle in perfect working order. The best safari guides are a fund of knowledge and can identify virtually every species of tree and plant as well as the many birds and animals encountered during a safari. The Zimbabwean guides are as good as any I have met in Africa and it generally takes two to three years to qualify.

John was born in what was then Rhodesia and joined the National Parks Service as a cadet ranger at the age of eighteen, after National Service. During the eight-year war that culminated in the country's winning its independence as the new nation of Zimbabwe in 1980, John was a member of the Selous Scouts, an elite team of trackers attached to the Rhodesian army. He helped to maintain a presence in Mana Pools as part of the Parks Service and spent the better part of six years in the bush, relishing the time in the wild, the camaraderie, parachuting into trouble spots, the pursuit....

But all that was in the past now and John lived very much in the present. He wanted to move on, didn't need to regale people with stories from the old days – no heroics. He treated everyone, black or white, with fairness and respect.

By the time he left the Parks Service in 1981, John had risen to the rank of Warden of Mana Pools National Park. Over the years he had become increasingly office-bound, involved more and more with administration and spending less and less time out in the bush. Tired of the confinement, he left to set up a safari camp called Chikwenya with Rob Fynn as his partner. Chikwenya is situated in the Sapi safari area on the eastern boundary of Mana Pools National Park, overlooking the Zambezi. The camp accommodated twelve people and offered visitors a range of safari options – walking, game drives and boat trips on the river.

During the off-season at Chikwenya John began operating long-haul canoeing safaris with Eddie Rous. John had canoed since 1968 and kept his own canoe at camp, occasionally taking people out with him on the water; Eddie was the first to see the potential of doing this commercially. Canoeing Safaris, as it was known in those days, ran its first canoe trip in 1982-3, and eventually gave birth to Shearwater, the company that had taken us white-water rafting.

Today as well as operating safaris from a mobile camp at Mana Pools in the north of the country, John and his partners have a concession on the boundary of the Matusadona National Park in western Zimbabwe, bordering Lake Kariba. Here they specialize in walking safaris. Their operation is affiliated to the Campfire Management project which seeks to help the local communities benefit from revenue generated by wildlife utilization, be it in the form of hunting, game-cropping or tourism. The concession is part of an 'intensive protection area' and John and his partner Alistair Hull provide additional manpower for anti-poaching patrols. Fortunately Lake Kariba is 30-40 km (19-25 miles) wide, so it is difficult for poachers to cross undetected.

It is hard to describe quite how enjoyable it is to be in a canoe. What a difference from sitting cooped up in a vehicle! Even with your head and shoulders popped out of a roof-hatch, it always feels as if you are isolated and distanced from the sights and sounds of Africa. Hunkered down in a light-weight fibre-glass canoe, a paddle in your hands, the combination of exercise and game-watching is irresistible – relaxing yet enervating. Sometimes you glide over water as smooth as ice, but when the wind gets up you find yourself paddling hard into choppy waves. John made it all look easy, moving the canoe along with the minimum of effort. 'Don't fight the water,' he advised. 'Use your legs to balance, press down with your feet, I'll act as rudder from the back here to steer us through.' I was reminded of the sight of North American Indians racing in long war canoes, perfect harmony between oarsmen and water, the canoes almost singing as they swept forward, the oarsmen's blades flashing, strong arms

*This page: A female saddle-billed stork* (Ephippiorhynchus senegalensis) *preening. Very large, silent bird with enormous, slightly upturned bill, females are distinguished from males by having yellow eyes rather than brown; the male is larger and has a yellow wattle on either side of the base of the bill. Saddle-billed storks frequent large inland waters: swamps, rivers, dams, pans and flood-plains, where they feed on frogs, fish and insects.*

*Opposite top: Little egret* (Egretta garzetta) *fishing. Egrets belong to the same family, Ardeidae, as the herons but differ from them in having entirely white plumage.*

*Opposite bottom left: Black-shouldered kite* (Elanus caeruleus) *perched on a bush, watching for prey. They feed primarily on insects, small reptiles and rodents, and are often seen hovering over grasslands.*

*Opposite bottom right: Egyptian goose* (Alopochen aegyptiacus) *with twelve young goslings. Egyptian geese are large, noisy birds, often seen in pairs along rivers or at the edge of marshes. Predators such as large snakes, mongooses and birds of prey take a heavy toll of the young, which is why they produce such large broods.*

rotating the paddles from one side to the other without pause. It was perfection to watch.

John had no compunction about drinking from the clear waters of the river, something that you would never do further upstream where it is more polluted. He would pass me his cup balanced on the end of his paddle. It was hot out on the river and the water tasted sweet and clean.

The birdlife was prolific among the narrow channels which snaked through the dense reed-beds mid-stream. There were open-billed storks and great white egrets, pied and malachite kingfishers, saddle-billed storks and fish eagles. New to me was the beautiful white-crowned plover, with its white breast and distinctive yellow wattles – not to be confused with the larger wattled plover, which I was used to seeing in Kenya and which has a dark breast.

Paddling a canoe along Africa's rivers is certainly one of the most tranquil and relaxing experiences I have known. But the dark side for most people is embodied in the fear of ending up in the water – victim of an attack by hippo or being swept up in the vice-like jaws of a crocodile. The chances of a nightmarish encounter with either of these giant creatures seemed remote, but I had had enough close calls with hippo on land not to want to engage their wrath in the water, particularly after reading an article in a local wildlife magazine describing an attack by an enraged hippo on a tourist taking a canoe safari in Zambia. The man's leg had been amputated in hospital after a gruelling journey taking many hours. They had travelled without a first-aid kit and had no rifle or radio. Although many a tale is told around campfires of those unfortunate enough to have fallen victim to such an attack, animals generally do everything possible to give humans a wide berth. In most cases hippo just want to be left in peace and any excitement is usually the result of a miscalculation on the human's part.

In Zimbabwe the sun is up an hour earlier than in East Africa, emerging from the haze as a giant orange orb at 5.40 each morning. I awakened to a dawn chorus of Cape turtle doves and red-eyed doves cooing, mingling with the strident calls of white-crowned plovers and the plaintive whistles of water dikkops drifting up from the river's edge. Eager to be out searching for something to photograph before breakfast, I joined John and Alistair for an early-morning game drive. Troy, the young Zimbabwean camp manager, acted as our driver-guide. Here on land the wildlife eked out an existence within walking distance of the waterholes. Baboon and impala came to drink daily, as did the greater kudu, which were somewhat shyer and lingered around the fringes. Not far from camp we found a pair of young male lion sprawled in the open, their yellow manes short and wispy, not yet fully grown.

To our great excitement a group of five female wild dogs had taken up residence at Ruckomechi during our stay, regularly cavorting through the shallows of the waterhole behind camp, drinking and wallowing in the mud to keep themselves cool. The young females must recently have emigrated from the pack in which they were born, forced to search for new males if they were to mate.

Waking early one morning I spied the five wild dogs from the window of my room. The troop of chacma baboons which nightly roosted among the clump of trees at the edge of camp watched as they wandered past. The dogs hardly even bothered to glance at the baboons as they left the safety of the *Acacia albida* trees and sauntered into the open. I grabbed my camera and crept on my hands and knees towards where the dogs were lying. They didn't move, seemingly unconcerned as I approached. Then one of them got up and walked towards a herd of cow elephants and calves, causing a half-grown bull to turn and mock-charge her, full of bluster. The cow elephants suddenly caught my scent; one of them turned towards me and charged. I quickly moved behind a tree and she stopped, head high, ears outspread, before continuing on her way with the rest of her family.

I crawled forwards, barely 9 metres (30 ft) from the dogs. Still they lay where they were. John and Alistair joined me. Usually busy making sure that their clients were in the best position to take pictures, they only rarely had the opportunity to take photographs for themselves. I 'hoo' called, imitating the plaintive contact call uttered by a wild dog when it has become separated from the rest of its pack. The dogs looked up, bat-ears cocked with interest. I had to keep reminding myself that we had already filmed wild dogs at Mombo, and that our priority now was the river.

One of the key sequences we had hoped to record while filming with John was drifting in our canoe towards a herd of elephants as they crossed the river. This is a regular event along the Zambezi – the problem, of course, is finding the place where they are going to choose to do it.

As so often happens, we saw what we wanted on our very first day out in the canoe. A group of five bull elephants had waded into the deepest section of the river and were cavorting about, rearing up on to each other's backs, throwing water and generally behaving as calves would in similar circumstances. We were able to approach very close, but unfortunately, as the boat carrying cameraman Mike Fox chugged over to film us, the elephants turned and swam back to shore. One of them wheeled round to face us as he hauled himself out of the water, towering over us from the top of the bank. The light, the elephants, the position of our canoe – everything had been perfect, except that the other boat had not been able to respond quickly enough for Mike to film us and the elephants in the way that he would have liked. We tried again on the next two days, but without luck.

In the meantime we set to work filming one of the carmine bee-eater breeding colonies. Carmines are glorious birds, with crimson plumage, dark blue crown and turquoise rump. They nest along the same stretches of river year after year and the noise of a large colony is almost deafening. Monitor lizards are attracted to the nest sites in the hope of finding eggs or hatchlings on which to prey. Monitors can grow up to 2 metres (6½ ft) long and are related to the Komodo dragons of Indonesia, the world's largest lizards. Formidable predators with conical crushing teeth, monitors are particularly partial to crocodile eggs and can destroy the contents of a nest unless the female is vigilant and guards her brood. When a monitor lizard came to investigate one of the carmine bee-eater colonies that we had been watching, the birds immediately mobbed the predator, swooping down on it en masse to drive it away, pecking at it with their sharply pointed bills and screeching in alarm – an effective form of group defence which caused the lizard to continue on its way.

With so few days in which to complete our film, John suggested that we try for the elephant sequence further downstream in the Mana Pools area. He had seen groups of bulls crossing over to the Zambian side of the river most afternoons when conducting canoe safaris with clients, and he felt sure that we would find what we wanted. But because of the drought the water level in the Zambezi was only a metre or so (3-4 ft) deep in places, making it difficult for the motor boat transporting the camera crew to navigate. To cut travel time between locations to a minimum, we set off early the next morning in one of the power boats, with a second boat going ahead towing the canoes. Just as John had promised, when we arrived there were already elephants feeding along the fringe of one of the islands of vegetation close to shore on the Zimbabwe side as we arrived.

Once the camera crew were ready John and I paddled quietly towards the six bulls, our oars dipping gently into the shallow water until we glided alongside the elephant's pillar-like legs. I could see every wrinkle of their thick hide. One of the younger bulls was busily yanking up great trunkfuls of water hyacinth – a beautiful purple-flowered plant with succulent leaves – pulling it across the tip of his left tusk and snapping off the muddy roots before swallowing the rest of the plant. By this process the bull had gradually worn a notch in his tusk. Eventually the tip would break off from his 'lead' tusk, as it is known, but as tusks continue to grow throughout an elephant's life it did not matter.

As we drifted with the current an old cow buffalo, her hips withered with age and shrunken by drought, glared across at us. It is unusual to see a cow on her own unless she is accompanied by a newborn calf and is leading it from cover back to the herd. At first I thought she must be a bull – her horns were enormous and swept low and then sharply up at the ends. A small group of cattle egrets with golden buff crests scuttled around her feet, feeding on insects churned up by her movements. The cow eyed us suspiciously, lumbering aggressively towards the canoe. But as soon as we moved away a little she walked into the shallows and lay down to cool off. Old and decrepit as she was, here she was safe from attack by lions, though crocodiles were always a threat.

There was one bull elephant that stood out. He was huge, with heavy, symmetrical tusks, towering over the other males and dwarfing us as we edged forwards. John held up his finger to test the wind, making certain that it was blowing our way so the bulls would not catch our scent. He coughed and tapped the side of the canoe with his

*Opposite: Crocodiles kill more people than any other large animal in Africa. They can grow up to 5.5 metres (18 ft) in length and weigh over a tonne. They are known to live for at least seventy to eighty years, and may live for as much as a hundred.*

paddle to ensure that we did not startle them. The elephants knew we were there, but showed no sign of alarm. Then the big bull suddenly moved forwards. Totally unconcerned by our presence, he strolled no more than 3 metres (10 ft) from the front of the canoe. I took two or three photographs as he passed, the moist tip of his thick, wrinkled trunk curling towards me to investigate my scent, massive feet churning the water frothy and white. He strode majestically onwards through the shallows to continue feeding on the next island.

With experience you learn to judge how close you can get to a wild animal, and that in turn depends not only on the animal but on whether you are in a car, in a boat or on foot. You learn to know how far you can push the limits, to evaluate the risks, to read the signs. But there are times when the animal decides to cross that line. Then all you can do is try to stay cool; don't panic; too late now to back off for fear of making things worse, startling the animal and destroying the trust. For a photographer there is always a tendency to throw caution to the wind in an effort to get the ultimate shot – even when it could cost you your life. The underwater photographer David Doubilet perhaps summed it up best when he said, 'I had no fear of the shark; I had a fear that I wouldn't capture the picture…. Sometimes you feel as though you would jump into their mouths if it would mean a better photograph.' On this occasion John and I could only shake our heads in disbelief. We were both mesmerized by the scene we had just witnessed.

Here, with the great wide river dotted with islands and speckled with animals, Zimbabwe is at its most magnificent. As we watched from the shore, a herd of buffalo, perhaps two hundred of them, spilled over the bank and charged across the water, forsaking the dry, grassless plains for the lush, island vegetation where food was plentiful. Troops of chacma baboons and parties of impala in their hundreds gathered to drink at a narrow lagoon along the shoreline, seeking safety in numbers – more eyes and ears to keep watch for the predators that might be lurking in the shadows.

John loved being on foot even more than being in a canoe. Tracking is his forte – reading the signs and sounds, bringing the place alive with his knowledge or stalking to within a few metres of a black rhino. He could follow the track of any animal, even when I couldn't tell there was a track at all. A slight bend in a piece of grass, a pebble shifted barely a millimetre out of position might tell him of the animal's passing. He could distinguish whether a track was more than a day old or only a few minutes in the making. Through John's eyes the ground at my feet came alive. He pointed, painting mental images: here an elephant had paused, swishing its trunk in half-circles to pick up some dry earth for a dust bath; over there it had dozed, spittle dripping from the tip of its trunk and leaving damp spots on the ground. The spoor was that of a female accompanied by a young calf.  Even without the presence of a calf John could have told that it was a cow because the footprint was less creased and crinkled than a bull's. We examined a dry pan – the earth split into massive pillars of mud, gaping cracks that would snap an antelope's leg in two if it stumbled, causing such creatures to avoid these places. Only elephant, hippo and buffalo, their massive imprints sunk deep in the mud, dared walk across the shrinking pool in its final days.

We moved quickly now to intercept a herd of buffalo that had been resting, chewing the cud. They were plodding towards a place along the bank where they could reach the river and drink. John led me to a massive termite mound around which we played hide and seek with the herd, the excitement mounting as we smelt the heavy bovine odour drifting on the wind towards us. As we peered around the mound a baboon barked in alarm and the herd stopped, tattered droopy ears twitching with anticipation. One of the cows at the front of the herd raised her wet, bulbous nose into the air. Neither of us moved. Then they lumbered forward again and were gone.

Later that day we made our way back to the river and climbed into our canoe. The river was deceptive; as calm and flat as a sheet of ice one moment, as rippled and fractious as the ocean the next. The weather could be just as fickle, changing within a few minutes from a clear blue sky to hazy and overcast. As we paddled back upstream black storm clouds brooded ahead of us, pressing down over the Zambian Escarpment, which rose steeply above the river to the north. The wind picked up, damp and heavy, and in its wake a dust storm blew in from the east – tearing across the dry land and devouring the fragile topsoil. Dust and sand from the islands whipped into our faces as we paddled for the shore, the strident screaming of a pair of African skimmers ringing in our ears. The gull-sized birds swooped low over our heads, intent on protecting their two freckled eggs, streaked and speckled with brown and laid in a saucer-sized depression in the sand among a tuft of grass and hippo dung.

It had been impossible to shelter from the heat in the middle of the day and all of us felt weary. The sun set like molten gold, its reflection spilling across our wake as we hurried for camp. The darkness was gathering fast and we knew that the camp staff would be worrying that we had got mired on a sandbank or had mechanical problems with the boat.

I gazed across the wide expanse of the Zambezi below Ruckomechi tented camp and marvelled at the timelessness of Africa. Livingstone's immortal words about Victoria Falls came easily to mind: 'Scenes so lovely must have been gazed upon by angels in their flight.' Today those same scenes echo a time long before the ivory hunters and slave traders ventured into the interior. Everywhere I looked there were animals – pristine wilderness. How different things might have been if Victoria Falls hadn't thwarted Livingstone's ambitions for the great Zambezi.

As we stepped ashore a lion grunted in the distance, answered by another far away. Then everything was still.

# SERENGETI: LAND OF ENDLESS SPACE

*If the great beasts are gone, man will surely die of a great loneliness of spirit.*
**Chief Seattle of the Nez Perce, 1884**

Occasionally one finds a place in the wild of such beauty and intimacy, harbouring such a variety and abundance of animal species, that one longs to stay. The Masai Mara in Kenya is one such place. I still remember the sight of two male lions, heads turned into the wind, their manes billowing, as I drove along the edge of the riverine forest flanking the Mara River. I was as 'green' as they come, but had been entrusted to the safe hands of Joseph Rotich, a Kipsegis guide who knew the Mara intimately. Joseph had spotted the lions from nearly 2 km (more than a mile) away. He hadn't even bothered to reach for the battered pair of binoculars perched along the dashboard of the ancient Landcruiser. He just knew it was lions.

Joseph told me that the two males were part of the Marsh Pride, a group that I was to follow intermittently for the next eighteen years. He chuckled to himself, smiling at my excitement as we sat without speaking in the regal presence of Scar and Old Man. Joseph had seen it all before – this instant love affair with Africa's wild places, this wanting to stay. He probably knew then, as I did, that nothing would deter me from fulfilling my ambition to make a life for myself among Africa's great predators.

In the epilogue of my last book, *Kingdom of Lions*, I wrote, 'If I had only one day in Africa I would spend it here, in the Masai Mara.' I was expressing an honest opinion about a place I still feel can provide people with the safari experience for which I was searching when I left England for Africa twenty years ago. That sentence wasn't written with the benefit of hindsight, either, nor because of the knowledge I now have of places such as Musiara Marsh, where the Marsh Lions could so often be found – once I knew where to look for them. Nor was it said because with Joseph's patient forbearance I had entered the secret world of Leopard Gorge and Fig Tree Ridge, realizing my dream of producing a book about a leopard called Chui and her two young cubs.

Rather it was a reflection of the fact that anyone who chooses can hire a car in Nairobi and set off for the Mara – a rugged five-hour drive away over pot-holed tarmac and dust-deep murram, passing wheat fields ploughed deep into pristine game country for kilometre after kilometre. The effort soon pales into insignificance in the

*The Gol Mountains lie to the east of Serengeti National Park and are the roosting site and breeding grounds of thousands of pairs of Ruppell's griffon vultures, which each day launch themselves on thermals, travelling up to 150 km (100 miles) in search of the wildebeest migration.*

face of such splendour. Suddenly you are there, winding your way past some of the most beautiful country I have ever seen. The blue of the granite hills, the lusty green of ancient woodlands hugging the narrow track before opening out into a broad vista of land and sky near a place called Aitong. The massive hill guards the eastern edge of the Masai's northern rangelands, where I used to watch the Aitong Pack – at the height of their fortunes some forty wild dogs, streaming across the rolling green country that is so typical of the Mara, the dust and the mayhem turning golden with the dawn, the blue of the Siria Escarpment looming 180 metres (590 ft) above the plains to the west.

With the escarpment as your guide and a four-wheel-drive vehicle there is nowhere you cannot explore. At times the animals are so thickly dotted across the land that Grant's and Thomson's gazelle seem like shoals of fish as they race away, their pure white bellies flickering in the light. Herds of toffee-brown impala cluster at the edges of the plains under the watchful eye of a territorial male, snorting and using his magnificent lyre-shaped horns to ward off rivals. The females move on, grazing and browsing, mingling with the acacia thickets, harvesting the kidney-shaped seed pods. Topi, larger and darker than the impala, are numerous here in the Mara – one of only two areas in Kenya where this handsome relative of the hartebeest is to be found. They are more numerous than their cousins, the *kongoni* or Coke's hartebeest, which lack the plum-coloured thighs, and are somewhat heavier, with bracket-shaped horns. Both species have the habit of standing atop the termite mounds that dot the plains, living statues advertising their presence to others of their kind while keeping watch for predators. And it is predators, above all, that people come to the Mara to see.

If you dreamed of lions, then this is the place to see them, and cheetahs and leopards too, as well as the many spotted hyaenas and jackals. It was hardly surprising, then, that when producer Keith Scholey and I first discussed the making of *Dawn to Dusk*, he felt that one of the programmes should feature the Masai Mara. After all, it had been my second home all these years, and had provided countless BBC film crews with spectacular wildlife footage. Keith was somewhat taken aback when I said I would rather not focus on the Mara in this series. Not that I doubted that we could make an exciting programme there; it was simply that so much had been done already. I wanted to do something different. And anyway, who would act as my guide in the Mara? The obvious choice would have been my old friend Joseph Rotich, who never failed to conjure up something new and exciting to enthral me. But sadly Joseph had died in 1989 at the age of seventy-five.

If it wasn't to be the Mara then I could think of nowhere better to film than Tanzania's Serengeti National Park, which is part of the same ecosystem. When Keith suggested wildlife film-maker Alan Root as my co-host for the programme my heart quickened in anticipation. Joseph Rotich had worked as head driver for Alan's safari company Root and Leakey, which Alan and Richard Leakey had formed in the 1960s and sold in the 1970s. Alan knew the Serengeti as well as Joseph knew the Mara. He

*The Serengeti–Mara lion population has recently been badly affected by an outbreak of canine distemper which almost certainly originated among the domestic dog population in the surrounding areas. Hundreds of lions have died as a result, though the population is now recovering.*

had explored every inch of the country during the last forty years, and provided a link to Bernhard and Michael Grzimek, the German father-and-son team who had been responsible for bringing the Serengeti and its great herds of wildebeest and zebra to a wider audience through their wildlife books and films.

If I was asked to name the books that had done most to reinforce my passion for natural history, then the Grzimeks' book *Serengeti Shall Not Die* would be high on the list, as would *The Last Place On Earth*, by the American author Harold Hayes. Both books are about the Serengeti, that land of endless space named by the Masai, nomadic cattle people of the high steppe who put fear into the hearts of the other East African tribes as they migrated south along the Nile during the fifteenth century.

The Grzimeks had gone to Tanganyika, as it then was, in the 1950s to try and save the Serengeti National Park from changes proposed by the British colonial administration in their attempts to appease the Masai, who had lived in the area for the last hundred years and made regular incursions into the park to graze their livestock and to cut firewood. They also used it as a thoroughfare for cattle rustling. They had never accepted the idea of being excluded from the park in the first place – land was not something you *owned* in the way that you owned cattle. Land was a gift from God to the people. Now the Masai were demanding that large areas of the park be returned to them so that they could find sufficient grass and water for their scrawny cattle.

Aghast at the proposed boundary changes and fearful of the consequences for the annual migration of plains game, the Grzimeks determined to try and count the Serengeti's animals before any changes could be made. They hoped to provide the authorities with an inventory of the park's animal numbers, and plot the path taken by the huge herds of migratory wildebeest and zebra which roamed well beyond its boundaries. If they failed, the Ngorongoro Crater Highlands and eastern plains would be given back to the Masai, reducing the size of the park by a third. There was no time to waste.

First the Grzimeks learned to fly. They then purchased a Dornier DO-27 high-winged aeroplane, a larger version of the Fieseler Storch communications and artillery-spotting planes used by the German army during the Second World War. The aeroplane was painted with zebra stripes to make it more visible from the air in case they had an accident. The Grzimeks flew across Africa to the Serengeti in 1958, and there began the work that was to ensure them a place in history.

But tragedy was to mar their efforts. I was eleven years old when Michael Grzimek crashed to his death after colliding with a Ruppell's griffon vulture above the Salei Plains to the west of the Ngorongoro Crater. The impact of the vulture-strike bent the right wing of the plane, blocking the rudder cables and causing the machine to dive in a steep right-hand curve. There were no other passengers.

Michael was buried the following day on the rim of the Ngorongoro Crater. That same year, 1959, Bernhard Grzimek published the book that was to make himself and his dead son – and the Serengeti – famous the world over. In death, Michael created a moving epitaph for the Grzimeks' efforts to save the Serengeti and its animals for posterity. A stone monument stands at the edge of the Ngorongoro Crater, marking an opening in the surrounding forest. The site provides a perfect view of the crater floor which to this day still teems with animals, just as the Grzimeks had hoped. A bronze plaque bears the words:

*Michael Grzimek*
*12.4.1934 to 10.1.1959*
*He gave all he possessed for the wild animals of Africa, including his life.*

Soon after Michael Grzimek's death, and before the results of his work could be made public, the colonial government announced their final decision on the Serengeti. The eastern portion of the plains and the Ngorongoro Crater Highlands were to be excised from the park and made into the Ngorongoro Conservation Area. Though the intention was to safeguard both the interests of the Masai pastoralists and the wild animals in the Conservation Area, the Governor, Sir Richard Turnbull added, 'Should there be any conflict between the interests of the game and the human inhabitants, those of the latter must take precedence.' But all was not lost. Extensive new tracts of land were added to the park in the north and south-west. As the size of the Serengeti's migratory herds expanded – particularly once rinderpest or cattle plague was eradicated in the 1960s – the northern extension connecting the Serengeti to the Masai Mara proved vital to their well-being during the dry season.

Bernhard Grzimek dedicated the rest of his life to saving Africa's animals, and when he died in 1987 at the age of seventy-seven he was granted his wish to be buried next to his son, overlooking the Ngorongoro Crater. But all those years ago the Grzimeks' story and that of the Serengeti seemed to me as good a reason as any to fast-forward my school years and enter the real world promising Adventure with a capital A, an outdoor life, working in one of the last truly wild places – Africa. Though it took me a little longer than I might have wished, in 1987 I wrote *The Great Migration*, celebrating the continued existence of the Serengeti and its animals.

Michael Grzimek had already made an award-winning film called *No Room for Wild Animals* in 1957, but he was relatively inexperienced as a cameraman. When he and his father arrived in the Serengeti, they asked the Senior Warden, Myles Turner, if he knew of anyone who could operate a movie camera. At the time Alan and Joan Root, who lived in Kenya, were beginning to establish themselves as wildlife photographers. Alan was working for Armand and Michaela Denis, the Belgian couple whose television series *On Safari* I had watched with such avid interest in England. Alan was much the same age as Michael, and in many ways they were like brothers – both shared a love of the wild, of creatures great and small, of life. They were both fearless and determined pilots – the Red Baron and the Battle of Britain flying ace – and one can only imagine that after Michael's death Alan's presence must have helped to ease the pain for Bernhard Grzimek. They remained friends over the years, and spoke highly of one another. The film of *Serengeti Shall Not Die* – much of which Alan filmed – went on to win the Grzimeks an Oscar for the Best Documentary Film.

East Africa has tended to make celebrities out of its wildlife watchers – or perhaps it is the animals that have made them famous. Our fascination with the natural world is mirrored in our preoccupation with the people doing the watching. The work sounds glamorous and exciting, spiced with danger. And the more powerful and enigmatic the creature, the greater the public's interest. Lions (George Adamson and George Schaller), elephants (Iain Douglas-Hamilton and Cynthia Moss), gorillas (Dian Fossey) and chimpanzees (Jane Goodall) have all bestowed fame, if not fortune, on the people that have studied and helped to protect them. So too have the animals of Africa brought out the best in Alan Root.

When I first arrived in Kenya, Alan had just completed his epic wildlife film *The Year of the Wildebeest*. It is a breathtaking piece of work which has survived the test of time: I still watch it with total involvement. The grunting, bellowing herds of wildebeest are the architects of the Serengeti Plains, swarming across the vast green oceans for as long as the rain keeps falling. When the rains stop, the 'migration' vanishes again into the woodlands, moving north during the dry season as far as the Masai Mara, where the wildebeest and zebra roam around until the short rains of October release them once more to the south. Onwards they march, always it seems at the double, over hillsides and across rivers – nothing can stop the herds from following their sensitive noses. Their instincts guide them unerringly back to the Serengeti's short-grass plains in time for the cow wildebeest to drop their calves – all 400,000 of them in the space of a few weeks. The annual cycle continues as it has for the last two million years, secrets of its past exposed among the fossil beds of Olduvai Gorge. This is the last of

*Opposite: Alan Root is considered by many people to be the greatest wildlife film-maker of his generation.* The Year of the Wildebeest *and* Castles of Clay *remain classics. Alan has always been fascinated by reptiles such as this monitor lizard and lost one of his fingers as the result of a bite from a puff adder.*

the great land migrations – one and a half million wildebeest, hundreds of thousands of gazelle, a quarter of a
million zebra – an army of animals on the move. The
thunder of hooves, the echo of the herds – no
sight in Africa can compare with this.

Alan is everywhere in the film – but never
seen. Running to position a camera concealed in the shell of a tortoise, creating a
stunning low-level view of the wildebeest's mad passage across the plains and
through the thorn thickets. He is there
again, this time up to his neck in the
water as the wildebeest and their calves
cross Lake Lagarja, documenting the
scenes where 1,500 calves become separated
from their mothers in the confusion and
drown, leaving another 1,500 orphans milling
about in the bush. Up, up and away he floats
quietly over the herds in his hot-air balloon as the wildebeest leave the plains, or sweeps past them in his aeroplane.
No one has done it better.

There is one sequence in *The Year of the Wildebeest* that I
always remember. Two male cheetahs enter frame, stalking side by side, their faces
impassive, riveting in the intensity of their gaze. The cheetahs are hunting wildebeest,
selecting a young calf from the herd. They creep forward, stride for stride, shoulders
almost touching, mirror images in perfect unison of thought and movement. It is
mesmerizing stuff – compulsive television watching. My son David was so taken with
the scene that he asked me if it had been done by a computer creating two identical
images. But it is more than just the pictures. The narration accompanying Alan's films
also bears his mark. He writes with clarity and humour, simplifying everything until
words and pictures form a completely comprehensible whole.

My first meeting with Alan Root confirmed all that I had heard about him. It was
1977, and I had recently come to live at Root and Leakey's Mara River Camp in the
Masai Mara. I had barely found out what four-wheel drive meant, let alone how to
apply it. I can remember feeling that I must be one of the luckiest people alive as I
drove across the rolling plains and acacia country to the north of the reserve one beautiful clear morning. Suddenly I was jolted from my reverie by a horrifying roar from
somewhere beneath the bonnet of the Land-Rover. My first thought was that the engine must have blown up; perhaps I had forgotten to check the oil. How on earth was
I going to break the news to the managing director, Jock Anderson? The previous
week I had been forced to explain how the passenger door had been caved in by a

cranky old bull buffalo that had stood up out of a mud wallow and charged the car. As my mind spun in circles, the wheels of 'Oscar Charlie', Alan Root's Cessna aeroplane, came into view a few metres above the bonnet of the car.

I hurried over to the grass airstrip and was greeted by Alan, who was grinning hugely to himself. There is an infectiously boyish enthusiasm about Alan. As we shook hands I noticed that the index finger of his right hand was missing – the legacy of a bite from a puff adder that had almost cost him his arm; just one of many scars that bear testimony to a life lived close to the edge.

Alan may not look the part of the intrepid explorer – in fact he looks more like an academic, with his beard and spectacles. But I can think of few people I would rather be with in a tight spot; his courage and ingenuity have kept him alive. He is so utterly self-assured in his manner, and in what he has to say, that it creates a physical presence of considerable dimension. Alan doesn't take chances so much as defy the odds. He is undoubtedly one of a kind.

School must have been miserable for Alan, his thoughts consumed with discovering the nest site of some new bird species or tracking down yet another cobra without getting bitten. He left school at sixteen and by eighteen was making a precarious living as a wildlife cameraman. In 1962 he made a film for *Survival*, Anglia Television's newly launched wildlife series. The film focused on the Ngorongoro Crater and the long-standing controversy over the impact of the Masai and their livestock on the wildlife. The producers back in London were delighted with Alan's footage and offered him a string of assignments. The turning point for Alan and Joan was in 1967, when their film on the Galapagos, *The Enchanted Isles*, was given a Royal Première and won a number of awards. It became the first natural-history show ever to appear on American network television. Now the Roots found themselves in the enviable position of being able to make the films that they wanted to make, and they would be involved at every step, producing, writing and overseeing the editing themselves. To this day there are few cameramen who have attempted to do this and fewer still who have been successful. But Alan never looked back.

Alan's love of wild places and of the creatures that inhabit them is a reflection of his own fascination and zest for life. He wants to know why things happen when they do, how they happen, what makes things tick. Though Alan is not a scientist by training, he knows as much – if not more – about natural history than the best of them, absorbing the essence of the scientists' work and then simplifying it into language that can be understood by his audience. As a field man he has few peers. Any questions he cannot answer prompt a terrier-like search for solutions. He not only sees the more obvious details of an animal's behaviour, he also has a talent for digging up obscure and little-known facts or animal characters to illustrate the complex web of life that is always such a feature of his films, exploring the interrelatedness of everything.

For years Alan and Joan's base in the Serengeti was a decrepit shack at the Serengeti Wildlife Research Centre. Entering any of the houses in this run-down and dilapidated

*Overleaf: Each year during the dry season the wildebeest journey from the Serengeti to their dry-season pastures in the north and west. If they are to reach the lush grasslands of the Lamai Wedge and Mara Triangle they must first cross the Mara River, which bars the way north. Wildebeest are strong swimmers, and though thousands may drown or be trampled underfoot when the river is swollen, the majority cross safely.*

centre was like going into a university squat – clothes flung carelessly on the floor, cups and plates unwashed, covered with grime. There was a sense of impermanence, of passing through. But Alan's house always gave the impression that someone actually lived there. Old weaver-bird nests and a trellis of creepers formed a natural tapestry on the walls. Books lined the bookcases; bronze sculptures of cheetahs and baboons by Alan's good friend Jonathan Kenworthy found the perfect setting here. It was evident that the Roots really loved being part of the Serengeti – not just using it.

Nothing bores Alan more than yet another workman-like film on lions or elephants. If it isn't new or better, then it isn't worth doing. Alan has made a habit of achieving 'firsts'. He was the first fully to document the migration of the wildebeest, visiting the Serengeti over the course of fourteen years before he felt he knew enough to complete the film. He and Joan were the first people to fly over Mount Kilimanjaro, the highest point in Africa – 5,896 metres (19,340 ft) up in the sky – in a balloon; and the first to establish a commercial ballooning operation carrying tourists on early-morning balloon safaris across the Masai Mara. Their film on the extraordinary nesting habits of the yellow-billed hornbill revealed many hitherto unknown facts about hornbill breeding biology and chick development, employing time-lapse photography – another of Alan's hallmarks – to speed things up.

Mazima Springs in Tsavo provided audiences with the first clear view of the underwater world of the hippo, an adventure that ended when a two and a half tonne bull hippo bit through Joan's face mask and shattered the glass, leaving her stunned but miraculously unhurt. Alan was not so fortunate. The bull turned on him, biting right through his calf. He was lucky to survive and spent weeks in Nairobi Hospital, recovering from the effects of gas gangrene and waiting for the fist-sized wound to heal.

When I studied the footage of Alan and Joan swimming underwater with the hippos at Mazima Springs, all my instincts for personal survival screamed at me that they were mad. But as a photographer I shared the feeling of exhilaration that envelops you when you visualize a particular shot – suddenly there it is, right in front of you, and you just have to get it. To stay at the top you have to be adventurous, to take risks – and, yes, you have to be a little bit crazy.

But perhaps the Roots' most difficult project, and the one that many people think of as their best, involved the least glamorous of characters, proving Alan's long-held belief that your subject doesn't have to be big to be interesting. Scattered across Africa's grassy savannas and acacia-bush country are countless termite mounds, the 'castles of clay' which provided the title for Alan's superb film on the life of a termite colony. Termites are the earthworms of Africa. Within a colony there are millions of soldiers and workers, all the offspring of a single king and queen who can lay up to 35,000 eggs in a day to replenish her nation. Through a complex division of labour among its citizens, a termite colony assumes the complexity of a higher organism.

Filming them was to test all of Alan's considerable ingenuity, as well as his patience and tenacity. The mounds had to be illuminated with the most modern surgical lamps

– anything else would simply melt the termites into a blob of fat. With the help of a Kenyan scientist who had been studying termite colonies, Alan was able to document every aspect of their lives, providing insights into termite biology and behaviour that were unknown to science. Alan has always maintained that he is not a camera buff, that his technical knowledge of photographic equipment is pretty basic. Though this may indeed be true, it has never hampered his work; he always knows enough to get the job done. Maybe he just means that he doesn't spend much time cleaning his cameras. *Castles of Clay* was acclaimed around the world and was nominated for an Oscar as Best Documentary in 1978.

Much about Alan is a contradiction, though in recent times he has mellowed and admits to finding a sense of peace and enjoyment away from filming. Many people felt that his films would suffer after his break-up with Joan. But his latest film – on the Zaire rain forest – seems set to rival *Castles of Clay* for sheer wizardry.

In 1994 Alan was honoured with a lifetime's achievement award by Wildscreen – the wildlife film-makers' 'Oscars'. Fittingly, the award was presented to Alan by Sir David Attenborough, who made no attempt to hide his whole-hearted admiration for Alan's skills and accomplishments. It was both strange and touching to see this tough, courageous man finally succumb visibly to the emotions engendered by the moment. Looking back over his years in the bush, Alan paid tribute to his long and successful partnership with Joan and to the happiness of a new life with his second wife, Jenny.

Others have followed in Alan's footsteps, portraying Africa's wild places with varying degrees of success; yet for me Alan still stands out for his masterful story-telling. Not only does he capture superb images of his animal subjects; he also manages to relate them to something bigger – he sees more, the whole. His photographic skills are such that you are barely aware of the techniques he has employed. Instead you become part of the story, so involved with the characters that you forget that it *is* a story – as you watch it becomes reality.

Sometimes Alan's lack of sentimentality is shocking in its honesty. Standing up and banging the drum in the name of conservation is not his style: he is an extrovert, yet somehow shy. In the end it doesn't matter that Alan chooses not to get involved publicly with conservation issues. His films speak for themselves, promoting wonder and concern for the wilderness in equal measure.

All of the other programmes in *Dawn to Dusk* had focused on a particular place and its wildlife. My role was to witness whatever we saw and to share it with a knowledgeable guide who had a particular connection with the area. But this programme was rather different – in my mind it was as much about Alan Root as it was about the Serengeti. Initially none of us was confident that Alan would even agree to be involved. For the last six years he had been battling with the logistics of making films in Zaire – the heart

of darkness – with a wealth of secrets waiting to be unlocked from within its steamy jungles: the Congo peacock, water genets, elephant shrews, chevrotains – just the right combination of impossible subject matter and daunting environment with which Alan likes to challenge himself. By comparison, *Dawn to Dusk* might seem pretty tame. Alan is known to have very strong views on what makes a good wildlife programme.

Until recently he had avoided including people in his films, seeing them as an unwarranted distraction from the thrust of his story. He had also studiously avoided becoming the subject of anyone else's film. It wasn't that he was averse to publicity – more that he was suspicious of being taken advantage of and determined not to be part of anything that didn't match his own high standards. As he put it, 'I don't want to act as a glorified taxi-driver to fly you around the Serengeti.'

Keith Scholey assured Alan that our reason for wanting to involve him was simply that he knew the Serengeti better than anyone else. Unfortunately we wouldn't be able to incorporate any of Alan's stunning wildlife footage. That would just complicate our efforts to give viewers a sense of *us* being in Serengeti *now*. Many of Alan's programmes take a year or more to complete, and may involve months of planning to get a single perfect shot. With less than two weeks in which to complete filming, it would be impossible to do justice to Alan at work.

We planned to film with Alan in March – a key month in the Serengeti. It is during February and March that the cow wildebeest give birth to nearly half a million calves out on the short-grass plains. As Alan proved long ago in *The Year of the Wildebeest*, you have to fly like a vulture over the herds really to appreciate the enormity of the spectacle, soaring over the short-grass plains and the ancient volcanoes of the

Ngorongoro Crater Highlands. Millions of years earlier the volcanoes had given birth to the plains, cloaking them with ash-rich soils which in turn created a rock-like hard pan of calcium carbonate beneath the surface, prohibiting the growth of trees, but allowing short grasses to flourish. The wildebeest prefer these mineral-rich grasses, which contain high levels of calcium, sodium and potassium – all vital ingredients for healthy growth. Here on the open plains there are fewer lions and leopards than in the woodlands, and during the rains the herds spread across the grassland until it is black-ened by their presence. The visibility is such that the herbivores can spot a predator from several kilometres away. But nature always strives to maintain a balance between the predators and their prey, and the Serengeti Plains are home to wild dogs and spot-ted hyaenas who do not rely on much stealth to gain a meal. They simply run and run, exhausting their prey until it slows sufficiently for the mob of predators to anchor it and pull it apart.

So we would fly over the short-grass plains, circle Oldoinyo Lengai, last of the active volcanoes, then drop down through the gorge leading to Lake Natron, breeding ground for hundreds of thousands of lesser flamingoes. Keith Scholey warned me that there were some surprises in store for me. With Alan on board that could mean any-thing. I would just have to wait and see. After Keith's gleeful announcement in Botswana that Abu should pick me up with his trunk and hoist me into the air, I was ready for anything, or so I thought.

The last time I had been to the Serengeti was during a month-long safari through Masailand with my wife Angela to collect material for a book on the Masai people of Kenya and Tanzania. Masailand is one of the last great strongholds of wildlife, but as the twenty-first century beckons, the future of the Masai and that of the wild animals is cloaked in uncertainty. Before entering the park Angie and I drove to the foot of Oldoinyo Lengai – the Masai's sacred mountain of God, which still at times spews ash from its cone, recreating the drama of the birth of the Serengeti Plains. Four wild dogs passed through camp the following morning, their huge bat ears twitching with curi-osity, noses sifting the wind for our scent. We watched them turn away and disappear into the distance – where had they come from, where were they headed for, I won-dered? That night we camped in the shadow of the Gol Mountains, where thousands of pairs of Ruppell's griffon vultures roost and nest on sheer cliff-faces. Each morning the birds rise with the thermals, lofting into the sky, soaring from one thermal to the next, searching for carcasses to feed on. The vultures can climb closer to the centre of a thermal, in far tighter turns, than even the best sailplane, travelling up to 320 km (200 miles) to keep within reach of the migration, wherever it might be.

During our stay in Serengeti I took time to talk to the scientists at the Serengeti Wildlife Research Centre. The original building had been located at Banagi, near the old game warden's house, and was named the Michael Grzimek Memorial Labora-tory. In 1966 a larger Research Institute was established 6 km (4 miles) from Seronera, the park headquarters. Here scientists from all over the world gathered to

*Overleaf: There are more than 400,000 Masai living in Kenya and Tanzania. Many Masai still cling to the old ways, but with land now a precious commodity they are being forced to adopt a more sedentary way of life. However, Masailand still harbours some of the world's most spectacular wildlife areas, none more so than the Serengeti.*

study the Serengeti and its wildlife. Research on lions and cheetahs stretches back thirty years, and many of the mysteries of the wildebeest migration have been explained by the painstaking collecting of data and the wonder of modern computers. But the old-time wardens such as Myles Turner were never convinced by the science, clinging to the idea that all the money poured into research would have been better applied to management and protecting the Serengeti from poaching. He had his reasons. Perhaps as many as 200,000 wildebeest and zebra are killed each year for their meat. The large herds of elephant and buffalo have been reduced by 75 per cent, the area's 700 black rhino slaughtered. Some would say that it was all a waste of time; that ultimately the animals are doomed. But the work of the Grzimeks immortalized a dream – that this last wild place would prosper and continue. And in many ways it has. The migration that so impressed itself on the Grzimeks currently numbers 1.6 million wildebeest – larger than at any time in living memory, and ten times the number in existence when the Grzimeks flew over the herds.

Questions, always questions for which to find answers. I wanted to know more about the wildebeest migration. Would their number continue to increase? And what about the gazelles – had their population crashed from competition with the wildebeest and zebra, as had been feared? In recent months the famous Serengeti lions had been stricken by canine distemper spread by the hundreds of domestic dogs that roam freely with the Masai herdsmen. The epidemic had reached the Mara, where veterinary surgeons had mounted a campaign to inoculate the Masai dogs in an attempt to stem the disease among the wild predators. The lion population would recover in time. It was the land itself that needed protecting if the animals were to survive.

The Serengeti has outlived the Grzimeks; yet their dream remains intact. The Tanzanian government has honoured its pledge to try and protect its wild lands against encroachment and is still committed to holding the poachers at bay, against all the odds and despite being one of the poorest nations on earth. Meanwhile, the Masai living in the Ngorongoro Conservation Area find themselves trapped in a rapidly changing world. Their diet is no longer primarily the blood, meat and milk of their livestock. Today they subsist – like the majority of Africans – on the products of cultivation, on maize meal. This they must buy from their neighbours, often at exorbitant prices. Officially they are still prohibited from cultivating in the Conservation Area, even though illegal cultivation is a fact of life in some places, and always has been. The authorities are struggling to find a solution that will keep both the people and the conservationists happy. I am reminded of the words spoken nearly forty years ago by the British Governor, Sir Richard Turnbull, who promised that the priority must be the needs of the people. Bernhard Grzimek always maintained that the animals could not vote. How right he was. But there is always hope: as Martin Luther said, 'Even if the end of the world is coming tomorrow, today I shall plant a young apple tree.'

It would have been easy to dismiss the Grzimeks as sentimentalists, 'bleeding hearts' among conservationists. But Bernard Grzimek was a realist, a practical man. Yes, he wanted to save the animals. But he understood, long before it became current doctrine, that the future lay in the hands of the Africans, particularly those who lived close to wildlife. He made personal contact with many of the leaders of the newly independent African states and impressed upon them the importance of wild animals, encouraging them to develop tourism as a means of giving an economic value to this effort. He never gave up the struggle. Nor should we.

*Men are easily inspired by human ideas, but they forget them just as quickly. Only Nature is eternal, unless we senselessly destroy it. In fifty years' time nobody will be interested in the results of the conferences which fill to-day's headlines.*

*But when fifty years from now a lion walks into the red dawn and roars resoundingly, it will mean something to people and quicken their hearts whether they are bolsheviks or democrats, or whether they speak English, German, Russian or Swahili. They will stand in quiet awe as, for the first time in their lives, they watch twenty thousand zebras wander across the endless plains.*

*Is it really so stupid to work for the zebras, lions and men who will walk the earth fifty years from now? And for those in a hundred or two hundred years' time?*

For those who have visited the Serengeti for themselves and the millions of people who have sat enthralled at the sight of all those animals portrayed through the sharply focused vision of an Alan Root wildlife special, the answer must surely be no.

# ACKNOWLEDGEMENTS

I consider it the greatest privilege to have been granted permission to live and work in the Masai Mara National Reserve, Kenya, for most of last twenty years. In this regard I would like to thank the Kenya Government and the Narok County Council who administer the reserve. Masai pastoralists roamed the Mara–Serengeti long before the area was opened up to tourism, peacefully co-existing with wild animals for centuries. While many other parts of Africa have seen their wildlife resources dwindle, Masailand still harbours the finest game-viewing areas in the world. Hopefully the transition from nomadic pastoralism to individual landownership will still enable the animals to survive.

I am particularly grateful to Keith Scholey, an old friend from the days when I lived at Mara River Camp and now the Executive Producer of the BBC's *Wildlife on One* series, and to Alistair Fothergill, Head of the BBC Natural History Unit, who conjured up the idea of *Dawn to Dusk* for me to present, and then helped ensure that it happened.

As a bit of a greenhorn when it comes to presenting to camera, I was incredibly lucky to be working with experienced and sympathetic producers. Talking into a camera lens as if it is your best friend takes a bit of getting used to, to say the least. But Keith Scholey, Robin Hellier, Sara Ford and Mike Gunton were all quite outstanding to work with. Robin Hellier was the Executive Producer of *Dawn to Dusk*, as he had been of the live transmissions *Africa Watch* and *Flamingo Watch*, both of which were broadcast from Kenya and which I helped to present. Robin is one of those rare individuals who combines the utmost professionalism with the ability to listen to other people's points of view. He is the ultimate team player and the most unassuming and delightful person to work for. I'm still trying to discover how he does it.

Diana Richards, the Production Manager for the series, was also brilliant. She always tried to ensure that everybody was happy and well looked after, while setting standards of efficiency that are hard to match. With Diana close at hand I hardly had to think for myself - except to remember what to say. And when I was desperate to retrieve some camera equipment from England at a moment's notice over a weekend Diana managed that too. Thank you!

Marguerite Smits van Oyen worked as a researcher on the series and provided me with excellent background reading for many of our safari destinations as well as helping to co-ordinate our trips in the field and back at base in Bristol. Sophie Neville also worked as a researcher and went on recces to Namibia and to Abu's Camp in Botswana, compiling a wealth of material in the form of voluminous scrapbooks illustrated with her photographs and handwritten notes. Thank you both for all the valuable reference material you provided to help me write about these destinations.

During the course of filming *Dawn to Dusk* and writing this book, I was able to visit Uganda, Tanzania, Zimbabwe, Botswana, Namibia and South Africa, all of which provided me with memorable safaris. Wherever I went I was greeted by friendly people, who made both filming and visiting their countries a pleasure – they couldn't have been more helpful. Some of these people are mentioned elsewhere in the book, but I must not forget Tim and June Liversedge who welcomed me back to the Okavango Delta in Botswana after an absence of twenty years. They are currently completing high-definition and 35 mm films on the wild dogs at Mombo. Tim's cameraman Dave Hamman had previously worked at Mombo Camp and was particularly helpful during our stay, providing us with detailed background information on the history of the Mombo Pack and its daily movements. Sandor Carter helped make our stay with the elephants at Abu's Camp particularly special, as did Michael Lorentz, Managing Director of Elephant Back Safaris. Pilots Carel Jansen van Vuuren and Greg Moss flew us on some unforgettable flights while we were in Namibia, enabling us to take aerial photographs. In Tanzania, Tony (Anton) Collins provided me with a fascinating introduction to the ecology of Gombe National Park. In the Queen Elizabeth National Park (QENP), Uganda, Daniela de Luca and her field assistant Onen introduced me to their study subjects – a troop of banded mongooses. At Mweya (QENP), Chief Park Warden Abdullahi Latif was most helpful, and Wilhelm and Ursula Moller welcomed us to their home and briefed me on the relocation of chimpanzees from the Entebbe Zoo to an island in QENP. And at Murchison Falls National Park, Shaun Mann and Max Linner, the Chief Park Warden, generously shared their knowledge of the area and made one of the park's boats available to us during our stay. Professor Derek Pomeroy was a fund of information during our visit to Makerere University in Kampala. Adrian Treves introduced us to the primates of the Kibale Forest, where he is studying vigilance behaviour in red colobus and red-tailed monkeys. And in South Africa I was finally able to catch up with Gus Mills, Chief Research Officer in the Kruger National Park, who has for years co-ordinated the wild dog project in the park, and spent a fascinating couple of hours with him and his wife. To these people, and the many others who extended their hospitality to us, thank you all.

In Kenya, Jock Anderson, the managing director of East African Wildlife Safaris, has been a great friend to me over the years and continues to allow me to use his office in Nairobi, where Stephen Masika helped to keep me supplied with mail, messages and vehicle spares. Jock still offers his clients the kind of private tented safari that really brings the African safari experience alive.

My wife Angela has become an integral and indispensable part of my work (and my life). She is an accomplished photographer and illustrator in her own right and worked on a number of the pen and ink drawings in this book. Somehow Angela manages to co-ordinate much of our work while running a home in Nairobi and looking after the needs of our children. Only with her gentle urging and help have I been able to complete this project – and the many others – within the necessary time scale.

Our neighbours in Nairobi, Frank and Dolcie Howitt, have been a tremendous support to us, helping to make up for the fact that our own families live so far away. Not only are they two of the kindest and most hospitable people we know (their house is always full of visitors), but they are always there when we need them most, even if it is just for a good cup of tea and a cake or a beer and a chat. We could not ask for more.

Both Angela and I have family living in England who have been an unfailing source of inspiration and encouragement to us. There is always a warm welcome awaiting us at Joy and Alan Seabrook's home in Hindhead, and at the home of Angela's brother David and his wife Mishi. My sister Caroline has been wonderfully hospitable to us at her home in Inkpen, and my only regret is that my brother Clive and his wife Judith are invariably out of the country when we visit. My mother, Margaret Scott, is now in her eighty-sixth year, and has throughout my life inspired me with her courage and humour. My sincerest thanks to you all.

Among our friends in England, Dr Michael and Sue Budden have been the most marvellous support ever since our first meeting at Kichwa Tembo in the Masai Mara in 1984. Nothing has ever been too much trouble and no request has gone unanswered, whether it entailed sending computers and printers for repair, shopping for camera or car spares or ferrying us to and from Terminal 4 at Heathrow. Michael and Sue are avid conservationists and keen photographers and share our love for Africa, particularly the Mara-Serengeti. Martin and Avril Freeth and Pippa and Ian Stewart-Hunter always have a bed and a warm welcome waiting for us whenever we visit London.

Caroline Taggart has co-ordinated and edited all my previous books with her special brand of friendly professionalism. Her editorial skills and enthusiasm have been indispensable, never more so than since she went freelance as an editor. Somehow Caroline manages to cut back on the words when necessary without making it obvious that she has done it. Her own love of Africa has contributed enormously to all my projects.

I feel very fortunate to have be published by Kyle Cathie, now of Kyle Cathie Ltd. We first worked together in 1984 when Kyle was at Hamish Hamilton and I was producing *The Leopard's Tale*. It just goes to prove what Kyle and her small

team of professionals can achieve, where attention to detail and a commitment to ensuring quality isn't sacrificed is always the priority. My thanks also to Commisioning Editor Sheila Ableman at BBC Books who helped to make it all work as a joint publication.

It has been a pleasure to join forces with a designer of the calibre of Geoff Hayes, who also designed my two latest *Safari Guides to East African Animals and Birds* and was prepared to listen to my views and blend them with his own creative skills.

Mike Shaw, my literary agent at Curtis Brown, and his personal assistant Sophie Janson have been tremendously supportive during this project. If you are thinking of writing a book, get an agent!

My grateful thanks also go to Kevin Gilks of Lonrho East Africa, Malcolm Bater of Toyota Kenya and Chris Elworthy of the camera division of Canon UK for the loan of equipment.

## DAWN TO DUSK: PRODUCTION TEAMS
This book has been written as a companion volume to a six-part television series bearing the same name. The BBC Natural History Unit in Bristol is recognized throughout the world for its innovative and informative portrayal of the natural world. Presenting the *Dawn to Dusk* series allowed me to work with some of the world's leading documentary crews and wildlife professionals, all of whom were generous in sharing their years of experience with me. Likewise my co-hosts were chosen for their intimate knowledge of the subject matter of each film, and all of them gave generously of their time in answering my many questions about their work. My thanks to you all.

**Botswana: Elephant Back Safari**
Producer: Keith Scholey
Production Manager: Diana Richards
Production Secretary: Catherine Mockridge
Documentary Cameraman: Mike Fox
Wildlife Cameraman: Gavin Thurston
Camera Assistant: Jenny Budd
Sound Recordist: Mike Lax
Presenter: Jonathan Scott
Co-Presenter: Randall Moore

**Botswana: Painted Wolves**
Producer: Robin Hellier
Production Manager: Diana Richards
Production Secretary: Catherine Mockridge
Documentary Cameraman: Mike Fox

Wildlife Cameraman: Hugh Maynard
Camera Assistant: Jenny Budd
Sound Recordist: Mike Lax
Lighting Assistant: Dale Hancock
Presenter: Jonathan Scott
Co-Presenter: Richard Goss
Guides: Alan Wolfromm, Ian Mitchener, Mike Penman

## Tanzania: Man's Closest Relative

Producer: Robin Hellier
Production Manager: Diana Richards
Production Secretary: Catherine Mockridge
Documentary Cameramen: Chris Openshaw
Wildlife Cameraman: Bill Wallauer
Camera Assistant: Andrew Thompson
Sound Recordist: Adrian Bell
Presenter: Jonathan Scott
Co-Presenter: Charlotte Uhlenbroek

## Namibia: Africa's Last Wilderness

Producer: Mike Gunton
Production Manager: Diana Richards
Production Secretary: Catherine Mockridge
Documentary Cameraman: Brian McDairmant
Wildlife Cameraman: Kim Wolhuter
Camera Assistant: Mike Carling
Sound Recordist: Graham Ross
Presenter: Jonathan Scott
Co-Presenters: Jean-Paul Roux, Juliane Zeidler, Blythe Loutit,
Rudi Loutit
Pilots: Carel Jansen van Vuuren, Greg Moss

## Zimbabwe: The Great Zambezi

Producer: Robin Hellier
Production Manager: Diana Richards (Base)
Researcher: Margeurite Smits van Oyen
Production Secretary: Catherine Mockridge
Documentary Cameraman: Mike Fox
Wildlife Cameraman: Kim Wolhuter
Camera Assistant: Jenny Budd
Sound Recordist: Mike Lax
Presenter: Jonathan Scott
Co-Presenter: John Stevens
Guide: Alastair Hull

## Tanzania: Serengeti: Land of Endless Space

Producer: Sara Ford
Production Manager: Diana Richards (Base)
Researcher: Marguerite Smits van Oyen
Production Secretary: Catherine Mockridge
Documentary Cameramen: Chris Openshaw
Wildlife Camerapersons: Mark Deeble, Victoria Stone
Camera Assistant: Andrew Thompson
Sound Recordist: Adrian Bell
Presenter: Jonathan Scott
Co-Presenter: Alan Root

# BIBLIOGRAPHY

Listed below are articles from scientific journals, popular magazines and books on which I have drawn as reference material or which I felt might be of interest as further reading. I hope that the various authors will forgive me for any inaccuracies or simplifications that I may have made in interpreting their work.

Bannister, A. & Johnson, P., 1979. *Namibia: Africa's Harsh Paradise*. Hamlyn Publishing Group Ltd: London

Barritt, D. 1994 (Oct). *Sealing their Fate*. Style. CTP Ltd: Johannesburg.

Bartlett, D., and Bartlett, J. 1992 (Jan). *Africa's Skeleton Coast*. National Geographic, Vol. 181, No. 1

Blixen, K. 1954. *Out of Africa*. Penguin Books: Harmondsworth.

Branch, B. 1988. *Field Guide to the Snakes and Other Reptiles of Southern Africa*. New Holland: London

Briggs, P. 1994. *Guide to Uganda*. Bradt Publications: Buckinghamshire.

Brooks, M. 1994. *Chairman's Report: African Rhino Specialist Group*. Pachyderm, No. 18

Chadwick, D.H. 1991 (May). *Elephants – Out of Time, Out of Space*. National Geographic. Vol. 179, No. 5

Chatwin, B. 1988. *The Songlines*. Picador: London.

Collins, A. 1988. *Gombe National Park*. Mombo. No. 4

Concar, D. and Cole, M. 1992 (Feb). *Conservation and the Ivory Tower*. New Scientist

Coulson, D. 1991. *Namib*. Sidgwick & Jackson Ltd: London

Delort, R. 1992. *The Life and Lore of the Elephant*. Thames and Hudson: London.

Estes, R.D. 1991. *The Behavior Guide to African Mammals*. University of California Press: California.

Gavron, J. 1994. *The Last Elephant: An African Quest*. HarperCollins: London.

Goodall, J. 1979 (May). *Life and Death at Gombe*. National Geographic. Vol. 155, No. 5.

.......... 1990. *Through A Window*. Weidenfeld & Nicolson: London.

Grzimek, B. and Grzimek, M. 1960. *Serengeti Shall Not Die*. Hamish Hamilton: London.

Hayes, H.T.P. 1977. *The Last Place On Earth*. Stein & Day: N.Y. 10510

..............1981. *Three Levels of Time*. E.P. Dutton: New York.

Heminway, J. 1983. *No Man's Land: The Last of White Africa*. Dutton: New York.

Hodgson, B. 1982 (June). *Namibia: Nearly a Nation?* National Geographic. Vol. 161, No. 6.

Jackman, B.J. and Scott, J.P. 1982. *The Marsh Lions*. Elm Tree Books: London.

Jacobson, D. *The Electronic Elephant: A Southern African Journey*. Hamish Hamilton: London

Leopold, A. 1987. *A Sand County Almanac: And Sketches Here and There*. Oxford University Press: Oxford.

Lessing, D. 1993. *African Laughter*. HarperCollins: London

Linden, E. 1992 (March). *A Curious Kinship: Apes and Humans*. National Geographic. Vol. 181, No. 3.

.......... 1992 (March). *Bonobos, Chimpanzees With a Difference*. National Geographic. Vol. 181, No. 3.

Lindeque, M. & Erb, P.K. 1995. *Research on the Effects of Temporary Horn Removal on Black Rhinos in Namibia*. Pachyderm, No. 20

Loutit, B. 1995. *Rhino Protection in Communal Areas, Namibia*. Pachyderm, No. 20

Matthiessen, P. 1991. *African Silences*. HarperCollins: London

Miller, C. 1972. *The Lunatic Express*. Macdonald & Co.: London

Miller, P. 1995. *Jane Goodall*. National Geographic, Vol. 188, No. 6.

Mills, G. 1995 (Oct/Nov). *Kruger's Wild Dogs*. AirTales. Vol. 2 No. 5.

Moore, R.J. and Munnion, C. 1989. *Back to Africa*. RMP cc: Sandton, South Africa.

Morell, V. 1995. *Ancestral Passions: The Leakey Family and the Quest for Humankind's Beginnings*. Simon & Schuster: New York.

Patemen, B. 1985. *Gombe Stream National Park*. Swara: Vol. 8 No. 2

Pearce, F. 1991. *Green Warriors: The People and the Politics behind the Environmental Revolution*. The Bodley Head Ltd: London.

Roodt, V. 1995. *The Shell Guide to the Common Trees of the Okavango Delta and Moremi Game Reserve*. Shell Oil Botswana (Pty) Ltd.

Santiapillai, C., and Ramono, W.S. 1992 (Dec). *Jungle four-wheel drive*. Geographical Magazine. The Royal Geographical Society.

Seeley, M. 1994. *Namib Bulletin: Desert Research Foundation of Namibia*. Number 11.

.............. 1995. *Namib Bulletin: Desert Research Foundation of Namibia*. Number 12.

Schaller, G.B. 1974. *Golden Shadows, Flying Hooves*. Collins: London.

Scott, J.P. 1985. *The Leopard's Tale*. Elm Tree Books: London

........... 1988. *The Great Migration*. Elm Tree Books: London

........... 1989. *Painted Wolves*. Hamish Hamilton: London

........... 1991. *The Leopard Family Book*. Picture Book Studio: London.

........... 1992. *Kingdom of Lions*. Kyle Cathie Ltd: London

........... 1996. *Jonathan Scott's Safari Guide to East African Animals*. Kensta: Nairobi

........... 1996. *Jonathan Scott's Safari Guide to East African Birds*. Kensta: Nairobi

Teede, J. and Teede, F. 1995. *African Thunder: The Victoria Falls*. Russel Friedman Books: Johannesburg.

Uhlenbroek, C. 1996. *A Study of the Structure and Function of Long Distance Calls Given By Male Chimpanzees in Gombe National Park*. PhD thesis, University of Bristol.

van Lawick, H. 1977. *Savage Paradise*. Collins: London.

van Lawick, H. and van Lawick-Goodall, J. 1970. *Innocent Killers*. Collins: London.

Wallauer, B. 1995. *A Tale of Two Families*. Jane Goodall Institute: World Report.

Williams, H. 1989. *Sacred Elephant*. Harmony Books: New York.

Williams, T. 1995 (Aug/Sept). *Follow-up on oiled penguins*. On Track: the environmental magazine. Penta Publications: Sandton, South Africa.

Willock, C. 1978. *The World of Survival*. Andre Deutsch: London.

Wilson, E.O. 1992 (Nov). *Living with Nature*. U.S.News and World Report Inc: Washington, DC.

Zimmerman, D., Turner, D., and Pearson, D. 1996. *Birds of Kenya and Northern Tanzania*. Princeton University Press.

# INDEX